The Making of a Code
The Issues Underlying AACR2

Papers Given at the International Conference on *AACR2*

held March 11–14, 1979

in

Tallahassee, Florida

Sponsored by the School of Library Science

Florida State University

Edited by
Doris Hargrett Clack

Chicago
American Library Association
1980

Library of Congress Cataloging in Publication Data

International Conference on AACR2, Florida State
University, 1979.
    The making of a code.

    Bibliography: p.
    Includes index.
    1. Anglo-American cataloguing rules—Congresses.
2. Descriptive cataloging—Rules—Congresses.
I. Clack, Doris H. II. Florida. State University,
Tallahassee. School of Library Science. III. Title.
Z694.A151567   1979   025.3'2   80–17496
ISBN 0–8389–0309–6

Design by Muriel Underwood
Composed by Modern Typographers
    in Linotype Times Roman
Printed on Warren's Olde Style,
    a pH neutral stock, by
    Chicago Press Corporation,
and bound by Zonne Bookbinders, Inc.

Contents

iii

Part 3

Access Points

Part 4

Looking beyond the Rules

Appendixes

Editor's Preface

In the spring of 1979 the School of Library Science at Florida State University, Tallahassee, sponsored an International Conference on *AACR2* (the second edition of *Anglo-American Cataloguing Rules*), which had been published just a few months earlier.

The anticipation and the anxiety about the code, experienced by librarians in the United States, Canada, and the United Kingdom, were relieved with its publication; nevertheless, questions of "Why this rule?" lingered on. The efforts of the Canadian Committee on Cataloguing/Comité Canadien de Catalogage, the Library Association–British Library Committee on Revision of AACR, and the American Library Association Catalog Code Revision Committee (CCRC) to solicit input from various library groups and to keep the library community informed of the decisions of the Joint Steering Committee for the Revision of AACR (JSC) merely served to intensify interest, not only in the rules themselves but also in the theoretical basis for the rules.

The final decisions for revision of *AACR* were made by the JSC, which took into consideration the many proposals, suggestions, and concerns received from various sources. The deliberations were long and arduous as the art of compromise was refined. Such was the making of a new code.

There are new rules, old rules, and changed rules. It was the deliberations that preceded the final rule statement that concerned the sponsors of the International Conference on AACR2. It was clear that, at least in the United States, most libraries would rely heavily upon the interpretation of rules by the national library in implementing the code and would, more than likely, apply the options so adopted by the national agency. With implementation delayed until 1981, the interim could be used to develop positive attitudes toward the code and thereby make acceptance and implementation less problematic. Thus the idea of this conference was conceived and developed.

The objectives of the conference were fourfold:

1. To provide librarians with an opportunity for dialog with the individuals directly responsible for the revision of *AACR*.
2. To provide an opportunity for individuals to discuss the various rule changes and thus gain a better insight into the theory behind the rules.

3. To provide an opportunity for individuals to exchange ideas about the code to increase their understanding of the impact of the code on library operations and user expectations.
4. To explore avenues for implementation.

A "quality conference" was assured by the selection of quality speakers and participants. Speakers included representatives of the JSC: Joel C. Downing, Ronald Hagler, Frances Hinton, Peter R. Lewis, Elizabeth L. Tate, and Ben Tucker; a coeditor of *AACR2*: Michael Gorman; and select members of the CCRC: Neal L. Edgar, Barbara J. Gates, Åke Koel, Joan K. Marshall, and Gordon Stevenson.

To provide a balanced, objective view of the code, Seymour Lubetzky and S. Michael Malinconico were also invited. Dr. Lubetzky, the dean of Anglo-American cataloging code revision, brought to the conference the wisdom of more than a quarter of a century of study of cataloging principles and work with code revision. Mr. Malinconico, representing a more futuristic view, brought a wealth of knowledge of modern technological capabilities and experience in library automation.

The conference was designed to attract catalogers and library science educators who, more than likely, would be expected to assume the responsibility for explaining the rules, that is, the reasons why certain rules were retained and others changed, what alternatives were examined during the revision deliberations. It must be emphasized that the purpose of the conference was not to teach cataloging or to teach the rules. The focus was on the "why" of the rules. The fourteen contributors and the 231 participants, thus, played equally deciding roles in the content and the structure of the conference.

The papers covered the genesis of *AACR2*, implications of the rules for automation and for the international community, and implementation of *AACR2* at the Library of Congress, as well as an overview of the entire code and a close scrutiny of each chapter in relation to the alternatives investigated and the logic behind the final decisions. The papers in this volume follow very closely the content of the oral presentations but not the exact order or wording, since most of them were rewritten for publication.

Acknowledgments

Many people worked long and hard to make the conference the success it was. Although the editor of these proceedings was directly responsible for the organization and administration of the conference, cooperation and support were rendered by many others. These include the faculty of the School of Library Science, Florida State University (FSU), especially John N. DePew, Phyllis Van Orden, and Adeline Wilkes, who assumed active roles in all phases of planning and execution, and to Liz Casey, Betsy Mallicote and David Presley who assisted with the typing.

Equally generous help was received from Maggie Dunaway, Center for Professional Development and Public Service at FSU; Martha Birchfield and Carolyn Padgett, FSU School of Law Library; William Quinly, FSU College of Education.

Expressions of appreciation also go to the following students who participated in the conference and contributed significantly to its success: Frances Benham, Patricia Bingham, Nada Brilliante, Mary Bryant, Sue Ann Clemons, Stephen Dornseif, Terry Gordon, Hsiao-Yu Ying, Laura Kimberly, Madison Moseley, Peggy Reed, John Rivest, Cindy Ruth, Marilyn Seymour, and Billie Wood.

Special thanks go to Terry Gordon and Barbara Kaden, who assisted in transcribing information from the audio tapes.

The understanding, patience, and cooperation of my husband, Harold, and my sons, Harold Levi and Herek Lerron, also helped make this book possible.

Part 1

Generalities

The Politics of Catalog Code Revision and Future Considerations

PETER R. LEWIS

It is prudent to begin by establishing terms. The classic definition of politics is "the art or science of government," but that won't really do for what I want to look at. To the classic definition, *Chambers' 20th Century Dictionary* (which I keep by my bedside as an essential aid for those wittily difficult Sunday-paper crossword puzzles that North America still doesn't know it's missing) adds another: "(*U.S.*) Manoeuvre and intrigue."

That is a bit closer, but it seems a bit cynical to me. Besides—although I don't doubt that here and there in all three author countries, while *AACR2* was in the making, there were sometimes what I once heard an excitable British cataloger call "shirt-sleeved men, plotting in smoke-filled rooms"—it is of the essence of such intrigue that chairpersons like me are excluded, and I saw too little of it to make any comment at all.

Somewhere between these two definitions is the activity that constitutes the *Realpolitik* of a professional undertaking like a uniform code of catalog rules. The nearest I can get to a generalized definition that will cover that area is "the pursuit of optimal conformity with a desired pattern of behavior." It won't get me into Bartlett's *Familiar Quotations,* I know, but that is what I will stick with for the purposes of this paper, even though there have been times—both before and since publication of *AACR2*—when I have been sorely tempted to describe what has been going on as (in an earlier attempt of mine at an Oscar Wildean epigram) "the pursuit of the satisfactory on behalf of the unsatisfiable."

The Interedition Years, 1967–1975

The best way to consider the future of code revision is to examine the past.

When the 1967 *Anglo-American Cataloguing Rules* were first published, in its North American and British texts, I had still to make my first transatlantic flight, and I was not in a position to make observations on the immediate effect of their publication on practicing catalogers on this side of the ocean. But I still remember vividly the excitement that was stirred up in Great Britain. For us, it was the beginning of a new epoch.

I doubt if, even in our headier moments, we saw it as a revolution of any kind. But there was a very strong sense of liberation for a generation of catalogers, tethered until then by the ball-and-chain anachronism of a code of rules first formulated in 1908, for, on our side of the ocean at least, most libraries—like the *British National Bibliography*, our major source of centralized catalog data—were still implementing the original Anglo-American Cataloging Code.

You must have felt something of the same sort in North America, even though an eighteen-year relaxation of our sixty years' hard labor was available to you through the *ALA Cataloging Rules* and the LC *Rules for Descriptive Cataloging* of 1949. There always seemed to me, anyway, a certain air of well-controlled jubilation about the preface and introduction of *AACR1*, suggesting that the editors and chairmen of committees themselves shared our feeling that the achievement was in some way epoch making.

If *AACR1* (1967) was the stuff of which new epochs are made, the "millennium" to follow was certainly cut short of its thousand years. In no time at all the forces of the Association of Research Libraries and the Library of Congress, with superimposition, had brought to bear on the rejoicing scene the sober economics of both the mammoth card catalog and the inventory of printed cards in the Navy Yard.

The repercussions of this decisive attempt to restore as far as possible an earlier status quo were, of course, felt not only in the United States but throughout the Anglo-American countries as a whole. At that time, we in Britain had a national library which was institutionally indifferent to the collective processing problems of research libraries generally, and in the British National Bibliography we had a centralized cataloging agency which was not flattened down by a warehouse full of printed cards for sale. It was easier for us to move toward full-hearted adoption of *AACR,* and the drag put on us by American conservatism, in the sphere of international cooperation, was very irksome. Besides, the expediencies which informed the North American text, and the uncontrollable effects of superimposition, flawed those qualities of principle and consistency which catalogers most admired in *AACR* as a whole; and perhaps we in Britain, being that much nearer to the Paris in which took place in 1961 the seminal International Conference on

Cataloguing Principles, were the more disappointed that agencies representative of the sixty years of Anglo-American cataloging tradition, which had played such a weighty role in making the Paris Principles a force in the bibliographic world, should now retreat so unscrupulously from their own canons.

A former British prime minister was fond of remarking that "a week is a long time in politics." But sixty years is a short time in the progress of cataloging, which moves along at glacial, if not geological, speed. The reasons why this is so are at the very center of the politics of catalog code revision.

In cataloging, all changes cost money. The larger the catalog in which the changes are introduced, the more they cost. That is why there is always a powerful conservative lobby among the administrators of the largest and richest libraries when the revision of cataloging rules is under consideration.

But failure to keep cataloging practice in line with changes in the characteristics in the documents in our libraries, and with the expectations and needs of document users in those libraries, leads to increasing inefficiencies; and so the long-term costs of avoiding catalog changes may be as high as those of accepting them, although this is not easy to demonstrate in library budgets. Either way, the longer the changes are deferred, the more they cost, and it may be that instead of letting even twenty years go by (let alone the sixty) between revised codes of rules, the proper method is to carry out revisions promptly. As the gardening books say, one should mow the lawn "little and often." In that case, there will be those who feel that even the ten years between the first and second editions of *AACR* are too many.

When the Joint Steering Committee for Revision of AACR was set up, we saw our task as a relatively modest one. There was no revolutionary fervor. We had not expected to have enough time to do more than make marginal adjustments to the texts of 1967, although, as it turned out, we did a lot more than that; and although we were all catalogers enough to gaze enraptured at the big shiny balloons of new ideas that were floated toward us during the three years of the project, we were also administrators enough to wield the spike of cost-benefit and to puncture all but the sturdiest of those balloons.

In other words, however different in appearance *AACR2* is from *AACR1*, it is the political factors above all that have already reduced to a virtually irreducible minimum the real and essential changes in principle and practice that *AACR2* introduces.

When all the pressure groups and lobbies and caucuses of the catalogers had expended their efforts on us, it was the long-enduring political tyranny of the retrospective file that determined, above all else, how far the editors and the committee could go to meet the revolution, which, if it hadn't been started in 1967, had certainly taken over since. It was not, of course, a catalogers' revolution. In most respects it was a technological revolution and it began to take hold within a year or two of 1967. This was the period when the computer got hold of the cataloging process, when the MARC record was born, when the first cooperative and centralized networks got on the drawing boards, and when the machine-readable data file attained an identity and recognition as a type of library document in itself. It was also the period when the supremacy of the printed book as the staple of the library collection began to be challenged by the range of what we were then learning to call "new media" and "nonbook materials," and in which the numerous bibliographic problems posed by these materials raised some fundamental questions relevant to catalogs for printed books which the 1967 code, like its predecessors, seemed almost unthinkingly to have taken for granted.

Above all, perhaps, in the ten years since the first edition, there has been a growth and a development in all kinds of library and information services on a scale that was not easy to anticipate before 1967: a growth and a development often culminating in the redefinition of the role of the national library and the national bibliographic services in relation to library services and bibliographic services generally. All of these factors have had effects on the assembly, the transmission, and the exploitation of bibliographic information, both within libraries and between them, on a scale greater than *AACR* could have predicted and "catered for" during the years when it was being formulated.

It also has to be said that even if these developments had not taken place, *AACR* in 1967 posed some problems as a compromise text. It was a compromise, for example, between Lubetzky and Spalding—between the acceptance of the 1961 Paris Principles and the inertia of the large and long-established research library catalogs. It also imported some of the unresolved problems from the 1949 ALA code and *Rules for Descriptive Cataloging in the Library of Congress*. So, notwithstanding its many excellences, the 1967 code had its conflicts and its inconsistencies, which, if everything else had been stable, could have been lived with for quite a few more years, but which sooner or later would have to be put right.

Then there was the fact that, for all the close cooperation between the British and the American cataloging committees in those years, there was still an authorized divergence of practice enshrined in the existence of two texts and in the alternative rules and the options which both texts offered us. Indeed, there was no less of this than there had been in the

1908 Anglo-American code. In an era when the exchange and the cooperative assembly of bibliographic information between national libraries and other agencies is assuming greater and greater importance as part of their role, the cost of mechanization means that the exercise of options and the divergences from the standards are luxuries that few people can now afford. This is now a familiar paradox when we remember that the computer is supposed to increase flexibility, not diminish it. In some respects, the divergences between the two texts grew worse in the years immediately following 1967. Just before publication of the first edition—that is, in 1966—the American Library Association and the (British) Library Association signed a memorandum of agreement that they would keep in touch with each other about amendments. The actual wording of the relevant clause was this:

After completion of the revised codes, each Association shall keep the other informed of proposed changes in the cataloguing rules. Each Association will give full and fair consideration to changes proposed by the other, and will attempt to make those changes mutually acceptable; but joint agreement shall not be a prerequisite to the establishment of the new rules in the country proposing a change.

In fact, in North America some amendments had already been made to the text in the interval between its publication in January and that of the British text in December, which the British had time neither to discuss with the Americans nor to incorporate undiscussed in their own text. For a few years there was a regular annual discussion of proposed amendments under the umbrella of this memorandum. It took place at the Descriptive Cataloging Committee's meetings during the American Library Association midsummer conference. In those days I attended, as often as not, as representative of the Library Association. The Library of Congress was there, as was the Canadian Library Association, though neither was actually party to the memorandum. I have to say that it was an unsatisfactory business. The proposals for amendment under discussion mostly originated in the Library of Congress, and were sent to us only a few days before the meeting. A lot of time was spent on flights to the United States, improvising our position without benefit of full consideration by our own Cataloguing Rules Committee which had been set up for this purpose. At the meeting itself, the Library of Congress advocated its case, the Library Association representatives urged either a contrary case or a modified approach to the problem, and the Descriptive Cataloging Committee acted as a kind of jury—at least the Descriptive Cataloging Committee members were the only people who had a vote, and they voted on the motion at the end of the discussion. Neither the Library of Congress nor the Library Association had any vote. The Canadians had no vote either; and they acted as a kind of liberal Mercutio, courteously offering a plague on both our houses and suggesting to the Descriptive Cataloging Committee that we should be looking at other problems altogether.

For the British, at that time, there was a basic belief that the code should be given a few years to settle down before we started amending it again, whereas the Library of Congress, which was, of course, operating a public catalog service across the whole spectrum of bibliographic conditions in the world's literature, soon began to discover ambiguities and inadequacies in the rules, which it was understandably anxious to put right as soon as possible. The tendency that we disliked about this was that the Library of Congress so often wanted to put things right by going back to an earlier practice which *AACR* clearly had meant to move from. So it happened that in most instances both sides agreed to differ, and the memorandum and the agreement that were supposed to keep us closer together led to a situation which threatened to drive us further apart.

There was no area in which this was more apparent than in the treatment of nonbook materials. The Library of Congress became rapidly involved in the documentation of some of the new media, but not the whole range, and began to propose piecemeal changes to some of the rules in Part III. Others had already decided that this problem had to be tackled as an integrated whole; so we in Britain declined, *a priori,* to discuss LC's proposed amendments at ALA meetings, and said that we would not accommodate them in the British text. We went off and drafted our own revised version of Part III as a whole, which became known as the LANCET Rules; and before we had finished that, the Canadians produced their *Non-Book Materials,* under the byline of Jean Riddle Weihs and her colleagues. Based primarily on the existing texts of *AACR,* the Canadian manual had an impressively authoritative steering group; and they created a certain dismay in the political arena when, first in the field, they sought recognition for their text by ALA as an authorized standard.

While all this was going on, the curious thing was that with the passage of time those parts of the original texts where in 1967 there had been an agreement to differ—that is, where there were variant rules between the North American and British texts—came closer together. The reason was that the North American text variants which represented late compromises on behalf of LC and other big research libraries were beginning to feel the strain. Since the British, as I have explained, had not felt the necessity for these compromises in the first place, the two texts began to resemble each other more in major respects as the North American fell back to an earlier state of grace. Eventually the North Americans abandoned rule 98, that most notorious and significant throwback to an earlier epoch, providing for the continued entry of churches and the like under place instead of name.

This voluntary retirement from the die-hard trenches occurred after Seymour Lubetzky published his proposal that the centenary year of ALA be celebrated by the publication of a single text code, modeled largely on the British text, and by the complete abandonment of super-imposition in the Library of Congress.[1]

At the same time, the British had now got round to the belief that it was time to make some revision of the 1967 texts. This was partly to make it possible for the newly formed British Library to adopt the uniform practices prescribed by the rules and so play the leading national and international role in the development and encouragement of bibliographic standards that its predecessor, the British Museum, had been unable and unwilling to do before 1967; and partly because the growth of networks and of international exchange of bibliographic information made it very desirable to reach a much closer reconciliation of practices within the English-speaking community in the future—that is, to eliminate as many as possible of the differences between the two texts and of variants and options within both texts; and partly because, after six or seven years' experience of using *AACR,* there was a clearer recognition of the directions in which developments were needed to provide adequately both for the mechanization of the catalog record and for the new media of the documents which catalog records describe.

Almost simultaneously with the British Library's declaration of interest in this field, the American Library Association put forward a formal proposal for a revised edition of *AACR.*

Grass Roots and the International Arena

I don't really know, even now, quite how and why this happened. My guess is that there was simply a burst into action of cumulative dissatisfaction at the grass-roots level of the practicing catalogers for whom

---

1. Seymour Lubetzky, "1976 minus 6, 5 . . . ," *Library Journal* 96 (Feb. 1, 1971): 450–451.

RTSD (Resources and Technical Services Division) is the main political platform: dissatisfaction with some of the rules, maybe; dissatisfaction, certainly, with some of the ways in which the rules were being applied or interpreted, and with what was being done to them in one way or another. I base this guess on my observation of the great eagerness and energy with which CCRC and other constituent bodies in ALA subjected the 1967 texts, and later the draft texts of *AACR2*, to comprehensive critical examination and review in the incredibly short time which was all that the timetable of the project allowed.

The main thing that my experience in the chair of the Joint Steering Committee for Revision of *AACR* taught me, in fact, is that in the United States librarians care deeply about the practice of cataloging as a professional craft in greater numbers per library than their counterparts elsewhere. Passions are readily engaged on such questions as (to pluck one out of the air) the corporate main entry of maps, in a way that can frighten the innocent bystander. I myself remember with deepest pleasure (still mingled with awe) a packed and passionate RTSD program meeting one summer, long before the *AACR2* project began, in which I added to the passion with a short paper bearing the most esoteric title of any paper I have ever heard of, let alone written myself. It was called "Early Warning Generic Medium Designations in Multi-Media Catalogues." I can tell you that it was better received in Chicago, where the conference was that year, than it would have been in London; and later it even made *LRTS* [*Library Resources & Technical Services*].

Wherever passions are engaged, political activity follows. There were times when this activity in the ALA constituencies led to incidents which threatened to bring the whole project to an abrupt halt; but even so, I found myself envious of the concerned and committed atmosphere in which, on this side of the ocean, our colleagues thrashed out their positions and defended them to their fellow librarians before bringing them to the international forum of the Joint Steering Committee. As Michael Gorman commented in his recent paper in *LRTS,* when you have appreciated the way in which this revision project was tackled by them, you can no longer sustain the belief that our cataloging codes are framed by persons remote from, and ignorant of, the realities of day-to-day cataloging.[2]

I am not saying that the other author bodies did not work with equal seriousness and commitment, but only that in Britain we did not

2. Michael Gorman, "The *Anglo-American Cataloguing Rules,* second edition," *Library Resources & Technical Services,* 22, no. 3 (Summer 1978): 211.

often encounter the warmth of conviction that leads to the kind of orchestrated lobbying and debate that accompanied the Americans' work almost from start to finish of the exercise. The one exception perhaps was the issue of the rules for nonbook materials and the defense of the LANCET rules at the time when the Joint Steering Committee was negotiating with IFLA for the general international standard of bibliographic description, the *ISBD(G)*. I still cherish the rhetoric of an editorial in *Audio-Visual Librarian* in which, as the chairman of that committee, coming back from Paris with an agreement on *ISBD(G)*, I was likened to Neville Chamberlain coming home from Munich in 1938 with a worthless treaty and calling out feebly "Peace in our time."

Now the reference to IFLA and *ISBD(G)* raises a political question of some importance for the future of catalog code revision.

The *International Standard Bibliographic Description for Monographs* had already been incorporated into the text of *AACR* by means of published amendments, but our editors faced a real difficulty in coming to grips with an ongoing program of *ISBD*s for nonbook materials, for serials, for cartographic materials, and so on, all going on at IFLA under the general designation "UBC—Universal Bibliographic Control." We were able to resolve the problem by negotiating, with the IFLA Committee and the chairs of the ISBD Working Parties, the creation of a generalized *ISBD*, the *ISBD(G)*, which was accepted as the basis both for *AACR* and the more specialized *ISBD*s that have since begun to emerge from IFLA. This achievement, and the consequently integrated and standardized framework for the systematic description of all library materials in *AACR2*, we regard as our principal contribution to the fulfillment of the objective that our main funding agency, the Council on Library Resources, enjoined on us: a contribution to the development of an international cataloging code.

But there remains a general problem in the relation of national and international codes of cataloging rules to international standards. I am referring not only to the *ISBD*s but to such other things as the ISO standards for romanization, IFLA's revision of *Names of Persons,* and its sponsorship of Eva Verona's *Corporate Headings*—with all of which, whether they be standards, or quasi standards, or pseudo standards, *AACR2* has had to achieve a sustainable relationship, if not an accommodation. We certainly haven't solved this general problem by the solutions we found in *AACR2*. Sooner or later, we have to find a better way of organizing the international standardizing effort and coordinating it with our valid national and regional requirements.

The Machinery of Decision Making

The aspect of this international game that should most concern us for the future is "Who gets to play?" and "Who picks the teams?"

The membership in the decision-making groups in the *ISBD*s and similar areas is almost inevitably self-selecting, and without serious constituency responsibility related to the specifics of catalog code revision. There are real difficulties of sustained involvement and democratic process for a body like the Joint Steering Committee for Revision of *AACR*, whose constitution was designed primarily to facilitate feedback and consultation with constituencies of institutions and individuals actually engaged in cataloging and bibliographical data handling.

I won't spend any time detailing the machinery of consultation and decision making by which the revision of *AACR* was carried out at the international and the national levels. It is briefly described in the preface of *AACR2,* and those who want more detail about the committees and constituencies can find it in the article by Carol Kelm (who acted as secretary to the Joint Steering Committee) in the Winter 1978 issue of *LRTS.*[3] There are just a couple of things worth drawing to your attention.

One is the constitution of the Joint Steering Committee during the exercise. The organization of interests was such that each of the five nominated author bodies had one vote.[4] This meant that there were two votes in the United States' interest, two votes in the British interest, and one in the Canadian interest—a built-in majority, so to speak, for North America on all issues in which the represented institutions had common cause; but not for the United States alone, because its voting strength was balanced by any two of the three British and Canadian votes. Since achievement of one of our principal aims (merging the two texts) precluded any agreement to differ, and since we were' working within a much shorter time span than our predecessors, the vote was clearly a very important method of resolving conflicts of view or interest.

The balance of voting power was really quite elegant, not only in terms of national interests of the three countries but also, for example, between the three national libraries whose interests were involved. To

---

3. Carol R. Kelm, "The Historical Development of the Second Edition of the *Anglo-American Cataloguing Rules," Library Resources & Technical Services* 22, no. 1 (Winter 1978): 22–33.

4. The five nominated author bodies of *AACR2* are the American Library Association, the British Library, the Canadian Library Association, the Library Association, and the Library of Congress.

win any vote, all three had to vote on the same side; and because the Canadians' single vote had to cover all their interests, a decisive national libraries' vote had to carry at least one professional association along with it. The Tripartite Meeting, which set up the Revision Project initially in 1974, did its work in this respect as thoughtfully as any of our nations' founding fathers.

That, in the event, it need not have expended so much thought on it is a tribute to the maturity and enlightened self-interest of the represented institutions and to the qualities of the individuals who represented them—a tribute which (because, at the beginning of a conference, a number of them have the opportunity, in following me at the lectern, to expose my ignorance and prejudices) I am especially happy to pay.

I don't mean simply that those who represented the national libraries were above ganging up on the professional associations (though, in fact, I don't believe they ever did so), or that ALA always pulled its punches—that were "Sunday punches" because of the sheer weight of numbers that supported its positions on some issues, compared with the rest of us (indeed, it made very effective political use of its strength in this respect from time to time). The important thing, as it turned out, was that even our narrowly chauvinistic interests were much more compatible one with another than we had expected them to be. I don't think, for example, that anybody lost out at all, in nationalistic terms, because of the merger of the North American and British texts.

It was only on such particularly British obsessions as the recent changes in our local-government areas, or on what an eminent American librarian not long ago called "the elitist baggage of British titles of nobility," that we sometimes detected a certain impatience on the part of our administratively more stable democratic and republican colleagues, who felt perhaps that we could legislate whatever way we liked, if only they did not have to listen any more to Philip Escreet and Peter Lewis talk about it. I think we perhaps felt the same about such things as the United States Court Rules, which for some reason aroused similarly strong feelings in the Catalog Code Revision Committee.

The other constitutional point I want to refer to is the position of the editors. The 1974 Tripartite Meeting got this wrong, primarily because it didn't (at that time) appreciate that the groundswell of catalogers' dissatisfaction (of which I've spoken) was going to force a much deeper consideration of the 1967 texts than had been anticipated, and also because of the obligation that the Council on Library Resources was to place on us to plan for a larger international audience than we had first intended.

Paul Winkler was, of course, a "natural" to follow Sumner Spalding to the editor's chair. But in retrospect, the idea of having Michael Gorman as no more than a kind of *chargé d'affaires* of the British text is ludicrous. It very soon became clear that if all the ground was to be covered in the time available, there would have to be a much more equal distribution of responsibility between the two. And as the importance of protecting British text interests rapidly faded, the division of responsibility quickly, and most satisfactorily, reflected the particular specialties and talents of two editors who, if I may say so, rose magnificently to the challenges which JSC placed before them.

There is one other aspect of the editors' role I should like to draw attention to, and that is their accessibility.

Most of the time that he was active as editor, Michael Gorman was living in England and maintaining his desk at the British Library. He was a full member of the British equivalent of CCRC (which, in our case, included representatives of the national library as well as representatives of the association), and we had him to every meeting in London he could get to. His contributions were crucial to our appreciation of what was practicable and what was desirable, not only in our own but in our North American partners' positions. So his accessibility enabled us readily to separate the issues we needed to stand on from those we should abandon or could concede; and this was a principal reason why the British tally of documents submitted to JSC was so much smaller, and clogged the agenda less, than anybody else's.

By contrast, it seems that, initially, positions were created and discussed at LC without taking formal advantage of the availability in Washington of the editor from Processing Division; and it was only at the end, with all important decisions made and huge publication pressures on the editors (now both in the United States), that LC pushed aside protocol to come to the rescue. (I may say that *AACR2* wouldn't be published yet, if it hadn't done so.)

I well understand the propriety of a careful distinction between "editorial freedom" and "national library policy"; and maybe this traditional manifestation of it is a necessary element in the domestic politics of LC's relations with other library and librarians' interests. But hearing now of LC's later difficulties in fully standing by the final text, which its representatives and agents did so much to create, my chief thought is that the library community as a whole may be paying a very high price for its insistence on LC's scrupulosity.

The Future of AACR

"The only thing we learn from history is that nobody learns anything from history." I hope this is not inevitably true, though there is such a sense of *déjà vu* about the responses to *AACR2* in some quarters that one fears an earlier repetition of the recently completed exercise than sensible and far-sighted libraries should be asked to go through.

So far as the author bodies of *AACR2* are concerned, it will be for the newly reconstituted JSCAACR to determine how soon and how far the amendments and revisions which *AACR2* will surely need, sooner or later, should be undertaken. When anything more radical than mere amendment is needed (e.g. a third edition), JSC will have to persuade the trustees of the common revision fund, formed from the royalties on sales of *AACR2* and the abridged edition, to fund it. Since the trustees are also the three professional associations, there will have to be an element of democratic approval, as well as international harmony, to bring a third edition about.

I hope, at least, that the new JSC, giving seats with voting rights to the editors and required to justify its ambitions to the trustee associations, will provide a more effective political machinery for a balanced evolution of *AACR* than its predecessor, the old Memorandum of Agreement of 1966. Keeping JSC in existence in this manner also offers the only hopeful way, at the moment, of collectively influencing developments on the wider international front, in the best Anglo-American traditions of service to library users through the provision of bibliographic data in the most helpful, possible way.

It is easy to be carried away politically by the prospect of worldwide networks and the products of powerful computers. Let us not forget, in our discussions this week, that the purpose of all our professional politics is, in the end, to achieve the best possible service to mankind through the use of our libraries.

The Fundamentals of Bibliographic Cataloging and *AACR2*

SEYMOUR LUBETZKY

As one who was involved in the revision of the former ALA rules and the development of the first *AACR,* which is now to be superseded by a second one, I am glad of the opportunity to comment on the basic differences between the two and their implications for the character and effectiveness of our catalogs. Having had occasion to discuss the merits of some of the major aspects of *AACR2*—the *ISBD,* the ambivalence toward the main entry, and the entry of serials without regard to their special condition of authorship—as I have had at the two ISAD institutes on cataloging, held in 1975 and 1977, when the present edition was still in progress, I shall not go into them here again, except as they may be relevant to the characterization of the general idealogy of *AACR2,* with which I primarily wish to concern myself here.

To begin, I think I must say that no one who peruses *AACR2* can fail to be impressed with the meticulous craftsmanship of the work. The anatomy of the subject matter, the coordination, subordination, and general organization of the rules, and the precision and clarity of expression represent a remarkable achievement. As one who had deplored the aberrations from principle in many of the rules of *AACR1,* adopted in the interest of compromise, I am happy to see those aberrations addressed—though not always entirely to my satisfaction—as in the treatment of serials, on which I shall touch later. A sound code must be based on a solid ideological foundation, as was recognized in the previous revision and to which that revision also contributed. Now what about the fundamentals of *AACR2*? In the opening paragraph of the preface to the present edition we are told that "in spite of the changes in presentation and content which it introduces," *AACR2* remains "firmly based" on "the same principles and underlying objectives as the first edition," published in 1967. Had that been the case—that is, had *AACR2* really continued to be based on the objectives and principles of *AACR1* and had it been devoted to improvements "in presentation and content" as needed—the result might well have been the best code of cataloging as yet. But it is apparent that other considerations, having nothing to do with objectives and principles of cataloging, have prevailed to cause *AACR2* to compromise the objectives and principles of *AACR1* much more deeply than did the aberrations in *AACR1,* the original cause of *AACR2.*

What is the first, basic question to consider in setting out to evaluate or prepare a code? It is, of course, the question that was at the center of the grand debate on Panizzi's rules for the catalog of the British Museum at the hearings held by a royal commission in 1847–49. The critics of Panizzi's rules, it will be recalled, argued that the principal purpose of a catalog is to tell one "that such and such books are in the library" and that it should therefore be a simple thing to make a list of the names and titles under which a given book might be sought. For this reason they regarded Panizzi's elaborate rules as exorbitantly complex and dubbed them "a magnificent mistake." Panizzi, however, countered (in effect) that the essence of a book is the *work* it contains, that a person in search of a book is actually in need of the *work* conveyed by it, that that work may be found in the library in different editions or translations under different names or titles, and that the catalog advocated by his critics would thus serve to disperse the editions or translations of a work and the works of an author—a result that would ill serve the needs of a reader. For, Panizzi insisted, "a reader may know the *work* he requires; he cannot be expected to know all the peculiarities of the different *editions;* and this information he has a right to expect from the catalogues." That is to say, an adequate catalog, concerned about the actual *needs* of a reader, must be designed to tell one not only whether the particular book he or she seeks is in the library but also what other editions of the work and what other works of the author the library has. That was the object of Panizzi's rules.

This, then, is the first question that must be deliberated and resolved, for the answer to it will profoundly affect the nature of the problem and the course of cataloging. Are we to have a catalog that has been designed to tell only what books the library has and nothing more, as the opponents of Panizzi's rules argued? Or are we to have one that also takes cognizance of the intrinsic relations of the books to one another and relate them accordingly, so that a person in search of a particular book would be informed at once of all the editions and translations of the work and of the other works of the author which the library has, as well as of other related works, as Panizzi contended? At the debate on his rules, Panizzi's view was upheld by the royal commission and his objective has been followed, though with some variations, in Anglo-

American cataloging. In the preparation of *AACR1,* that objective—
and the method evolved by Panizzi and Cutter to accomplish it—was to
be carried out consistently and systematically. That method required
that a publication be entered under the name of the author of the work,
that the author be represented in the catalog under one particular name,
that under that name all the editions and translations of a work be "arranged" together under the original title, and that this be followed by a
clear and concise description of the publication. Accordingly, *AACR1*
dealt with these questions in this order to produce the basic or "main"
entry on which the desired catalog was to be based.

On opening *AACR2,* we note a conspicuous difference in the general structure of the code and the terminology used—suggesting a
"fresh" orientation toward the problem of cataloging. The new code
begins with an elaborate "Description" of the materials cataloged and
follows with "Headings," characterized as "access points," to be added
to the descriptions to facilitate their location in the catalog. This will
readily be recognized as the approach advocated by those who would
ignore the traditional objectives of cataloging as explained before, who
would abandon use of the traditional "main" entry, designed to represent a book as an edition of a particular work, and replace it by a "title
unit entry" to represent the book as such, with multiple "access points."
This approach might be described as a modern variant of that advocated by Panizzi's opponents, requiring that a catalog should tell only
"that such and such books are in the library." Indeed, we are told that
abandonment of the idea of the main entry was earnestly considered in
preparation of *AACR2* (0.5), and had that prevailed, *AACR2* would
have marked an ideological atavism in cataloging. We are also told, however, that the idea "has not been embodied in the rules largely because
of the lack of time to explore the considerable implications of such a
change." Thus *AACR2* provides that one of the entries under the "access points"—that is, the one under the author heading—should be
treated as the main entry to represent the publication as an edition or
translation of a particular work by a particular author and to relate the
publications under this heading accordingly.
In the previous Anglo-American codes the main entry was also the
basic or unit entry on which all other entries were based, so that a publication appeared in *all* entries as an edition of a particular work. This
is not the case in *AACR2,* where "added entries provide access to
bibliographic descriptions" (21.29A)—that is, where publications are
represented as individual bibliographic entities and not as editions of
particular works. It seems that, faced with conflicting demands, on one

hand are those who continue to view a publication as an edition of a particular work and continue to use the traditional main entry as such. On the other hand are those who view a publication as an individual bibliographical entity and would use a title unit entry with multiple "access points" to represent it as such in the catalog.

AACR2 chose an incongruous compromise—that is, generally following the latter view but also providing for the former, in part, under one of the "access points." To make *AACR2* quite acceptable to the adherents of the title unit entry, they are officially absolved from the provisions of the main entry and are advised that they may use the rules only "as guidance in determining all the entries required in particular instances" (0.5). But adherents of the traditional main entry are here presented with a code that exhibits a split ideology on the basic question of whether a cataloged book is to be viewed and represented in the catalog as an individual entity or as an edition of a particular work by a particular author.

The second basic question follows directly from the answer to the first. Unlike *AACR1,* the main entry is used only as one of the "access points" and not as the basis of all other entries. Since *AACR2* also prescribes the use of main and added entries and since the first rule is that the main entry is to be under the name of the author of the work, the next question is What constitutes authorship in cataloging? Turning to the *AACR2* glossary, we are surprised to find "Author. *See* Personal author," suggesting that our traditional concept of authorship, embracing both personal and corporate authorship, has apparently been drastically changed and that the principle of corporate authorship, heretofore the prize feature and special contribution of Anglo-American cataloging, as evidenced by impressively increased recognition abroad at the International Conference on Cataloguing Principles (held in Paris in 1961), is now suddenly no more. Corporate bodies do continue to exist and to have a potential responsibility for certain "categories" of works which are indeed treated exactly as works of corporate authorship.

The mention of "corporate authorship" is scrupulously excluded from *AACR2,* as an idea to be shunned. Thus while *AACR1* sought to replace the individual rules for separate types of works by general principles, based on the varying conditions of authorship of the works, *AACR2* proceeds in the opposite direction. The principle of corporate authorship is replaced by an arbitrary list of "categories" of works which should be entered under the corporate bodies that issue them. There is no indication of what these "categories" have in common and why they should be treated differently than other categories of works. There is no indication that the principle of corporate authorship was abandoned in

AACR2 in the conviction that this was necessary to improve the ideology of the code or the effectiveness of the catalog. Rather, it seems that this, too, was done to make *AACR2* more widely acceptable abroad among those whose narrow and literal concept of authorship is not compatible with their view of the world of corporate bodies. If so, we have not yet learned from the experience of the previous revision that politics and principles do not mix, and that the pursuit of universal acceptance by people of varying views, objectives, and needs is bound to lead to adoption of the lowest ideological denominator in cataloging.

The concept of corporate authorship is necessarily a part of the general concept of authorship, and it would therefore seem that that is the place to begin. Given a clear definition of what constitutes authorship, it should be possible to determine whether that concept is, or is not, equally applicable to individuals as well as to corporate bodies. But a review of the definitions of "author" in the successive editions of our cataloging rules will reveal a persisting and murky ambiguity of the idea, which should briefly be noted here.

Since Cutter first defined "author" and set forth "the principle of corporate authorship," it is of interest to compare his definition with that in *AACR2* and note their implications for the principle of corporate authorship. Cutter defined "author" simply, but not very perspicaciously, as "the person who writes a book." By this, however, he did not mean literally "who *writes* a *book*" but figuratively: "who *creates* a *work*." Having used the word "writes," he found it necessary to specify in a subsequent rule that a person who writes down, say, the speech of another person is not to be considered the author of the speech; the speaker is. His indiscriminate use of "book" to mean "book" sometimes and at other times "work" has been a great source of confusion in cataloging.

The *AACR2* definition of "author," given more fully preceding the general rule for works of personal authorship (21.1A1), is considerably more elaborate but hardly more lucid. It says: "A personal author is the person chiefly responsible for the creation of the intellectual or artistic content of a work," by which is also meant simply the person who creates a work, as is evident from the examples that clarify the definition:

Writers of books and composers of music are the authors of the works they create; compilers of bibliographies are the authors of those bibliographies, cartographers are the authors of their maps; and artists and photographers are the authors of the works they create.

The phrase "responsible for the creation" has been the cause of much confusion in determining authorship of a work prepared by an employee of a corporate body at the direction, on the time, and at the expense of that body. Who, in such a case, is to be regarded as "responsible for the creation" of the work? The individual who prepared the work or the corporate body which directed and caused the preparation of the work that otherwise might have never come into being? And what is the meaning of "the intellectual or artistic content of the work"? Is it something other than "the work" itself? Would anything other than the ambiguity of the definitions be lost if it were reduced to the simple statement "A personal author is the person who creates a work"? It would seem that this would express more clearly the intent of both Cutter's and the *AACR2* definitions of "author."

However, aside from the ambiguity of the definition, there is also the question of its essential adequacy. There can be no quarrel with the fact that a person who *creates* a work is the *author* of that work, simply because the term *author* is synonymous with creator. But is the creation of a work the single and paramount determinant of authorship? There is a large and growing number of works in libraries, such as "autobiographies," speeches, articles, even novels, that are written by ghost writers for others, represented as the authors. Are the ghost writers who actually created the works or the individuals under whose names the works were published to be considered chiefly responsible for the content of these works and to be treated as their authors? A most prominent example, Washington's *Farewell Address* is said to have been written for him by Hamilton. Is it to be entered in the catalog under "Hamilton" as the author of the famous address?

Merely to ask the question is to answer it—and call attention to the fact that in reality it is not the person who *created* the work but the one under whose name the work is published that is regarded as chiefly responsible for it and treated as its author, excepting cases of erroneous or fictitious attribution.

Recognizing this situation, *AACR1* provides that ghost writings should be treated as the works of those under whose names they are published. This provision serves to complement and modify the definition that the author is the person who *creates* the work. *AACR2* has no specific provision for ghost writings. Instead, it incredibly includes as an example a "ghosted" autobiography under the name of the biographee as author (21.4A), in disregard of its own definition of "author" as the person who *creates* a work.

It should be apparent that, realistically, the paramount criterion of authorship is not who really wrote the "autobiography," the *Farewell*

Address, or any report, but who is formally represented as its author and, presumably, had assumed full responsibility for its content, whether written by him- or herself or by anyone else as his or her agent.

Obviously, this criterion is equally applicable to individuals as well as corporate bodies, and demands the equal treatment of individuals as well as corporate bodies as authors. Interestingly, this is also the foundation of Cutter's principle of corporate authorship, expressed as "Bodies of men are to be considered as authors of works published in their name or by their authority"—that is, of works for the contents of which they have presumably formally assumed responsibility, whether prepared directly by them or indirectly by an agent for them.

Cutter's principle of corporate authorship did not go unchallenged and his reply was reproduced in the later editions of his rules. He argued persuasively the rationale and the practical value of his principle. That principle has dominated Anglo-American cataloging since and has gained increasingly greater recognition abroad. To abandon this valuable principle in an edition of Anglo-American cataloging rules, which historically should have celebrated the centennial of Cutter's rules, is a deplorable miscarriage of ideological justice.

The inadequacy of the definition of "author" in general and abandonment of the principle of corporate authorship have also had a deleterious effect on the treatment of serials—that is, works intended to be continued indefinitely by successive parts or editions and therefore subject to change of personal or corporate authorship. The *AACR1* rule for serials specifies a list of types of serials, such as "a serially published bibliography, index, directory, biographical dictionary, almanac, or yearbook," etc., that should be entered under title. On the contrary, the governing principle in *AACR1* is that entry is to be based *not* on type of publication or work but *only* on the varying conditions of authorship. But if the rule is bad, at least the *"exception,"* which follows it, is of redeeming practical value. It prescribes that "if the title (exclusive of the subtitle) includes the name or the abbreviation of the name of the corporate body, or consists solely of a generic term that requires the name of the body for adequate identification of the serial, enter it under the body." The result of this exception prevents the inexorable growth of confusing accumulations of entries under such generic titles as "journal," "bulletin," etc., and their equivalents in other languages, and is what Cutter's principle of corporate authorship was practically intended to accomplish (among other results). But *AACR2,* abandoning the principle of corporate authorship and restricting the entry under corporate bodies to a few specified categories, will foster the growth of such accumulations which Cutter described as "chaotic collections of empirical entries."

Aside from this aspect, the very approach to the treatment of serials in *AACR2* is fundamentally wrong—a case of misapplication of a sound principle. *AACR2* has no special rules for the entry of serials, on the ground that serials represent a special type of publication and the rules of entry are based on conditions of authorship, not type of publication. This is one of the basic principles that was recognized and adopted in the preparation of *AACR1*. Although this is not quite consistent with the specification of certain "categories" of works for entry under their issuing corporate bodies, its observance in *AACR2* is all to the good. The fact is that serials are not merely a type of publication but also involve a special condition of authorship that requires special provision. Because a serial is intended, by definition, to be continued indefinitely, the person or corporate body that is originally or subsequently responsible for it is subject to change, and hence the appropriate entry of a serial is generally under its title.

However, this is not always the case. There are also serials which are not susceptible to change of the persons or corporate bodies responsible for them, and they should be treated like all other works for which a given person or corporate body is responsible. These include serials whose titles include the names of the individuals or corporate bodies responsible for them (e.g. *I. F. Stone's Newsletter, Library Association Record*) which obviously could not be continued by other individuals or corporate bodies without change of title and serials concerned primarily with the affairs of their issuing bodies, which likewise cannot reasonably be expected to be continued by other bodies without change of title, in which cases they would be treated as new serials. Under *AACR2*, even a serial whose title includes the name of the corporate body responsible for it will not be entered under the name of that body unless it belongs to one of the "categories" certified for entry under corporate body.

But what is much worse—indeed almost incredible—is that a serial that is subject to change of authorship is to have "a new entry" every time "the person or corporate body responsible for the serial changes." In this case, none could be regarded as responsible for the serial as a whole. For example, *Library Literature,* which has had—and presumably will continue to have—different editors responsible for it, is to have "a new entry" whenever the editor responsible for it changes. This appears as a case of bibliographical malpractice, perpetrated unwarrantedly on a serial which required merely a simple entry under title. This is hardly an improvement on the faulty rules for serials in *AACR1*.

As a footnote to one of the earlier observations, it should be noted that while the subject of ghost writings received no special attention in *AACR2*, "spirit communications" did, and on this subject *AACR2* differs pointedly from *AACR1*. Apparently skeptical of such messages and unwilling to lend them bibliographical credence, *AACR1* rules that "a communication purporting to have been received from a spirit should be entered under the medium or other person reporting the communication"—that is to tell the catalog user: the medium says so, and we are not in a position to confirm his or her claim. However, with mistrust toward none and unqualified faith in all, *AACR2* rules that "a communication presented as having been received from a spirit" should be entered "under the heading for the spirit"—thus concurring implicitly with the medium's claim. This will undoubtedly please the medium; but will it also please the spirit, to be held responsible for any statement made in its name by a medium without any chance for denying it? Perhaps the question is beyond the cataloger's ken—with the answer secreted in the domain of the spirits.

I began by praising *AACR2* as a work of meticulous craftsmanship and then proceeded to criticize its combined use of the title unit entry with the traditional main entry, its abandonment of the principle of corporate authorship, but not of the main entry, under corporate bodies of certain "categories" of works, and its failure to recognize that serials and other continuing works are often, though not always, subject to change of authorship—or of the person or corporate body responsible for it—and should therefore, in such cases, be entered under title. This may seem contradictory, but it is not. I think the praise is fully deserved, and so is the criticism.

The new code, like any other code, has two distinct aspects. Technically, reflecting the skills of its editors, *AACR2* is praiseworthy and leaves little to be desired. Ideologically, reflecting the disparate thoughts of the different members of the cataloging code revision committees that were responsible for the determination of its course, objectives, and principles, *AACR2* represents an attempted compromise of divergent views and ideas, and of political, technological, and ideological objectives, but a compromise unsusceptible to a coherent ideology based on the requirements of a sound catalog designed to serve the users of the library. And herein lies the essential difference between *AACR1* and *AACR2*—or, for that matter, between *AACR2* and all previous Anglo-American codes.

In fact, with the digressions from the fundamentals of traditional Anglo-American cataloging noted, what is there typically Anglo-Ameri-

can about *AACR2* any longer? *AACR2* began as a revision of *AACR1*
—a code of a defined character, of objectives susceptible to critical
evaluation, and of a respectable history—but ended up as a transformed
code that lacks the features, character, and integrity of *AACR1*, despite aberrations in some of its details. To implement *AACR2*, it was
suggested that our existing catalogs should be closed, with *AACR2* used
to begin new catalogs for a new era in cataloging. It is an incredible
vista. Should it come to pass, it will prove a grievous, historical, and
very costly mistake, and a dire setback to the progress of Anglo-American cataloging.

AACR2 and Automation

S. MICHAEL MALINCONICO

Other papers discuss the details and philosophy of the *Anglo-American
Cataloguing Rules,* second edition. I shall attempt to define the relationships that might exist between *AACR2* and computer-based technologies. The discussion will, as a consequence, ignore many advances
made by the new code which are unrelated to automation. We shall attempt to explore only the extent to which *AACR2* has succeeded in
incorporating modern technology into a set of prescriptions for bibliographic control. We shall recognize only the applications of that technology as we know them, or as we are likely to know them by 1981, and
so avoid indulging in solid-state fantasies.

   In the months that I have struggled with this paper I have found
myself repeatedly returning to the position that there is little causal relation between technology and cataloging principles. This seemed obvious
to me when I first started working on automated cataloging systems ten
years ago and first came across Seymour Lubetzky's writings. A decade
later it seems more obvious. There is, of course, a very pronounced cor-
relation between technology and the form and effectiveness of a library
catalog, and technology can either assist or hinder a transition from one

set of principles to another, but technological advances have not had, and cannot have, any influence on the principles on which bibliographic control is based. We can, of course, modify our basic objectives to articulate more smoothly with facilities made possible by advanced technologies, but this is better characterized as capitulation than as progress in harmony with a new ambience.

The objectives of bibliographic control and the functions to be served by a library catalog exist independently of the medium chosen to achieve those objectives. Computer technology, despite (or rather because of) its power and flexibility, is an enormously passive medium. Because of its flexibility, computer technology can be readily fashioned into a tool that can be used to achieve virtually any objective whose means we can clearly articulate. If a process is to be computerized, it must be very carefully analyzed and described in highly precise and unambiguous terms. In our analysis we may discover inconsistencies that we have long complacently accepted. We may discover within those procedures particular "sacred rituals" that contribute nothing toward the objectives they are intended to realize. This is all to the good. The discipline inherent in attempting to instruct an automaton to perform some particular function forces us to think more clearly about that function and about the ends we are seeking to achieve by performing it.

Less facetiously, there is a real danger. In our attempts to free a structure of its accretion of fortuitous circumstance we may find ourselves hacking away at its supports. This danger can be greately exacerbated by a euphoric sense of weightlessness. We can also run the risk of enhancing particularly attractive features of an edifice beyond the dictates of a sound sense of proportion or structural integrity.

Both metaphors probably apply to the recently completed exercise in the revision of the Anglo American Cataloging Rules. *AACR2* shows a greater coherence in its organization and design than does any previously created code. However, in an unsuccessful attempt to incorporate modern technology it also exhibits a perhaps unwarranted faith in a computer's ability to retrieve discrete items as a substitute for an automaton's lack of integrative abilities.

The new code has not managed to incorporate to any significant extent what has been loosely alluded to as "advances in the machine processing of bibliographic data." Michael Gorman, coeditor of *AACR2* and author of much of the seminal work on which its first part is based, has summarized the aims of the Joint Steering Committee for Revision of AACR. He enumerates these aims in order of complexity and achievement:

(1)   to incorporate already agreed revisions to AACR1;
(2)   to harmonize the British and North American texts of AACR1;
(3)   to incorporate international standards and international agreements;
(4)   to take developments in library automation into account; and
(5)   to incorporate changes arising from proposals for change coming from any source.[1]

Gorman then goes on to state: "The fourth aim cannot, in all frankness, be said to have been fully achieved."[2]

The reason why this aim was not fully achieved is not because of lack of ability or expertise of those who participated in the code revision process, or even because of a lack of general experience with automated bibliographic systems. The reason, quite simply, is because it was unrealistic to expect that automation would have any fundamental effect on a cataloging code. The effects of automation on bibliographic control will be made evident in the formats for machine representation of bibliographic data, and the nature of the systems implemented to manipulate those data, not in the codes developed to record and control bibliographic data. Computers will simply make it easier to accommodate principles that can only be developed in isolation from them; they cannot create new principles or modify existing principles. Despite the electronic *Tarnhelm* of automation, it seems unlikely that our technological *Nibelungen* will augment, modify, or otherwise gainsay the bibliographic principles articulated by Cutter and refined by Lubetzky. This is not meant to imply that those principles are immutable, only that they exist independently of any technology and hence cannot be modified by changes in technology.

AACR2 is not a major departure from *AACR1*. It primarily represents a more rational restatement of that code. In a sense, *AACR2* is not a new code; however, it is a different code. As such, it will result in dislocations in catalogs developed according to *AACR1* as interpreted by the particular practices of the Library of Congress. The extent of these dislocations has been estimated in various studies published by the Library of Congress. An initial study revealed that 37 percent of existing headings would require revision. If these changes were made, they would affect 49 percent of all cataloging records. This, clearly, was too great a dislocation for LC, or any other library without an automated authority

1. Michael Gorman, "The *Anglo-American Cataloguing Rules,* Second Edition," *Library Resources & Technical Services* 22 (Summer 1978): 209–210.
2. Ibid., p.210.

control system, to tolerate. Hence LC reexamined the *AACR2* options it would adopt; supported a proposal before the JSC to drop a prescription in the rules regarding the recording of the highest level in the hierarchy of corporate names; chose unilaterally to ignore certain other prescriptions in the rules; and chose to adopt a new, milder form of superimposition. The result was that the number of heading changes was reduced to 11 percent and the number of affected records to 15 percent.[3]

As might be expected, publication of a new code brings with it a sense that many of the nagging problems associated with the code it supplants have been solved and laid to rest. *AACR2* is not the first code that seemed to augur a bright new future for bibliographic control. The enormous preparation that went into the development of *AACR1* gave the same impression. Michael Gorman is quoted as saying of *AACR1*, "This is not only the best cataloging code we have, it is also the best we are likely to have for a very long time."[4]

Perforce, each new code brings with it some advance over the previous, superseded code. However, although it is fairly simple to revise errors in a code by publishing a new edition of it, one cannot so readily expunge the reflection of those errors in existing catalogs where a need for continuity will necessarily propagate them into the future. One important question that was not raised during the code revision process, and has not been satisfactorily answered since then, is whether substantial benefits result from *AACR2* to compensate for the dislocations (be they great or small) it will cause. The benefits with respect to automation seem not to be significant enough to serve as justification for the implementation of a new code.

There is, nonetheless, an important relationship between automation and *AACR2*. The relationship, however, is extrinsic to the code. The successes of automated bibliographic systems seem to indicate that new, more effective catalog forms will shortly be available to replace card catalogs. In order for these systems to operate effectively, and not be constrained by the inertia and problems of retrospective card catalogs, it seems desirable to close, or freeze, existing catalogs and start afresh. Thus it would appear desirable to synchronize both forms of

3. Library of Congress, "*AACR2* Impact" (mimeographed) (Washington: Library of Congress, 1978).

4. Quoted from the jacket of the British text by R. O. Linden in "Seminar on the Anglo-American Cataloging Rules (1967)," *Proceedings of the Seminar Organized by the Cataloging and Indexing Group of the Library Association at the University of Nottingham, 22–25 March 1965*, ed. J. C. Downing and N. F. Sharp (London: Library Assn., 1969).

dislocation—a new catalog form and a new cataloging code. In addition, the Library of Congress has found that its card catalogs are rapidly becoming virtually unmanageable and, hence, has found it necessary to freeze them and to attempt to start anew. For most of us who have become extremely dependent on the bibliographic products distributed by LC, this seems to portend yet another profound dislocation, which it would seem desirable to synchronize with those mentioned earlier.

The major flaw in this reasoning is an assumption that it will be possible to synchronize these three events. In fact, it is not! The official date on which LC will close its catalog is January 1, 1981. Other libraries, contemplating a similar move, are attempting to coordinate their plans to synchronize with this date. However, a close examination of the situation will reveal that LC actually began closing its card catalogs in 1968, and many other libraries did the same shortly after. At least, so matters will appear on January 2, 1981, at the Library of Congress. When LC starts its prospective catalog, it will not abandon the investment it has made in a MARC file it began building in 1968, which by 1981 will contain nearly 1.25 million records created under *AACR1*.

This store of bibliographic records presents an inertia that will transcend the implementation of a new cataloging code and a new catalog form. The effect of this inertia has already manifested itself in the decisions LC has made to ameliorate the impact of *AACR2*. Ironically, this inertia has even resulted in LC's decision to ignore certain provisions of *AACR2* which can be considered to be accommodations to the machine processing of bibliographic data. (We shall return to this point when we consider provisions of *AACR2* that can be attributed to automation.)

It would appear, in our zeal to hasten the future, that we are attempting to implement the future without making adequate preparation for it. It is obvious that bibliographic data in machine-readable form can far more easily be accessed, manipulated, modified, and reorganized than can bibliographic data inscribed on 3 by 5 inch unit cards. It is also obvious that bibliographic data in machine-readable form can serve as the basis for more effective catalog forms, be they in microform or online. However, are the facilities in place to realize either of these possibilities?

We indeed have the capability to create and manipulate individual cataloging records by computer. We have automated the process of creating and heading unit catalog cards that can be filed into card catalogs. We have effective online systems that permit access to discrete bibliographic records. We even have systems of limited sophistication that can create list-form catalogs with some semblance of a syndetic structure. However, with the exception of the New York Public Library and the Washington Library Network, systems have not yet been developed which can maintain a coherent catalog in machine-readable form with a controlled syndetic structure. Again, with the exception of the two systems just mentioned, we have not developed the systems that can permit the extensive modifications and reorganizations of existing data bases attendant to transition to a new cataloging code.

The most unfortunate aspect of *AACR2* is its timing. It would appear that, because automated authority control systems are feasible, and had even been implemented in some cases, the authors of *AACR2* perhaps had presupposed their general existence at the time of implementation of that code. Vision, confidence in the future, and optimism are laudable attributes; however, the line between optimism and delusion may not be overly broad.

Had adequate preparation been made—that is, had automated authority control systems been in place, particularly at the Library of Congress—the establishment of *AACR2* headings could have been carried out within the context of a coherent authority file. If machine-readable links are maintained between an authority file, within which *AACR2* headings are to be established, and the bibliographic file they are intended to organize, then the process of establishing new headings could be made identical with that of converting the retrospective file. That is, when an *AACR2* heading is to be established which is the analog of a previously established heading in the authority file, one would need to change only the existing heading rather than create a new one. If appropriate machine-interpretable links are maintained, each new heading of this kind would automatically convert the entire retrospective file. Had such systems been generally implemented before a transition to *AACR2*, any library, wishing to remain consistent with the Library of Congress, could do so simply by accepting the authority record corrections made by LC. A truly farsighted view would have sought to ensure that such facilities were in place before anyone began tampering with an imperfect code.

The foregoing approach would seem to have the deleterious effect of permitting headings that have been established according to different conventions to remain in a cataloging file for some time. However, under such a scheme the colocation function of at least the machine-readable catalog could be maintained while steady progress was made toward a uniform, consistent file. Obviously, the most organized approach would be to use the facilities of a linked authority system, which permits global changes to be made in a catalog, to make all of the necessary changes prior to implementation of a new code. This too would have been possible if a central agency, such as LC, undertook the task and issued all of its changes in the form of revised authority records.

The consequences of the first, admittedly somewhat awkward approach seem to be more desirable than the options that are left by a premature implementation of a new cataloging code. A realistic view of the situation would reveal that pitifully few institutions have the facilities in place that will permit them to make a transition to an alternative catalog form simultaneously with conversion to a new code. Spurious arguments about the pressing need for international cooperation aside, the not-too-distant future, when these facilities were in place, would have been the time for a new code.

Only a limited number of mutually exclusive choices will be open to most libraries in the United States when they implement *AACR2* in 1981. Clearly, they can choose to close their existing card catalogs or they can choose not to. If they choose the former, they again have two choices: (1) they can elect to make the new catalog entirely consistent only within itself or (2) they can choose to make it consistent with an existing catalog. It is clear that libraries with catalogs of any appreciable size cannot elect to follow the latter option by modifying an existing catalog to make it consistent with the new. Nor would it appear sensible to attempt to make a prospective catalog consistent with an existing catalog, as this contradicts the basic premise: it is necessary to close a catalog. Thus the only viable choice is to make the new catalog entirely consistent within itself, whether or not linking references are provided.

This, then, brings us to our second major choice: electing not to close catalogs. Here again we have both of the former subchoices, plus a third. (1) We can choose to make all new entries consistent with an existing catalog; (2) we could attempt to modify the existing catalog as necessary to make it consistent with new entries integrated into it; or (3) we could simply interfile new entries without giving any thought to consistency. The first subchoice—making all new entries consistent with an existing catalog—is moot, as it contradicts the basic premise that a new code was needed. The second subchoice—modifying an existing catalog to be consistent with new entries—is in all but rare instances totally impractical. This, then, leaves the third choice: interfiling without imposing consistency. This, however, is only a disorganized variant of the only viable option we have left after we choose to close existing catalogs, that is, making all new entries consistent only among themselves.

Thus it appears that, by whatever approach, we come to a single conclusion: If we are to implement *AACR2* effectively, we will need to make all new entries consistent only among themselves. Obviously, this can best be done by starting a new catalog and a new authority file.

Thus far the logic seems sound. With a bit of courage, we might permit reality to intrude into our ruminations. Few libraries have the automated facilities needed to implement a new catalog form; however, a great many libraries *do* have facilities, which they have come to find indispensable, that produce catalog cards. The major problem with card production systems is that they treat each cataloging record in isolation from the rest of the data base. That is, they are, in a sense, reflections of the limitations of card catalogs; they make very effective provision for the modification of individual records, if we wish to make them consistent with an existing data base, but they do not treat the opposite condition, in which it becomes necessary to restructure an existing data base to make it consistent with a new record which reveals a new and different practice.

Thus whatever choice is made by the vast majority of libraries that employ automated systems, they will necessarily create inconsistent data bases which may prove too troublesome to reconcile, when, eventually, they will have the facilities necessary to use them as the bases for alternative catalog forms. It has been advocated that temporary card catalogs be established until a complete transition can be made to a new catalog form, but this, obviously, will only serve to aggravate the problem. In fact, with the limited automated facilities available to us, the recommendation that we close card catalogs simultaneously with implementation of *AACR2* actually carries an implied suggestion that we close our retrospective machine-readable files as well. This may be a blessing in disguise. However, one might wish that the self-proclaimed architects of our bibliographic future would have been less cavalier with the enormous investment we have made (collectively) in these files.

This is not meant to imply that no accommodations are made in *AACR2* to the requirements of automated system. These provisions are most evident in that code's preoccupation with computer filing. The guiding principle behind the filing provisions in *AACR2* derives from one of the fundamental tenets of the filing rules developed by John Rather of the Library of Congress. The first published version of these filing rules indicates that their "first principle emphasizes the way a heading looks. These rules allow for only a few exceptions to the 'file-as-is' principle."[5]

---

5. John Rather, "Filing Arrangement in the Library of Congress Catalogs: An Operational Document" (provisional version) (Washington: Library of Congress, March 1971), p.vii. Abridged version published in *Library Resources & Technical Services* 16 (Spring 1972): 240–61).

Such a principle is very much in harmony with computer processes. A computer treats data in a sublimely literal manner. Each character or combination of characters, processed by a computer, is totally devoid of any meaning; hence a filing principle which prescribes that strings of characters be treated literally will obviously facilitate computer filing. In *AACR2* there is a systematic attempt to cast headings in a form which makes their filing readily apparent. The resulting headings, however, might appear somewhat odd to a human, for example:

> *United States Navy Fleet, 6th*
> *United States. Congress (87th : ...)*
> *World Peace Congress (1st : ...)*
> *Piano (2), 8 hands*

Tortured creations, such as

> *Cantata, sopranos (2), altos (2), orchestra ...*

might even evoke a smile. Nonetheless, such headings help ensure that they will be filed correctly by a computer without manual intervention. However, the amount of manual intervention required to file each of these headings correctly hardly seems a worthy cause for consternation. The New York Public Library has cataloged over 900,000 titles with its automated system, and an occasional manual filing form has caused no appreciable stir among the NYPL cataloging staffs.

The manner in which conference headings are established in *AACR2* has also been changed, presumably to facilitate their filing by computer. Under *AACR1* we would have had

> *International Geological Conference, 15th, Pretoria, etc., 1929*

Under *AACR2* we have

> *International Geological Conference (15th : 1929 : Pretoria, etc.)*

The obvious difference is the order in which place, number, and date are recorded. There is, however, a more subtle difference: the entire qualifying statement is enclosed in parentheses and the individual elements within the qualifying statement are separated by consistent punctuation (in this case a colon).

In general, *AACR2* is very consistent in this respect. All qualifiers are enclosed in parentheses, and elements within a qualifier are separated by consistent punctuation. However, one is left wondering whether this was not a solution in search of a problem. It would appear that the filing problems of numbered units could have been more effectively solved by data formats for machine-readable data. Punctuation, no matter how standardized, is hardly as effective for machine manipulation as explicit content designators. In fact, the MARC format has provisions for delimiters that explicitly identify number, place, and date of a conference name. Hence adequate facilities already exist in the MARC format to permit these data to be manipulated for filing purposes, a problem which *AACR2* has solved *de novo*. The net effect is that we now have redundant identification of the various qualifying elements associated with a conference name when represented in machine-readable form. Nonetheless, the order in which the elements of such heading are presented is of some value in making readily apparent to a user how a particular heading is arranged in a catalog.

Abbreviations in headings have always posed a filing problem for automated systems. The Library of Congress, early in its experience with MARC, began to drop abbreviations in headings when it found itself unable to develop the algorithms necessary to file them correctly. Among the earliest abbreviations to be dropped by LC were *U.S.* and *Gt. Brit. AACR2,* in order to avoid similar problems, has attempted, whenever possible, to avoid using abbreviations in headings. In general, *AACR2* sanctions only those abbreviations that are an integral part of a heading; otherwise they are not permitted. Thus England, Ireland, Scotland, and Germany will no longer be represented by *Eng., Ire., Scot., or Ger.* In addition, the abbreviation *Dept.* for department will no longer be used. However, LC will continue to use *Dept.* because of the number of headings that would be affected if it were to adopt this proscription of *AACR2*. This turn of events is particularly ironic. One can see very good reasons for dispensing with abbreviations such as *Dept.* in the context of an automated system; the irony is that LC has chosen, nonetheless, to continue using it because it appears too frequently in its MARC file: a machine-readable cataloging data base for which the proscription was intended.

To say that *AACR2* is unblemished by constraints of automated systems would also be far from the truth. I assume there is some good reason for modification of *AACR1* rule 66A, which prescribed that initial articles in corporate names were to be retained if they were required for reasons of grammar or *clarity*. *AACR2* rule 24.5A prescribes that initial articles should be retained only if they are required for grammatical reasons. The humble request that they be retained if needed for clarity has been dropped. Perhaps, in the opinion of the designers of

AACR2, a decision based on "reasons of clarity" was too subjective to entrust to the fallible judgment of catalogers. I would guess that the constraints of the LC MARC format, which makes no provision for the suppression of initial articles when filing, may have played at least an equal role.

Influences of automation can also be found in *AACR2* in more subtle ways. As a consequence of a desire to ensure uniformity of description and bibliographic record creation, *AACR2* places greater emphasis than *AACR1* on the concrete, physical entity-in-hand at the time of cataloging. However, this may also be due to the requirement of an automated system whose processes deal best with precisely defined items, and the inability of computing devices to deal with ephemeral relationships and abstractions. It may also be a consequence of a not unwarranted expectation that a computer can easily maintain explicit relationships among particular discrete items in lieu of relating them via an abstraction extrinsic to any particular item. The result seems to be an attempt to reduce cataloging judgment (whenever possible) to precise, mechanical decisions, and whenever possible prescriptions in *AACR2* have attempted to free themselves from dependency on context. When context must be acknowledged, it is done in very precise terms that can be programmed into a mechanical intelligence if necessary.

Whenever possible, prescriptions in *AACR1* which required the exercise of qualitative judgment have been made more stringent and mechanical in nature, or eliminated entirely. For example, whereas *AACR1* would have permitted one to ignore "slight changes," *AACR2* is in general more strict about the treatment of changes. This is very much in keeping with the intrinsic nature of computer logic. Computer processes will acknowledge a change of state with even the most minute provocation. Simple, binary decisions are made quite readily by a computer. On the other hand, more complex decisions, permitting a margin for tolerance, can become hopelessly complicated. Anyone who has attempted to program a computer to seek out a particular condition, say a search for all records containing "US," and has neglected to include in his search explicit mention that *U*-space-*S*, and *U*-period-*S*-period, or *U*-period-space *S*-period-space, etc., are also acceptable, will immediately recognize the inspiration for these more stringent prescriptions.

An example of this tendency can be found in the *AACR2* rule that governs the treatment of name changes, 24.1B, which replaces rule 68 of *AACR1.* The new rule is almost identical with the old. The only change seems to be the elimination of superfluous verbiage and a footnote. The footnote, no doubt, was thought to be too permissive. It suggested that if the change is so slight that the distinction between the names might be easily confused in citations or escape notice by users of the catalog, it may be preferable to enter all publications under the later form of name with a reference from the former.

Perhaps the point is that even though the distinction might escape the notice of a catalog user or be confused in citations, it is certain that it will not escape the notice of a computer's sublimely punctilious logic, nor is a computer apt to be "confused" by names that differ in only a very minute detail.

Of course, both forms of name will be connected with a "see also" reference. We can expect that, some time in the future, this network of relationships will be machine interpretable and, hence, will permit catalog access with unprecedented flexibility. But will such facilities be in place by 1981? It does not seem likely. Perhaps, however, the new code will serve to spur their development. If this is so, the trauma associated with *AACR2* will have been worth it. But must we take such drastic measures to facilitate progress? Is it really necessary to intensify an irritant before we seek a balm for it?

Perhaps a more obvious example of the faith vested by *AACR2* in a computer's ability to create a logical whole from fragmented parts can be found in the treatment accorded to uniform titles. Uniform titles represent abstractions; as such, they are anathema to a mechanical intelligence. Although *AACR2* makes more liberal use of this artifice than *AACR1*, it does so in a more controlled, concrete manner. An assiduous attempt is made to divorce prescriptions for uniform titles from any considerations deriving from context. The nature or content of any particular catalog is not a consideration in chapter 25 of *AACR2*. This is clearly an advantage if we are to exercise uniform control of bibliographic materials rather than simply the limited collection of a single library. However, chapter 25 also seems to attempt to limit even those influences of context which transcend particular catalogs.

Problems of context have been obviated by reducing the decision whether a uniform title is made a subordinate element of the title of a larger work to whether or not a part of a work has a distinctive title of its own. Ron Hagler has pointed out that *AACR1* rule 106A1 "had required the title of most parts to be cited in a uniform title as a subheading of the title of the whole."[6] *AACR2* requires uniform titles for parts of works to be established more frequently as independent entities.

6. Ronald Hagler, *"Where's That Rule?"* (Ottawa: Canadian Library Assn., 1979), p.114.

Presumably, the ability of computers to maintain machine-readable links among discrete entities, and hence reconstruct in this way the whole from its various parts, would be the solution to the problem posed by fragmentation. Without undue fear of contradiction, we can place our faith in the ability of computers to create and maintain such links. This ability has been demonstrated in systems developed as long ago as 1972 by the New York Public Library, and more recently by the Washington Library Network. But can we be sanguine that it will be generally available by the beginning of 1981 or, more specifically, that such a facility will be operational at critical centers such as the Library of Congress or the major bibliographic utilities? At least for the Library of Congress, it does not appear likely. One can only regret that nearly a decade of talk, and ostensibly work, on an automated authority control system at the Library of Congress has brought forth little more than a defective authority record distribution service.

AACR2's reliance on the syndetic structure of a catalog, and by association on a computer's ability to maintain and manipulate such a structure, might be interpreted as incorporating into a cataloging code advances made possible by automation. But is this really so? It would appear that fragmenting, just for the sake of being able to synthesize by machine, is somewhat akin to circular reasoning. Our existing bibliographic and subject analysis codes already provide more than adequate justification for such a facility.

Mainly for the sake of completeness, we should cite the most obvious example of *AACR2*'s presupposition of the existence of systems for automated control of a catalog's syndetic structure. As we all know, *AACR2* makes far more liberal provision for the use of pseudonyms as forms of entry than *AACR1* recognized formally. Thus if an author identifies himself in his works with several noms-de-plume, and none of them can be judged to be predominant, those works will be entered under the names appearing in them. I have intentionally distorted the language in the pertinent *AACR2* rule, 22.2C3, which does *not* speak of the entry of works; it merely refers to the manner in which *items* are to be treated. Perhaps the authors of the code were too self-conscious to speak of *works*. The following rule, 22.2C4, does make provision to avoid the scattering of editions of a work when they appear under different names; however, it is silent on the question of translations.

The various forms of an author's name can, of course, be related by a network of references. But it would appear that exactly the same amount of research will be necessary to develop this as would be required to establish an author under a single form of name. Thus the only advantage to the cataloger seems to be the greater stability of the heading. This seems an odd distortion of reality. The greatest advantage of *existing* automated systems is the ease with which they permit records to be modified; so why a preoccupation with the stability of headings? On the other hand, none of our existing systems provides the public catalog access facilities that seem to be taken for granted in *AACR2*.

In the case of pseudonymous authors, one can make a good argument for the wisdom of the prescriptions in *AACR2*. The problems of pseudonyms arise primarily in fiction, which is by and large the province of public libraries. Catalogers who work in such an environment must make provision both for readers who use the catalog and those who do not. Those who bypass the catalog and go directly to the shelves will find the material they are seeking only if it is arranged by some "Cuttering" device. Cross-references are scarcely a useful device. In general, these readers seek a novel that is cited in the popular media; they do not seem concerned with bibliographic research. Thus when they go to the place on the shelves where they expect to find Jean Plaidy's novels, they expect to see a whole array of them, not an obscure dummy book.

Perhaps the greatest fanfare surrounding the code revision process came from reports that proclaimed excitedly that the main entry was moribund. It was, and still is, difficult to interpret these reports, as there are at least two entities to which the term *main entry* might refer. The first, enshrined in the ALA glossary, refers to a unit card, or that single catalog entry which contains all the bibliographic detail concerning an item that we will include in a catalog; the second is a more abstract and useful concept, given its most precise definition by Professor Lubetzky. Quite simply, *it is the name we assign to a work*. This *name*, like any other, contains two elements: the first indicates the genesis of the thing named, that is, the agent responsible for its intellectual content, and the second identifies a particular issue of the agent that is responsible for the entity named, which serves to distinguish it from all others.

The concept of main entry as a unit card, duplicated and filed under all of its access elements, has little meaning in a computer-based cataloging system. However, the concept of main entry as the name of a work, being quite independent of any particular physical medium or technology, is not a concept that can be gainsaid by automation. Bibliographic relations, maintained in a catalog, do not refer to particular books. In general they refer to a larger abstract entity of which a particular book is only a single manifestation. Just as references in any formal context to persons are generally not made with particular sobriquets by which that person may have been known, they are made, rather, to his or her full name. It has been suggested that the concept of a single name for a work could be replaced by a complex of links among its various manifestations; but if this network of links is to be controlled, a focus, or center, must be provided for it. If we do this, we have only reinvented the concept of main entry under a different guise; if we do not, we will have, at best, a difficult time making decisions to incorporate additional manifestations of the unnamed entity into the network of relationships that defines it. The problem is ontological, not mechanical; hence its solution is not likely to vary with technology.

If we ignore the nature of the relationships that must be maintained, for whatever reason, within a catalog, it might appear that we could grant that in a multiple access file main entry is not an important concept. But even this position is not tenable. A catalog must exist in a larger world of scholarship and library use. A citation in one work, referencing another, must be able to name its referent. Until such time that we can expect all libraries and other suppliers of books (for example booksellers) will have their entire inventory accessible through an interactive system, bibliographers will continue to need to supply an unambiguous name for a work which can transcend its physical manifestations. Even if the named facilities were ubiquitous, we would need to tackle the problem of assuring a reader who comes upon two or more superficially different citations that the citations are indeed for the same work and, hence, he or she need not bother to search the catalog or a library's collections again.

Because of the difficulties inherent in applying rules relating to corporate authorship, and because of the oft-heralded ability of computers to retrieve a record by any of its access elements, *AACR2,* rather than attempting to solve the problem of corporate authorship, simply abandoned the entire concept. As a consequence, the vast majority of serials and series will now be entered under title. This immediately raises the problem of creating relationships among them, since the bibliographic name assigned to them will, in the overwhelming majority of cases, be ambiguous. The Library of Congress, which was one of the forceful proponents of title entry, discovered the problem after the code was finalized, and is now exploring several solutions. It is interesting that a code as logically constructed as *AACR2* contains no specific guidance on the matter of series added entries. Among the more creative solutions proposed by the Library of Congress is a recommendation that series tracings be constructed from title proper, qualified by statement of responsibility expressed in catalog entry form. Thus in lieu of corporate author main entry we will have a title/responsible agency statement, which to the untutored mind must seem remarkably similar to an author main entry.

I have saved for last the one aspect of *AACR2* which has often been represented as of major utility in the context of automated bibliographic systems—that is, the conscious attempt in *AACR2* to separate description of an item from the manner in which that description will be organized in a catalog. If, and when, automated authority control systems become generally available, this feature of *AACR2* will, no doubt, prove extremely useful. With its authority control system, the New York Public Library can change the form of a heading throughout an entire catalog with only a very simple transaction. The NYPL can in this manner completely reorganize a catalog. The only flaw in the scheme exists when such a change alters a form of main entry to something different from that which appeared on the title page of a book when it was originally cataloged. Thus we can be left with the situation, following a change made by an authority system, in which the relationship between the main entry heading and a particular bibliographic record is no longer readily apparent. *AACR2* obviated this problem by always requiring that a statement of responsibility be transcribed following the title proper. However, unless a more elaborate structure is built into the MARC format, this provision of *AACR2* will create a situation in which the title of a work can be completely obscured in a catalog display by a virtually identical statement of responsibility preceding and succeeding it. Nonetheless, it would appear that these problems can be solved, and the general idea of capturing all data that one will need for a bibliographic record with one handling of a book will prove to be an advantage when cataloging systems that incorporate automated authority control are generally implemented.

In conclusion, though we can find some traces of the influence of automation in *AACR2,* none of them seems to represent a major philosophical departure from the previous code. The one attempt at a major philosophical departure—abandonment of corporate authorship in favor of title entry—has already revealed major problems that cannot easily be rectified by existing automated systems. It is somewhat regrettable that the automated facilities on which *AACR2* would have relied are not in place, nor can they be expected to be in place when it is implemented. It is even more regrettable that adequate automated facilities that would have assisted us in making the transition to this code also will not be in place by 1981, thus placing in jeopardy enormous investments already made in machine-readable bibliographic files.

AACR2 may be a justification for automation, but it does not appear that automation can be a justification for *AACR2*.

AACR2: Main Themes

MICHAEL GORMAN

I have already published a general overview of the second edition of *Anglo-American Cataloguing Rules*[1] and so will not recapitulate the general observations I made there. Rather, I wish in this part of my paper to treat three main themes or major aspects of the second edition. By way of preface, I would like to state that this is truly a second edition of the *Rules* and not a completely new code of rules. Though the differences between the two editions are superficially great, they are, in many respects, differences in presentation and style rather than in substance or in ultimate results of the cataloging process. Mr. Malinconico in his earlier paper quoted me as writing (in 1968) that "this [*AACR*] is the best code we have or are likely to have." Maliniconico, as one of the leading opponents of *AACR2*, is trying to show that at least one of those who was responsible for *AACR2* has changed his mind on *AACR* and, by inference, is not to be trusted in his evaluation of *AACR2*. However, I still regard my observation valid, as I believe that the first edition of *AACR* and *AACR2* are manifestations of the same work.

One of the major aims of those responsible for *AACR2* was to "clean up" and make clearer some of the aspects of *AACR1* which seemed to all unbiased students to be anomalous or irregular. Viewed in this light, *AACR2* should be judged not just on its own merits but also as part of a continuum, as part of the "great tradition" in Anglo-American cataloging which stretches back to Panizzi, Jewett, and Cutter. Those who attack *AACR2* often ignore its place in that tradition by focusing on the supposed problems of this day and age, or misrepresent that tradition by contrasting the letter of, say, Cutter's rules with *AACR2* while ignoring the unity of spirit which animates those sets of rules and their predecessors and successors. Blinkered views of cataloging and petty legalism are common phenomena at all times, but in retrospect one finds that the broader vision prevails and carping critics are soon for-

---

1. Michael Gorman, "The *Anglo-American Cataloguing Rules,* Second Edition," *Library Resources & Technical Services* 22 (Summer 1978): 209–26.

gotten. Who now remembers the contemporary critics of Panizzi's rules, or Cutter's rules, or Lubetzky's great work? The first of my main themes is the integrated approach to the descriptive and author/title cataloging of all library materials. *AACR2* has picked up the beginnings of an integrated approach which can be found in *AACR1* and has, in my estimation, made a major breakthrough in that it provides rules for all materials that are not only detailed enough for the cataloging of each type for a general catalog but also provide a commonality of approach which enables entries for each and every type to coexist in the same catalog or data base. It is worth emphasizing that (in the words of the general introduction to *AACR2*) "these rules are designed for use . . . in general libraries of all sizes. They are not specifically intended for specialist and archival libraries." The rules are intended for use in general catalogs in general libraries. Archival collections of, say, manuscripts or motion pictures will require more detailed and more or different access points than those provided in *AACR2*, though there seems to be no good reason why the provisions of *AACR2* should not be taken as the starting point for such specialist cataloging. *AACR2*, then, must be viewed as a generalist code; as such, it has built upon the beginnings made in *AACR1* with a considerable degree of success. In studying the integrated nature of *AACR2*, we need to consider the descriptive element and the access points separately.

One of the fundamental concepts of *AACR2* is that the cataloging process is viewed as one in which the cataloger establishes a standard description of the physical object (the book, videorecording, map, etc.), using clues derived from that physical object, and then establishes the access points (headings and uniform titles), which not only provide access to the standard description but relate that description to the work of which it is a manifestation. The descriptive process is concerned with the object in hand; the assignment of access points is concerned with the work. The crucial distinction has led to the symbolism of putting the descriptive part before the access-point part of *AACR2*. That descriptive part (chapters 1–13) is based upon the ISBD(G),[2] which was drawn up by the Joint Steering Committee for Revision of AACR (JSC) and the Committee on Cataloguing of the International Federation of Library Associations (IFLA). This formula for all international descriptive cataloging was a direct result of the policy decision that was made for *AACR2*: all library materials would receive equal and consistent treatment in its descriptive rules. The ISBD(G) provides a framework for all

---

2. *ISBD(G): General International Standard Bibliographic Description* (London: IFLA Office for UBC, 1977).

descriptive cataloging in that it assigns an order to all the descriptive elements of a catalog entry and provides a consistent pattern of punctuation to delimit those elements.

I shall discuss some details of the ISBD(G) later in this paper, and will content myself here by observing that such an impartial framework is a necessary precondition for rules which deal even-handedly with all library materials. It made the general chapter/special chapters structure of Part I of *AACR2* possible and is, in my view, a triumphant reinforcement of the idea that the best practice comes from the best and most-thought-out principles.

The integrated approach to all library materials, as far as author and title access points are concerned, hinges upon the concepts of authorship and the work as an abstract entity with physical manifestations. The "general" rules on headings and uniform titles in *AACR1* (chapters 1–5) are dominated by ideas which stemmed from book cataloging. In a highly revealing introductory note to Part III of *AACR1* ("Nonbook Materials"), the following statement is made: "The rules for entry [and] heading . . . for books and book-like materials . . . apply also in the cataloguing of non-book materials . . . to the extent that they are pertinent and unless they are specifically contravened or modified by the rules in the following chapters." Thus one can see a simultaneous reaching for common principles underlying author/title access points and a fear that some of those principles will not apply to some types of material. In chapter 12 of *AACR1*, films are flatly and unequivocally to be entered under title, and chapter 10 of *AACR1* allows for the entry of manuscript collections under the person, family, or corporate body around which the collection is formed. Thus in these and other instances one can see that the general principles adumbrated in Part I of *AACR1* are not applied in all cases. *AACR2* has attempted to get away from the limiting ideas of "book authorship" which have to be modified for other materials and to achieve a general application of truly general principles to all materials.

Before I examine the application to some specific types of material, it is worth pointing out that in *AACR2* "authorship" applies only to persons. The idea of "corporate authorship," with its glittering and delusive attraction embodied in Cutter's rule 45 ("Bodies of men are to be considered as authors of works published in their name or by their authority") and *AACR1*'s rule 1 ("Enter a work . . . under the person or corporate body that is the author"), has been abandoned in favor of a more restrictive notion of corporate responsibility. Even Cutter's definition of corporate authorship is less than comprehensive (see pages 39–41 of his *Rules for a Dictionary Catalog,* 4th ed.), and he quotes a contemporary as describing corporate authorship as a "library superstition." Also, Panizzi's *Rules* restricts corporate main entry to some special cases (see rule 4 of the British Museum *Rules, 1936*). Even those who wish to restrict cataloging theory to a fundamentalist poring over the sacred texts can find evidence to support the view that *AACR1* and one or two other codes are aberrant in treating corporate authorship as a principle equal to personal authorship. The restriction of corporate main entry to the five classes set out in *AACR2* rule 21.1B2 is helpful in clarifying cataloging practice and in the application of rules for main entry to all library materials.

The rules in chapter 21 ("Choice of Access Points") of *AACR2* apply to all types of library material. For example, the provisions of rule 21.4A (which deals with personal authorship) are illustrated by a filmstrip, a set of slides, and a sound recording by a jazz pianist (among others). This last example is especially indicative in that the pianist (Earl Hines) is undoubtedly the person "chiefly responsible for the creation of . . . artistic content" of the recording and receives main entry in the same way and for the same reasons that one enters *Moby Dick* under the heading for Melville.

There is no example of a motion picture appended to rule 21.4A, but one can easily imagine such an individually produced item. This is not to say that the *auteur* theory of French film criticism should be extended to provide main entry under the director, but merely to point out that a motion picture for which one person is chiefly intellectually or artistically responsible is not inconceivable, and that in such a case main entry would be under the name of the person responsible. The reason why the vast majority of motion pictures will continue to be entered under title is not because motion pictures are different but because the authorship is "diffuse" (is shared by a number of persons who perform different functions).

Another interesting application of the general principles of authorship in *AACR2* is that of the rules for sound recordings (general rules 21.1–21.7 and specific rule 21.23). Sound recordings can be divided into two classes: those in which performers execute the work of authors (writers or composers) and those in which the performers are, to a greater or lesser extent, responsible for the artistic content of the recording. At one extreme one has, for example, a recording of James' *Turn of the Screw,* read by Sir Michael Redgrave—a clear case of single authorship in which the performance is secondary to the writing of the original work. At the other extreme, one has a sound recording of extemporaneous performances by a "traditional" jazz band—in this case the band is clearly responsible for the artistic content of the recording (see *AACR2,* rule 21.1B2). In between lie numerous complicated examples which are difficult to resolve. A practical solution, which is in agreement with the general principles of authorship, is found in *AACR2* rule 21.23.

These problems raise another interesting question of principle. Are performing groups (jazz bands, rock groups, improvisatory dance groups, etc.) that are responsible for the works they create "authors"? If they are, they cannot, by definition, be corporate bodies, because *AACR2* specifically escrews the idea of "corporate authorship." I believe that, in providing an integrated approach to the application of authorship, *AACR2* has hit upon, but not named, a different kind of authorship which is somewhere between personal authorship and corporate responsibility. I tentatively offer the term "collective personal authorship" to describe this condition.

The second of my main themes is the main entry concept. For two quite different reasons, a determined attempt was made during the construction of *AACR2* to do away with the main entry idea. The first reason appeared to be an attempt to provide a justification for the register index type of union catalog.[3] The second reason was the belief (held by many) that the main entry is an idea which has been overtaken by technology. The first reason was, at best, oblique; the second reason is rather more considerable. Put at its simplest, in an online catalog, where any access point gives equal access to bibliographic information, what is the point of the main entry? Even in a card catalog that uses alternative heading entries, what is the point of the main entry?

I wish to make two preliminary points on this issue. First, I know that Professor Lubetzky, the greatest Anglo-American cataloging theorist of this century, does not agree with the notion of doing away with the main entry. It gives me no pleasure to disagree with him, and I would like to advance the view that the important functions of the main entry can be carried out in a no-main-entry catalog or data base. In other words, the idea of doing away with main entry rules does not mean that the useful functions that the main entry performs will also be done away with. My second preliminary point is that the notion of doing away

---

3. As far as *NUC* is concerned, it was proposed that the *full* entries in *NUC* be arranged in a nonsignificant numerical order, and that access to the records arranged in that "idiot" order would be by way of author, title, etc., indexes. The result would be a register index. The obvious economy is that only the indexes would need to be cumulated and the individual full items would not need cumulation. In some persons' minds (not mine) this idea (which I do not agree with anyway) made headings unnecessary and brought forth the idea of the so-called title unit entry.

with author main entry does not imply replacing it with title main entries. This harmful proposition has obscured much of the argument
about main entries.

In my view, what should be proposed, and what fits the emerging
realities of the machine-readable cataloging age, is that the catalog record should be viewed as, first, a kernel standard bibliographic description, based on the physical object, and second, a number of appropriate
and equal access points derived by considering the authorship of, and/or
responsibility for, the work of which the physical objects are manifestations united by the standard title (or the uniform title). In other words,
for general purposes, all entries will be main entries.

There are, of course, numerous subsidiary functions which the main
entry performs. Some of these are useful, for example, furnishing a focus
point for subject entries and related work entries. Some of these functions are not entirely useful, for example, use of the main entry to construct "Cutter" numbers and use of the main entry to subarrange subject
and added entry files. Each of these functions should be reconsidered
and ways to meet those which are considered useful should be found.
For example, it would be simple to attach a rule to a no-main-entry
code that would say what one is to do in cases where one has to make
subject entries for a work or related work entries. Then the cataloging
of the more than 99 percent of works which do not need such entries
would not be confused by a rule which would apply to less than 1 percent. Such a code would meet all the classical aims of author/title cataloging in that all the records relating to one work or to the works of one
author would be collocated, without inhibiting other access or the other
aims of catalogs. For the first time, the first two sets of Cutter's objects[4]
would be met equally, without—as has happened in the past—the second set being achieved at the expense of the first. *AACR2* contains
main entry rules (in chapter 21) because the arguments against them
were confused and confusing. An echo of those arguments can be found
in the statement in the general introduction: "It is recognized, however,
that many libraries do not distinguish between the main entry and other
entries. It is recommended that such libraries use chapter 21 as guidance
in determining all the entries required in particular instances." Thus, in
my view, the inevitable abandonment of main entry is foreshadowed in
what may be the last main entry–based set of cataloging rules.

My third main theme is style and presentation of *AACR2*. Probably the most noticeable change between the two editions of *AACR* lies

---

4. Charles A. Cutter, *Rules for a Dictionary Catalog* (4th ed.; Washington:
Government Printing Office, 1904), p.12.

in the wording, order, and method of construction of the rules. I believe that some have been misled by these differences into assuming that similarly large changes in *substance* exist between the two editions. Changes in substance should, of course, be judged by the results which the rules achieve rather than by their form. Too little attention has been paid to the form of cataloging rules and, I believe that this inattention has been unfortunate for a number of reasons. It is a well-established fact that if a rule is expressed in a confusing manner, different catalogers will come up with different results, and as cataloging rules are increasingly used in cooperative ventures, such inconsistency in application is increasingly undesirable. Cataloging rules are not written by lawyers but are often subjected to legalistic scrutiny, and such scrutiny yields the most diverse results when the rules are long, complex, and clotted with redundant verbiage. Cutter asked for "plain rules" plainly expressed. It is unfortunate that only Lubetzky's draft rules[5] (which were, of course, never used widely in practical library cataloging) approached Cutter's ideal. Instead, in our cataloging rules we find complex rules expressed in seemingly endless sentences constructed upon neo-Teutonic lines. These almost Jamesian rules (with none of James' elegancies) have proved to be a burden to the student, a trial to the cataloger, and a menace to shared cataloging.

Another problem in the presentation of rules has been the presence (or absence) of examples or their aptness (or inaptness). Examples abound where they are not needed, have been herded together to illustrate related but different rules, and have exemplified outdated or rare conditions at the expense of the up-to-date and the relevant.

A final problem concerning the presentation of Anglo-American cataloging rules has been the differing uses of English in North America and the United Kingdom. Since it was determined at an early stage that *AACR2* was to exist only in a single text, this problem loomed rather larger than it did in the previous edition.

How has *AACR2* attempted to resolve these various problems? The first answer lies in the style in which *AACR2* is written. A basic editorial rule was that all the rules be written in the imperative mode (rather than in a mixture of the imperative and the passive, as in *AACR1*), and that they be written in short sentences within short paragraphs. An example of this change in style is the rules for the dimensions of a book:

---

5. Seymour Lubetzky, *Code of Cataloguing Rules: Author and Title Entry* (Chicago: American Library Assn., 1960).

AACR1. Chapter 6, revised.
141E1. The height of the work [*sic*] is given in centimeters, exact to within one centimeter, fractions of a centimeter being counted as a full centimeter. For example, a work [*sic*] which measures 17.2 centimeters is described as 18 cm. Miniature books, those ten centimeters or less in height, are described in millimeters, exact to the nearest millimeter. In describing bound volumes, the height of the binding is measured. In describing the height of a pamphlet inserted into a binder, the height of the pamphlet is given.

AACR2. Chapter 2.
2.5D1. Give the height of the volume(s) in centimetres, to the next whole centimetre up (e.g., if a volume measures 17.2 centimetres, record it as 18 cm.). Measure the height of the binding if the volume is bound. Otherwise, measure the height of the item itself. If the volume measures less than 10 centimetres, give the height in millimetres.

Thus we see that not only is the *AACR2* rule shorter (57 words instead of 83), without any loss of information, but its instructions are more direct and therefore more comprehensible. One problem which resulted from writing the rules imperatively lay in the treatment of options. In *AACR1,* such options could be contained in, and to a certain extent hidden by, the passive sentence structure. The approach that was chosen for *AACR2* is that of preceding an optional rule with *optional addition* or *alternative rule* and then stating the rule imperatively. Parts of rules embodying an option are stated imperatively and preceded by the word *optionally.* I believe that this solution, though it preserves the simple and direct structure of the rules, has led to misapprehension by some that *AACR2* contains a vastly increased number of options, which is not so.

An effect of the decision to write the rules in short' paragraphs is that the examples are associated more directly with the rules to which they pertain. This is an important aspect of the rules because the understanding of an individual instruction can be made much greater if that instruction is directly linked to pertinent and illuminating examples. A deliberate attempt has been made in *AACR2* to increase the quantity of examples and to raise their quality in at least two respects. There are certainly more examples, and a signal example occurs in the rules for recording the titles and statements of responsibility of books, where chapter 1 of *AACR1* (rules 133–134) had relatively few examples but chapter 2 (rule 2.1) of *AACR2* contains at least three times as many. The two major respects in which *AACR2* has sought to improve the examples are, first, that each section of the rules be exemplified in an equal manner and, second, that the examples be current and relevant. The equality of exemplification has been achieved by ensuring that all rules receive examples and that those examples cover all of the major points raised by the rule. The selection of more examples from nonprint materials and the deliberate replacement of relatively rare and out-of-date examples by those reflecting more commonly encountered instances and current realities has led to the achievement of the second part of this aim.

A significant difference between *AACR1* and *AACR2* results from submissions made by the U.S. Catalog Rules Revision Committee concerning the sexism implicit in the language of *AACR1* and, less blatantly, in the examples in *AACR1*. The sexism centered on such statements as "Enter a person under the name by which he is commonly identified" (*AACR1*, rule 4) and "the reader who does not already have in hand the exact citation to the work he is seeking" (*AACR1*, rule 144A), and on one or two rules which actually excluded women. An example of the latter is *AACR1* rule 49C1: "Add the word *Saint* after the name of a Christian saint unless the person was an emperor, king, or pope, in which case he is identified only as such." Margaret of Scotland, saint and Queen? Elizabeth of Hungary, saint and Queen-Regent?

As far as the examples are concerned, it is significant to note that women's names or works created by women are either in a small minority or not present. In *AACR2*, all statements and rules which exclude women have been replaced: "Choose, as the basis of the heading for a person, the name by which he or she is commonly known" (*AACR2*, rule 22.1A). "If a bishop, cardinal, archbishop, metropolitan, abbot, *abbess*, or other high clerical official . . ." (*AACR2*, rule 22.17C [my italic]). This decision proved to be easy to implement, contrary to fears that the abolition of sexism in *AACR2* might prove overly expensive. Even if it had been an expensive and time-consuming process, I believe that it would have been worth it, and there are two reasons for this belief. The first is moral, the second is political. The morality of the situation is surely clear: It is wrong to reinforce stereotyped notions of the relative roles of the sexes, and it is wrong to make a tool for use in a predominantly female profession if that tool ignores the existence of females as authors or library users (see quotations from *AACR1*, above). In addition, few people now doubt the potency of written codes, rules, or lists, either in reinforcing outdated attitudes or in raising the consciousness of groups as a whole. The effect of sexist cataloging rules may be considerably less than the effect of sexist subject headings (see

Sanford Berman[6] and Joan Marshall),[7] but the essential moral point remains. If for no other reason, *AACR2* deserves commendation for this stand on principle. The political reason for adopting a nonsexist policy is simple. An important school of "populists" in technical services espouses both principled causes and user-oriented cataloging (see, for example, Maurice Freedman's "Processing for the People").[8] The populist school has a natural and understandable hostility toward research library–oriented and centrally imposed cataloging rules. Meeting their principled objections to sexism not only makes *AACR2* more palatable but demonstrates that a set of cataloging rules can respond to moral imperatives and socially desirable aims. Thus a rare combination of the morally right and the politically expedient can be found in *AACR2*.

Reconciling British and American usage of the English language proved to be almost as difficult as reconciling the content of the rules. There was, for example, "the big *U*"—the one that lies, or does not lie, between *g* and *i* in "cataloguing" or between *g* and *e* in "catalogue." The answer, arrived at in *AACR2,* has to use Webster's *New International Dictionary*[9] as an arbiter. Where Webster's gives a British spelling as a permitted alternative, that has been used in *AACR2*; if only the American usage is given, that has been used in *AACR2*. Thus *AACR2* exists in one text only and has achieved a difficult reconciliation without sacrificing clarity.

The presentation and style of *AACR2* are vital to its understanding, important in its use, and noticeable to the most cursory reader. It is probably not exaggerated to state that use of *AACR2* in the future may stand or fall on the acceptability of its presentation.

6. Sanford Berman, *Prejudices and Antipathies: A Tract on the LC Subject Heads Concerning People* (Metuchen, N.J.: Scarecrow Press, 1971).

7. Joan K. Marshall, *On Equal Terms: A Thesaurus for Nonsexist Indexing and Cataloging* (New York: Neal-Schuman, 1977).

8. Maurice J. Freeman, "Processing for the People," *Library Journal* 101 (Jan. 1, 1976): 189–197.

9. *Webster's Third New Dictionary of the English Language, Unabridged* (Springfield, Mass.: Merriam, 1961).

Part 2

Description

General Description and Description of Books, Pamphlets, and Printed Sheets

MICHAEL GORMAN

The organization of *AACR2* is novel in a number of ways, including two which are essential to understanding the nature and content of the general chapter on description of library materials. The two important innovations are, first, the strict separation of descriptive rules from rules on access points and, second, the relationship between a general chapter, chapters on the description of specific types of library materials (chapters 2 through 11), and chapters on pervasive problems in description (chapters 12 and 13).

The separation of description and the provision of access points means that the descriptions which are formulated in accordance with the rules in Part I must be neutral in that they are absolutely independent of the separate and subsequent assigning of headings and uniform titles. This point has been explored earlier in this paper, but it has the particular effect of making the general rules both comprehensive and independent. The second major innovation is that of isolating all the rules which apply to all types of material and separating those rules from those which apply only to a specific type of material or to a pervasive condition.

This structure, inspired partially by the organization of the British LANCET rules[1] for nonprint materials, has had at least two desirable results. First, it has eliminated redundancy and repetition in the cataloging rules. Second, it has forced a searching analysis of our rules, because the effort to fit all rules into a logical structure necessitates such analytical inquiry. This analysis has led to a generalized consistency and a diminution of the largely unnecessary anomalies and peculiarities in the treatment of one material as opposed to another. One finds in

---

1. *Non-Book Materials: Cataloguing Rules* (London: National Council for Educational Technology, 1973).

AACR2, Part I, a strict division into truly general rules and particular rules which arise from the genuine differences between types of material and not from traditional or customary differences in the treatment of each material.

The main component of the logical structure of Part I is the framework contained in the *ISBD(G)*.[2] This all-encompassing framework, developed on lines familiar to all from the *ISBD* for books[3] and chapter 6 (revised) of the first edition of *AACR*, provides all the elements necessary for the description of any type of library material, assigns an order to those elements, and assigns a standard punctuation to enclose or introduce each element. The significant advance on the *ISBD(M)* is that the *ISBD(G)* is a universal framework in that descriptive records for any type of library material can fit into its provisions. This important breakthrough has made possible the achievement of the logical and consistent rules in *AACR2*. The pattern in the general chapter on description is repeated throughout the twelve subsequent chapters of Part I. This pattern is expressed in a rule-numbering pattern of considerable mnemonic value. Each rule number in Part I begins with a number indicating the chapter, is followed by a number corresponding to the area of the description with which the rule deals, and then, for specific rules, by a letter indicative of the elements of the description. For example, rule 1.4D deals with the name of publisher (etc.) element in the publication (etc.) area in the general chapter; rule 2.4D deals with the same element in chapter 2 (description of books, etc.); rule 3.4D deals with the same element in chapter 3 (description of cartographic materials); and so on throughout all chapters in Part I. This is the means by which the cross-referring essential to use of Part I is made possible.

Theoretically, this cross-referring in using the rules could be extensive and time consuming. In actual practice, it is unlikely that catalogers will have to refer to more than one rule in solving a particular problem. There are two reasons for this. First, catalogers who are versed in the rules will not need to use general instructions and will refer to these rules (as they have to all others) only for guidance on specific and out-of-the-ordinary problems. Ken Bakewell's thorough and excellent index will help here. Second, although general rules are not repeated in the specific chapters, they are exemplified. Thus the cataloger will be able to see the answer to many problems even though the rule is not

---

2. *ISBD(G): General International Standard Bibliographic Description* (London: IFLA Office for UBC, 1977).

3. *ISBD(M)* (1st standard ed.; London: IFLA Committee on Cataloging, 1974).

repeated. A good instance of this can be seen in rule 2.1B, where the examples illuminate a good proportion of the problems encountered in recording the titles proper of books, even though the rule is merely a reference back to the general chapter.

In describing the general chapter one has, of necessity, to describe innovations and changes in all descriptions because the general chapter not only contains all the rules of general applicability but also sets out the framework and punctuation patterns for all descriptions. I shall therefore review each area of the description and briefly indicate new rules or changes in practice, as well as the content of the rules in chapter 1.

The first section of chapter 1 (numbered 1.0) contains general rules dealing with sources of information, the framework of the description, and other matters such as language and the treatment of inaccuracies. The most important innovation in this section is contained in a rule on levels of detail in the description. Though I have described it as an innovation, the basic idea can be found in Cutter's "long," "medium," and "short" entries which he outlined in his rules over 100 years ago. Since many cataloging agencies do not make complete or even full entries, it seems only logical to try to achieve standard short and medium-length entries rather than make the content of those entries subject to the exigencies of a particular catalog or the whims of a particular cataloger. In the dawning era of bibliographic resource sharing, this measure of standardization becomes a vital necessity. The Nationally Acceptable Record, which is being discussed as a matter of urgency at the national level, is already being talked of as containing at least *AACR2*'s second level of description (see rule 1.0D). It is important to note that levels 1 and 2 are minimum levels and will allow the addition of any element deemed necessary in a particular case. The idea is that if one has catalog records in which the descriptive information has been formulated at, say, level 2, a common core of information will be found in each. Differences in the provision of *additional* information will not mar the essential standardizing concept.

The first area of the *ISBD(G)* is the title and statement of responsibility. This section of the general chapter (numbered 1.1) contains detailed rules on titles proper (including section titles), parallel titles, other title information, and statements of responsibility (a generalized name for what ISBD[M] calls "statements of authorship") for all materials. These rules contain innovations, such as a rule for "telescoped" titles (1.1B5), a rule on the treatment of initialisms in titles (1.1B6), and rules on the treatment of statements of responsibility when the item has parallel titles (1.1F10 and 1.1F11). In addition, this area contains a rule on the use of general material designations (found in a rudimentary form as "statements of physical medium" in some chapters of *AACR1*). In this rule (1.1C), general material designations (hereafter GMDs) are stated to be optional, in that they may be added to all descriptions, some descriptions, or none. There are two lists of GMDs. One is recommended for use in Britain and contains truly general terms; the other is recommended for use in North America and contains a mixture of general terms (e.g. microform) and less general terms in current use in the United States and Canada (e.g. filmstrip, game, diorama). This sole instance of failure to agree in *AACR2* is unfortunate but scarcely vital, since the use of any GMDs in British cataloging is unlikely, and since codes in machine records will supply a far better answer to the problem than do GMDs.

The second area of the *ISBD(G)* is the edition area. This section of *AACR2* (1.2) contains detailed rules on the recording of edition statements and the statements of responsibility associated with them. The striking innovation of the rules in 1.2 is the provisions they make for "subsequent edition statements." These cover the relatively uncommon but important case where a particular edition is revised and reissued. For example, a motion picture's "English-language version" may be shortened and reissued as a "school version." Rule 1.2D specifies that in such an instance the entry would contain "English language version, School version." Though most commonly encountered in books, this phenomenon also occurs in nonprint materials. Rules in 1.2 also allow for the association of particular statements of responsibility with the edition statements or subsequent edition statements to which they pertain.

The third area of the *ISBD(G)* is the material (or type of publication) specific details area. It contains details that are special to cartographic materials and serial publications. The general chapter does not deal with these specific matters, and the rules for use of this area are set out in chapters 3 and 12.

The fourth area of the *ISBD(G)* is the publication, distribution, etc. area. The most notable feature of this section in *AACR2* (compared with the "imprint area" of *AACR1*, chapter 6 revised) is that it accommodates the details of the publication *and* distribution of materials, and allows the option of naming the function performed by the publisher or distributor.

The fifth area of the *ISBD(G)* is the physical description area. As compared with *AACR1*, one sees a generalizing of the area into four elements:

Extent and specific material designation
Other physical details
Dimensions
Accompanying material

This generalization results, for example, in the following physical descriptions—for a book, a sound recording, and an object, respectively:

271p. : ill., ports. ; 21 cm. + 1 atlas
1 sound disc : 33⅓ rpm, stereo. ; 12 in. + 1 pamphlet
1 diorama (various pieces) : col. ; in box, 30 × 25 × 13 cm +
    1 sound cassette

These examples show that even in the area which differs most from one material to another we can achieve a measure of standardization and consistency.

Naturally, since chapter 1 contains only rules of general applicability, the rules relating to the physical description area in that chapter give only the outline of the area and its punctuation. Chapters 2–12 contain detailed specifications or sources of information and the content of this area.

The sixth area of the *ISBD(G)* is the series area. The striking changes between the rules in *AACR1* and *AACR2* lie in the fact that the rules on series are far more specific in that they deal with some elements of series statements which were either only lightly touched upon or ignored in *AACR1*. This increase in the prescriptions has been achieved by remodeling the series area to correspond to the title and statement of responsibility area where there is a correspondence. Thus the title proper of a series precedes parallel titles and other title information of that series, and these are followed by statements of responsibility relating to the series. The prescriptions for subseries follow the same pattern. Although there are a number of elements in the new series area, they are mostly concerned with the rare case and thus are unlikely to lead to series statements that are more complex than those we have encountered hitherto.

The seventh area of the *ISBD(G)* is the note area. In *AACR2* the most significant features of this area are that the notes are given a standard order across all materials (this order is set out in chapter 1) and the prescriptions on the form of notes are less rigid and leave more to the judgment of the individual cataloger or cataloging agency. Chapter 1 contains general rules on types of notes.

The eighth and last area of the *ISBD(G)* is the "standard" number and terms of availability. The corresponding section of chapter 1 in

AACR2 sets out the rules for recording international standard numbers (at present, these are ISBNs and ISSNs), key titles, and terms of availability (including price).

The last three major rules in chapter 1 of *AACR2* deal with supplementary items (1.9), made up of several types of materials (1.10), and facsimiles, photocopies, and other reproductions of print, manuscript, and graphic materials (1.11). Essentially, these rules summarize present practice and offer alternative but standard treatments for supplementary and multimedia materials.

Because chapter 6 of *AACR1* was revised to incorporate the provisions of the first standard edition of the *ISBD(M)*,[4] the corresponding chapter in Part I of *AACR2* (chapter 2) contains fewer differences in substance than do the chapters dealing with the description of other types of material. The descriptions resulting from the application of *AACR2* chapter 2 will not look unlike or be markedly different from the descriptions resulting from the application of *AACR1*, chapter 6, revised. The differences in approach between *AACR1* and *AACR2*, however, do make the rules look different and do cause minor changes in substance. For example, many of the rules in chapter 2 consist of brief references back to the general chapter rather than detailed instructions specifically tailored to books and other printed items. Other differences in the rules themselves are the large number of examples in chapter 2 and the brevity of the instructions when compared to those in *AACR1*. An example of the latter can be found in the relative prolixity of the rules on sources of information and the use of the title page in *AACR1* and the relative concision of the corresponding rules in *AACR2*, chapter 2.

Detailed changes between the two sets of rules include the following:

AACR2 chapter 2 does not require a number (occurring in a title) to be followed by its written equivalent (see *AACR1*, 134B4b).

The treatment of parallel titles differs between the two editions. In *AACR1*, detailed instructions are given on how many and which parallel titles are to be recorded. In *AACR2* the treatment of parallel titles depends on the level of description.

---

4. Now available as *ISBD(M)* (1st standard ed., rev.; London: IFLA International Office for UBC, 1978).

AACR2 allows the optional addition of the general material designation "[text]," following the title proper of a book, pamphlet, or other printed text item.

AACR1 allows the recording of an original title on a title page as a parallel title. *AACR2* restricts this to cases where the book contains some or all of the original text.

AACR1 somewhat cryptically indicates that an alternative title must be recorded as other title information. *AACR2* defines a title proper as including an alternative title.

AACR1 prescribed the addition of the "real" name for a person to a pseudonymous author statement in certain cases. *AACR2* does not make this prescription.

AACR2 deals with subsequent edition statements and their accompanying statements of responsibility (see 2.2D and 2.2E). *AACR1* is silent on this topic.

AACR1 dealt with illustration statements (135 F) and statements of the number of volumes (135 G) in the rules relating to edition. Both problems are dealt with differently and elsewhere in *AACR2*.

The treatment of the "imprint" in *AACR1* differs from the treatment of the "publication, distribution, etc." area in *AACR2* in a number of relatively minor particulars. For example, if the town in which an item is published is unknown, *AACR2* allows the interpolation of the name of the country or state in which the item is published or is thought to have been published. *AACR2* also deals with the recording of the names of distributors and distribution details in a more detailed and systematic manner than *AACR1*. Another difference is the treatment of dates of publication, which in *AACR2* is explicitly tied to the edition named in the edition statement.

The treatment of the pagination in the two editions differs in matters of detail and in the extent of treatment of the problems encountered in recording this information. *AACR1* restricted the counting of plates to "leaves of plates"; *AACR2* recognizes both leaves and pages of plates.

The series area differs in ways which have been mentioned earlier in this paper, but probably the most striking difference is the treatment of statements of responsibility relating to series. For example, *AACR1* would prescribe "*Its* Technical Memoranda *and* Special paper—Geological Society of America," whereas these would appear, according to

AACR2, as "Technical memoranda/Electrical Research Institute *and* Special paper/Geological Society of America."

The notes in *AACR2* are less rigidly prescribed and more exactly analyzed, compared to the equivalent rules in *AACR1.* A vivid example of this difference can be seen in comparing the rules on thesis notes in *AACR1* (146–147) with their equivalents in *AACR2* (2.7B13). Contents notes are also formulated differently between the two editions.

AACR2 contains a number of rules (2.12–2.18) on the description of early books which are not found, or are found elsewhere, in *AACR1.*

Cartographic Materials, Manuscripts, Music, and Sound Recordings

FRANCES HINTON

My assigned topic is really four separate and discrete topics, which have little relation to each other. Chapters 3 through 6 of *AACR2* contain the rules for description of cartographic materials, manuscripts, music, and sound recordings. The only theory involved is that which led to the development of *ISBD(G),* namely, that it is feasible to devise a framework for describing any object, that certain elements are required to describe and identify all types of material, and that a prescribed order of these elements is desirable, both for the convenience of the cataloger and for the exchange of information between different cataloging agencies.

The arrangement of rules in Part I of *AACR2* by *ISBD* area and element makes it easy to compare, for example, the chief sources of information for different types of material. It also facilitates the comparison of the provisions for cataloging specific types of material that are to be found in *AACR2* and the general standards for description of the same types of material that are found in *ISBD(CM)* and *ISBD(NBM).* Essentially, this is what I have attempted to do, at the same time pointing out the differences and similarities between these chapters and the relevant chapters of *AACR1*.

Part III of *AACR1* consisted of chapters on various types of "non-book" materials that included rules for the choice of entry as well as the rules for description. The rules for entry, heading, and description of books and booklike materials were to be applied "to the extent that they are pertinent and unless they are specifically contravened or modified by the rules in the following chapters." All chapters in Part III were somewhat less than satisfactory. They became even more unsatisfactory when chapter 6 was revised to incorporate the provisions of *ISBD(M)*, leaving catalogers of nonbook materials uncertain as to whether *ISBD* punctuation should be used, but even more uncertain of the appropriate chief source of information for the various areas of the description.

This flaw in *AACR1* was, in fact, one of the major causes of the code revision that produced *AACR2*. The flaw was not only the inadequate provision for the description and organization of entries for nonbook materials; even more, it was the basic orientation of rules that divided the universe of library materials into "books" and "nonbooks," with the tacit assumption that "nonbooks" are second-class citizens that must somehow be forced, as far as bibliographic description goes, into a booklike mold. The very fact that no term more general than "bibliographic" has appeared shows how far we are from acknowledging that any and all forms for transmitting information and culture are equal.

A basic feature of the *ISBD*s and *AACR2* is that the description of any type of material is derived from a chief source of information for the material that is being described. This chief source of information varies from one form of material to another but is normally the item itself, in preference to outside sources. The "item itself" is sometimes interpreted as including a label attached to an item or a container that is an integral part of the item.

Within an item, the part that supplies the most complete information is preferred over a part that supplies less information. This is not for any theoretical reason but to avoid the necessity of sprinkling the description with square brackets to indicate the interpolation of information needed to describe and identify the item.

The chief source of information for an atlas is the same as for any other book: its title page. For other kinds of cartographic material—maps, globes, etc.—the chief source of information is the entire item or its container or stand. If the item that is being described is in several physical parts, all the parts are the chief source.

Similarly, for the various types of sound recordings, the labels on a disc, tape, cassette, etc., are a chief source of information. The reel upon which a tape is wound or the cassette or cartridge which contains a tape may also be a chief source of information.

Manuscript texts and published music are more like books than other types of material. It follows, therefore, that their chief sources of information are similar to those for books. For both, the first choice is the title page. However, since a music title page is frequently merely a listing of works in a series, the rule specifies that the source that provides the most complete information shall be considered the chief source. The order of preference, if the title page is not the chief source, differs among books, early books, manuscripts, and music. Although the reason is not stated, and there is really no place that it could be made explicit, it seems to be the place that is most likely to provide the fullest information for a particular material. For example, the caption of music (i.e. the first page of the music itself) usually provides the most information if the title page does not suffice.

The first element of description is the title proper. This is transcribed from the chief source of information and is recorded exactly as to wording, order, and spelling, but not necessarily as to punctuation or capitalization.

Because maps frequently include a statement of scale in the title and because this is also part of the material specific area for cartographic materials, it is necessary to state explicitly that if the title proper includes a statement of scale, it should be transcribed as part of the title proper.

The title of a musical work frequently includes the medium of performance, the key, and the opus number. If the title, exclusive of these elements, is a generic term, indicating a type of composition (e.g. trio, symphony, string quartet, etc.), the cataloger includes the medium of performance, etc., as part of the title proper. Otherwise these are treated as other items of title information. The same principle is applied to sound recordings of musical works.

If an item has no title proper, the cataloger may need to supply one from another part of the item or from reference sources, or may need to devise one.

For cartographic material, the name of the area is always included in the supplied title. For music, a supplied title must include all the elements prescribed for uniform titles of music in the order prescribed by rules 25.25–25.36. The rationale is obvious. If these elements were not supplied in the title proper, they would have to be supplied elsewhere.

Because manuscripts frequently have no title and because there are many different kinds of manuscripts, chapter 4 has very detailed instructions for supplied titles. Reasonably enough, the supplied title for the manuscript of a subsequently published work is the title by which the work is known—in effect, its uniform title. For ancient, medieval, and Renaissance manuscripts one follows, when appropriate, the provisions for early printed books. Otherwise, we supply a title by which the work is known or devise a title that indicates the nature of the material.

Other types of manuscripts can be grouped in clusters and the data to be included in the title can be prescribed. For letters, etc.—any message sent from one person to another—supply a title consisting of the word *letter* (or *postcard, telegram,* etc.), the date of writing, the place of writing, the name of the addressee, and the place addressed. For a speech, sermon, etc., supply an appropriate word, followed by the place and/or the occasion of delivery. For legal documents, supply a word or brief phrase characterizing the document, the date of signing, the names of persons concerned (other than the person responsible for the document), and the occasion for the document (if it can be expressed concisely). These are the bits of information that are needed to identify items of this type. It is apparent that the necessary data are usually available in the item itself.

If more than one title is given in the chief source of information, the general rule directs the cataloger to record as the title proper the one that is given in the language of the item's content. Otherwise, the choice is based on the order of titles or the layout of the chief source of information. Although it is stated only in the glossary, a title that is not the title proper, but is in the same language as the title proper, is considered as other title information.

Of all the forms of material that are my concern, cartographic materials are the most likely to contain variant titles. *AACR1* chapter 2 explained in great detail that the information that usually is found on the title page of a book is arranged on a map to fit the available space and to suit the taste of the map designer. It gives explicit instructions for choosing among variant titles, preferring a title that appears within the borders of the map or a cartouche to a marginal title. In contrast, *AACR2* relies on the general principles of sequence or layout, adding that in case of ambiguity one should select the most comprehensive title. Incidentally, *ISBD(CM)* expresses this as the title deemed most appropriate by the cataloging agency. The difference seems to be that *AACR* attempted to provide instructions to cover every possibility in an abstract environment, while *AACR2* recognizes that the item that is being described provides its own guidelines.

A different kind of choice between different titles must be made if a collection is to be described as a unit. This decision was made before the cataloger began to develop the description, but only in chapter 3, Cartographic Materials, is there a rule entitled "description of whole or part." Since such a decision may be needed for many types of material, the rule really belongs in chapter 1. It affects the chief source of information for what is being described and determines the title proper. Basically, there are three kinds of collections. First, and simplest, are those that have a chief source of information that includes a collective title in addition to titles, with or without separate chief sources of information, for the component parts of the collection. Second are those with a chief source of information that merely lists the contents without providing a collective title. Finally, there are those with no chief source of information, other than the fact that the collection is described as a unit.

The first kind of collection presents no particular problem, although a secondary decision, to describe the individual parts as well, may be needed.

The distinction between the other two kinds of collections varies from one chapter to another. In part, this is a reflection of the way libraries tend to handle various forms of material, and in part it reflects the nature of the material. Rule 1.0A2, for items that lack a chief source of information, includes as an example a collection of pamphlets assembled by the library or by a previous owner and which are to be cataloged as a single item. There is no difference between this and a collection of manuscripts, yet the manuscript collection as a whole is considered a chief source of information, and the instruction for supplying a title is part of the general rule for supplying a title proper. There is no provision in the general chapter for supplying a collective title, although *ISBD(G),* in its rule for items that lack a collective title, says that when an item is made up of a large number of works but lacks a collective title, a concise descriptive title may be supplied. In *AACR2* the only chapter with this precise provision is that for cartographic materials, and there it is limited to an item that "consists of a large number of physically separable parts." Neither the chapter on music nor that on sound recordings suggests the possibility of supplying a collective title if one is lacking.

In general, if an item has a chief source of information that lacks a collective title but lists the titles contained in the collection, it is considered to have no title proper. The titles and statements of responsibility are recorded-transcribed—as they appear in the chief source of information. For cartographic materials and sound recordings, the options of describing the item as a unit or describing each separately titled component separately are presented as possibilities.

What underlying principles and conditions can we deduce from these rules and from our own store of information? Published collections are likely to have collective titles if they contain a large number of separate works. If they contain only a few separate works, the chief source of information frequently lists the contents without a collective title.

The form of material apparently affects the decision to catalog a collection that lacks a collective title as a unit, although the exact reasons for this are unclear. There is a tacit assumption in the rules that a single manuscript or volume of printed music will be cataloged as a unit even if it contains several separate works and lacks a collective title. On the other hand, there is an explicit assumption that a library will at least consider the possibility of cataloging the two sides of a sound disc or each of several maps on a single sheet separately. All of these are collections that are issued as such, whether because the author wrote two sonnets on a single sheet of paper or a record company put a different musical work on each side of a disc.

The form of material also affects its chance of being made by a library into a collection to be handled as a unit. Collections of manuscripts are so frequently cataloged as a unit that the title of chapter 3 is "Manuscripts" (including manuscript collections). It seems likely that the value of a collection that is formed around a person or a corporate body is considerably greater than that of its individual parts. The provision for supplying a collective title for a collection of maps implies that libraries frequently handle a number of otherwise unrelated maps of an area as a single item.

On the other hand, although a library may be equally likely to catalog a sound disc as a single item or to catalog each separately titled work on that disc as a separate item, it is most unlikely that any library would elect to treat a group of sound recordings as a unit unless the producer supplied a collective title for the group.

In general, other title information is transcribed from the chief source of information. If the title proper needs explanation, the cataloger supplies it as other title information. For example, if neither the title proper nor the other title information on a cartographic item contains an indication of the area covered, we add it as other title information. If a manuscript letter, speech, or legal document has a title that lacks any of the data specified for a supplied title, we add it as other title information.

Chapter 1 is emphatic in its restrictions on recording a statement of responsibility. Such a statement must appear prominently. It is recorded in the form it appears. If no statement of responsibility appears prominently, neither construct one nor extract it from the content. Do not include statements of responsibility that do not appear prominently. If such a statement is necessary, give it in a note.

In view of this emphasis, it is interesting that the rule for manuscripts includes the optional addition of the full name of the person concerned if the name is incomplete in the manuscript and a rule—not optional—directing the cataloger to supply the name or names of persons responsible for the manuscript (if known).

The rule for cartographic materials does not include one of the more curious provisions of *ISBD(CM)*. This is the arbitrary instruction to give the name of a corporate body before a personal name if both appear on the chief source of information and are not linguistically linked in the opposite order. This provision is presumably related to the expressed preference of map librarians for entry of cartographic materials under the heading for a corporate body rather than under the title or a personal name. In spite of the statement in *ISBD(G)* that the first statement of responsibility does not imply chief responsibility for the item, most people will probably continue to assume that the first name is the most important one and expect to see it used as the main entry heading. This is natural and understandable, and in most cases the assumption is correct since title pages, record labels, etc., are designed to give prominence to the name the publisher considers the most important. It does not justify manipulating the order laid out in the chief source of information, and I am glad *AACR2* did not fall into *ISBD(CM)*'s trap.

The question of including performers in the statement of responsibility for sound recordings was an occasion of great controversy. There was a clear split of opinion between those most familiar with "classical" music and those concerned with "popular" music. To some extent the arguments were based on the very practical consideration that including the names of individual performers results in an extremely lengthy descriptive paragraph. It was only gradually that it became apparent that the underlying difference lay in the fact that performers of classical music—and readers of stories or poems and actors in a spoken drama— are typically considered to be presenting in sound the intention of the composer or author. Performers of jazz and other types of popular music, on the other hand, are themselves performing an act of creation and must be considered at least partners in the performance of the composer's music.

An optional addition within the title and statement of responsibility area is the "general material" designation. If the library wishes, a word or words, indicating the general type of material being described, may be placed in brackets immediately after the title proper. If the item has no title proper (i.e. no collective title), the GMD follows the last of a series of titles by the same author or the last statement of responsibility pertaining to a group of titles by different authors. Two lists of GMDs are given, one for British and one for North American catalogers. For the types of material I am concerned with, only one type has different terms. The British list, as in *ISBD(CM),* prefers "cartographic material" while the North American list uses "map" or "globe," as appropriate.

Area 2, the "edition statement," is not used in describing manuscript texts, nor would it be used for nonprocessed sound recordings, which are to commercial recordings as manuscripts are to books.

Cartographic materials is one of the two types of material that use area 3, which is called generally the "material (or type of publication) specific details" area. For cartographic items, the precise name is "mathematical data" area. This information in *AACR1* was given as a note, but only if it had not been given in the body of the entry. In *ISBD(CM)* and *AACR2,* the statement of scale appears in area 3, even if it was already transcribed as part of the title proper or in other title information. The statement of projection is given only if it is found on the item, its container, or accompanying printed material. In *AACR2* the statements of coordinates and equinox are optional, while in *ISBD(CM)* a statement of coordinates is optional but a statement of equinox is required if applicable.

Variations in the "publication, distribution, etc.," area are those required by the type of material. For example, a manuscript has no publisher or distributor, so its date is the only element possible in this area. Even so, it is omitted here if, as in the case of letters and legal documents, it has been recorded in the title area. If the date of delivery of a speech differs from the date of the manuscript, it is recorded in a note, not in area 4. Similarly, a recording date, if it appears on a sound recording, is given in a note, not in area 4. The normal location for the copyright date on a musical work is on the first page of music; so it is not enclosed in brackets if it is taken from that page, even if the chief source of information is the title page. *AACR1* (245C) recorded a plate or publisher's number in the imprint if there was no publication, printing, or copyright date. *AACR2* records plate numbers and publisher's numbers in a note.

"Early" is an exceedingly ambiguous term—what is early for one type of material would be quite modern for another. It is also, apparently, an elastic term that cannot acceptably be defined, because the most complete instructions for describing "early published items" is in chapter 2. The cataloger is referred to rule 2.16 for early cartographic items (date not specified) and for music published before 1821. At the beginning of these chapters, reference is also made to chapter 4 for manuscript maps and manuscript music.

As might be expected, the greatest variation is apparent in the "physical description" area. The general instructions in chapter 1 tells us that if an item is available in different formats, we shall give the physical description of the item in hand. The same chapter directs us to give the number of physical units and the specific material designation of the item described.

Each chapter contains a list of specific material designations for the general type of material, and most provide for additional terms if none in the list are appropriate or if the item is a combination of forms (e.g. a map on a slide). Booklike materials, such as atlases, manuscript texts, or music not in score form, are described like books in terms of pages, leaves, volumes, or even columns if appropriate. Maps and plans can be very difficult to describe, but these rules give enough detail, in a commonsense manner, so that almost any combination of maps on the front and back of sheets, maps in sections, and maps on wooden blocks can be described. We have, at last, a definition of a miniature score that depends on the size of the music, rather than the paper on which it is printed, and specific instructions for music that is not a score. The specific material designations for sound recordings, which all include the word "sound" (sound disc, sound tape, etc.), were objected to because they seemed unnecessarily redundant. The option that saved the day was that if the GMD "sound recording" is used, the specific material designation can omit the repetition of the "sound" (except for a soundtrack film, which would be meaningless without it).

The last element of extent for sound recordings is the playing time. If the duration does not appear on the item, give an approximate time, if it can be readily established. Note that the duration for printed music is given in the note area.

Maps and sound recordings are similar in that more than one map can be printed on a single sheet and more than one separately titled piece can be recorded on a single disc or tape, etc. I do not recall any battles over maps, but there was violent disagreement over how one should express the fractional extent of a single band on a long-playing record. The final decision was a very general statement that the item is on one side of one disc, etc.

Other physical details for specific forms of material are material specific and, for the most part, are given only if they are considered significant. In many rules, this is expressed in terms of whether a detail is standard for the form or not. For example, a map is assumed to be printed on paper, a manuscript to be written on paper. If another material is used, record the type of material. Another consideration is whether a specific kind of equipment is needed to reproduce a sound recording. For example, always give the playing speed of discs, tapes, etc., but give the groove characteristic only if it is not standard for the speed (e.g. 78 rpm, microgroove, but not 33⅓ rpm, microgroove).

There was a good deal of discussion during the code revision process of the advisability of giving all dimensions in metric terms. In principle, this would have been desirable for the sake of uniformity. In practice, it seemed somewhat precious to insist upon a measurement that is not commonly used at this time in the three countries that prepared the rules. For forms of material that are commonly described in inches (e.g. sound discs), metric measurement is not prescribed.

For all kinds of material it is necessary to specify exactly what is to be measured and the order in which the dimensions are given. For each type of material the elaborateness of the rules is determined by the standardization, or lack of it, that prevails for that particular format. Materials that are usually stored on shelves are measured in terms of height alone, unless the width is greater than the height. It is evident that we assume the standard shape of a book, a manuscript, or a musical score is an oblong and that the larger dimension is its height. Round or circular items, as might be expected, have the diameter as the only dimension, specified as such. Many types of sound recordings are so completely uniform in size that it is not necessary to record their dimensions unless a particular item varies from the standard. Soundtape cassettes are an excellent example of standardization.

Recording the dimensions of maps and other two-dimensional cartographic items has one of the most detailed rules in *AACR2*. This is necessary because of the variety of ways in which maps are printed, because the size of the map is frequently quite different from the size of the sheet on which it is printed, and because maps are often designed to be folded into a smaller size.

There is nothing unusual in the rule for accompanying material in any of these chapters. Each merely refers back to the general rule in chapter 1. Nor is there any special provision for the series statement, unless one considers that the rule specifying that this area is not used for manuscript texts is unusual.

Although the actual notes that are appropriate for different types of material vary according to the nature of the material, the general order of notes is the same throughout these chapters. The first note concerns the nature, scope, or artistic form of the item. It is used to call attention to features that are not apparent from the description, such as the fact that a manuscript is a holograph or a carbon of a typescript, or the form of composition and medium of performance of a musical work. The second note gives the language, if it is not apparent from the description.

In general, notes follow the order of the areas of the description. Interpreted broadly, this results in giving the donor of a manuscript where another chapter might give the title of a previous edition. Although only cartographic items use the area for material specific details, a note, showing the place where a manuscript was written or the notation in a piece of music, is given in this location because such notes are in a sense material specific and do not fit comfortably anywhere else. Similarly, a note referring to published versions of a manuscript is given where a note relating to the distribution of a published item would appear. The duration of performance, on a piece of printed music, is given in a note, as is the duration of each part of a multipart sound recording that has no collective title and is described as a unit. A note on restricted access or literary rights to a manuscript is the equivalent of the note on the intended audience for other types of material.

Some notes that are described in chapter 1 are repeated only in the chapters for the specific types of material to which they pertain. For example, only the chapter on manuscripts contains a note referring to published descriptions of a manuscript collection, and only the chapter on sound recordings contains a note describing an item's availability in different formats.

Any item may need a contents note, or, rather, a contents note may be appropriate for any type of material. However, the nature of map collections (map sets) makes it essential to note both the state of the collection described and the composition of a complete collection.

Because maps, music, and sound recordings frequently have numbers assigned by the manufacturer that identify them but that are not the equivalent of ISBNs or ISSNs, a separate note area is provided for these. Because such numbers may be duplicated by another publisher, the number of a sound recording is preceded by the label name.

The note that gives the special features of the particular copy described or the holdings of a particular library is used in *AACR2* to replace the dashed-on copy number used in *AACR1*(246C) to show that the library has, for example, the number of scores and parts needed for performance of a musical work.

The location of the "with" note was a matter of some controversy. In *AACR1* 146, the "bound with" note was the last note for the first work in a volume but usually the first note for the second and subsequent works. In the original chapter 14, Phonorecords, a "with" note was the final note. In chapter 14 revised, Sound Recordings, a "with" statement is used as the first note. Other chapters did not mention "with" notes at all. In *AACR2*, a "with" note is the last note preceding area 8 "standard number."

The chapter on manuscripts has a separate rule for additional notes needed in describing ancient, medieval and Renaissance manuscripts.

The chapters on cartographic materials, music, and sound recordings refer to chapter 1 for the description of supplementary items and items made up of several types of material. The chapters on cartographic materials and music refer to chapter 1 for the description of facsimiles, photocopies, etc. In the chapter on sound recordings, this rule is replaced by one for nonprocessed sound recordings, which bear much the same relation to commercial recordings that manuscript texts have to published books.

At the beginning, I indicated that a major goal of *AACR2* was to regularize the description of all forms of library materials. How closely did we approach this goal for at least four types of material? What differences from *AACR1* resulted for this? And finally, what other differences can we detect between *AACR1* and *AACR2*?

One measure of *AACR2*'s success in overcoming *AACR1*'s book/nonbook orientation could be seen in comments on chapter 1. It was surprising how frequently reviewers of the typescript draft, and even members of the Catalog Code Revision Committee and the Joint Steering Committee, complained that chapter 1 lacked a particular provision that pertained only to printed books and that belonged to and was explicit in chapter 2.

The skeletal structure provided by *ISBD(G)* has resulted in increased uniformity in the descriptions of various types of material, chiefly because the elements of the description are given in a consistent order. Thus the difference between a description prepared according to *AACR1* and one prepared according to *AACR2* is likely to be the order in which the necessary details are given rather than the content.

The major difference between *AACR1* and *AACR2* is the extent to which *AACR2* omits the rationale for certain rules, which is a noticeble feature of *AACR1*. Perhaps because the rules for description in the North American text of *AACR1* were developed by the Library of Congress for its own use, they incorporated a good deal of material that is more appropriate to a manual for catalogers than to a code of rules. The Decimal Classification Division of the Library of Congress calls this sort of helpful advice "motherly notes." For better or worse, *AACR2* does not attempt to mother the cataloger, but assumes that a degree of common sense, applied to the task of describing a concrete object, will result in a recognizable description of that object.

Nonbook Materials: Chapters 7 through 11

RONALD HAGLER

Whether in the literature or in private conversation we call them audio-visual media, nonbook materials, educational or learning packages, or just nonprint, they have proved troublesome. Once aptly called "the librarian's Excedrin headache," they have annoyed us by not fitting on our bookshelves, or by requiring special equipment for their use, or by being fragile and subject to severe (even fatal) wear, or by not showing up in familiar bibliographies. We have long demonstrated a reluctance to accept them for what they are: not information which tried to become a book but couldn't quite make the grade, but equal partners with the more traditional formats in our collections.

The cataloger seems to have experienced a particular schizophrenia when faced with them. They have authors, but not quite, or quite always. They may have titles, but where? And oh! how *many* of them. Someone publishes and distributes them—if we could only figure out the complexities of *that* situation, we might have a little more confidence when filling in that part of a citation. As for their physical formats . . .

Yes, they have engendered deep mistrust among many of us catalogers. Not only do they refuse to conform to our notions of how they should identify themselves, they breed like flies and mutate like a sci-fi character. As soon as we felt we had solved a problem in their bibliographic identification, a variant would crop up. Is it any wonder that we have in the past sometimes tried to "divide and conquer" rather than apply our bibliographic skills to attempt true integration? Some of us, to the shame of our profession, were quite happy to leave their entire handling to the "media experts" down the hall. More frequently, though we admitted them into our libraries, we made sure that they and our books would not be represented together in the same bibliographic tools or catalogs.

Those who saw virtue in the integrated catalog found it a hard job to adopt the format for the cataloging of books to the cataloging of nonbooks; but perhaps the even harder job was adaptation, when the format seemed to require some change. Just how far apart should the rules for the different media be allowed to develop? Just how much should the rules for books act as a brake on the tendency to treat each type of material as an entirely different case?

Hindsight tells us that we started off on the wrong foot in this adoption/adaptation cycle. By beginning with the assumption that there must be some booklike bibliographic characteristics in every nonbook, we committed ourselves to creating title pages where none existed.

Like any generalization, the foregoing is partly unfair. To balance any untoward impression of naiveté or outright stupidity, one must remember that cataloging rules have never before been developed in advance of, or even contemporaneously with, the first appearance of a previously unknown medium of documentary communication. It took almost 150 years after the invention of printing before the bibliographic description of printed books could be said to have received systematic attention; and the title page was in existence for 250 years before its implications for that description, so obvious to us, were embodied in rules or recognized consistently in practice. This title page itself, sacred to us for so long, and its relation to a satisfactory bibliographic description are both in a constant state of change, as we have heard. In our more hurried age, we must risk groping in the dark as the nature, format, internal identification patterns, and use of the various nonbook materials settle and show a greater degree of predictability. Our users need catalog records *now,* not when media manufacturers have finally stabilized the identification of their products.

Variant Practices

Thus far, I have hastily sketched some background for the two most significant issues in nonbook cataloging: (1) In what kinds of libraries do these materials occur, and with what status or priority? (1) Whether or not they occur in conjunction with books, to what degree should their treatment be made consonant with that of books?

Familiar as we all are with the type of bibliographic organization embodied in, and typified by, the Library of Congress catalog entry, it may come as a rude reminder that differing rules for description and, to a lesser extent, for heading are still common in our own houses. Varying forms of citation for serials are the tip of the iceberg in the larger or special library. Although now defunct, the Wilson card provided in some respects a less full, in others a fuller description, than the LC card. Its domain was the smaller library. Again, it is but the most visible tip of an iceberg.

Such variations have, however, been disappearing or at least diminishing. What has caused the tendency toward greater uniformity is not so much, I submit, the realization that one of the several variants is somehow intrinsically the "best" for all libraries and all situations, but rather the realization that to have a single standard for purposes of cooperation is better than to have several incompatible ones. Thus the *content* of the rules becomes in a real way secondary in importance to their *existence* as a single standard. How else could one rationally justify the use in a small popular library of a cataloging code (need one name it?) which describes itself as designed to meet the needs of general (and almost by definition, large) research libraries? We have already heard how *AACR2,* designed for general libraries of all sizes (though still not for *all* libraries), incorporates three levels of description and a considerable number of optional practices. We seem to be coming full circle, with a single code meeting varying needs, but with the very important proviso that the variations are entirely compatible with one another, a feature which was not always true of previous divergent practices.

This problem of variant practices among different types and sizes of library has been a relatively minor one in North America in this century in the cataloging of books. In the cataloging of nonbook materials, it has been the besetting difficulty of both *AACR1* and *AACR2.* I see at least three reasons for this:

1. The very existence of the name "library" for collections of books of the most diverse types indicates the existence of a long unifying tradition. On the contrary, the various (for example) film collections—in schools, in national bibliographic agencies, in archives, etc.—have found little commonality of interest among themselves, and little need to cooperate with each other in formulating, among other things, common rules for bibliographic description and arrangement.

2. The benefits of a single cataloging standard over a diversity of such standards have been far less evident for the managers of nonbook collections. For most of the newer media, there are no listings comprehensive enough to be convincing models. Those we have follow patterns and formats which are not compatible with one another. Perhaps most important, there are few external sources of catalog copy which yet provide for most of the needs of nonbook collections: so high a proportion of the cataloging must be "original" that the chief economic benefit of an external standard cannot be realized.

3. Finally, the individuals who work as specialists in the newer media—those who feel most comfortable with nonprint—have frequently been unaware of traditional means of bibliographic control because of their different training. Some have even scorned those traditional means as irrelevant, and prefer to reshape the hubcap while reinventing the wheel.

Integration

This brings us directly to the second major issue: the degree to which the treatment of books should be the basis for the treatment of other materials. Traditional librarians are likely to regard this as a straw man, a non-issue. Of course it is desirable to unify, integrate, standardize— the devil take the individualist! But it cannot be denied that widespread resistance to *AACR1* Part III derived in large measure from the book orientation of that entire code, an orientation which made Part III irrelevant to some, and to others a series of damaging concessions. Belatedly, we came to the conclusion that the real problem was not integration but integration on the model of the traditional book.

Even the book-oriented were not entirely consistent in their application of the principle of integration. Take as an example a work that is republished without any change of content by a different publisher, who merely reproduces photographically the pages of the original. In its final form, *AACR1* prescribes that if the reproduction takes the physical form of a printed book, then the imprint of the reproduction is given in area 4, while the imprint of the original is given as a note in area 7. However, if the reproduction takes the physical form of a microform, the reverse is prescribed, the imprint of the original appearing in area 4 and that of the reproduction as a note.

When the film librarians say that "publication" for them is not a single concept and that separate (and not necessarily sequential) consideration needs to be given to the functions of production, manufacture, and release, I have sympathy for their view. I find it entirely conceivable that an investigation of the media, and of the way their varying content and presentation is approached by users, could result in a recommendation that the integration of cataloging rules for all media is undesirable. The reasons why recent cataloging history has seen an increasingly powerful current in favor of integrating the rules for all types of materials are diverse, but the trend is unlikely to be reversed. Economic factors that favor greater standardization—the development of machine-readable formats, the increasing acceptance of multimedia approaches to knowledge by students and the general public, and of course the greater media awareness of librarians—are all part of this trend.

If *AACR1* was a multimedia code (I used this as shorthand for a code covering many media), it was certainly an imperfect one. How close it came to not being one at all. It was only in the last stages of its preparation that it was finally decided to include Part III in the North American edition; the British edition reproduced it with obvious and stated reservations. The content of this part came almost directly from the rules developed by the Library of Congress through the 1950s in conjunction with a number of specialist associations. They originally dealt only with a few specified types of material for which LC produced catalog copy for its own purposes, and very few of the materials covered by *AACR2* chapters 7 through 11 were among these.

Still, *AACR1* strongly represented the case for integration in cataloging. It was an early, and very strident, complaint in 1967 that the new rules had failed to rise to the opportunity of liberating the nonbook media from the procrustean bed of rules designed for books. This, combined with the stated research library orientation of *AACR1,* was almost sufficient to destroy its credibility among those who were struggling with the cataloging of school media collections, on the one hand, and specialist archival collections on the other.

Steps toward *AACR2*

The Library of Congress itself made the first major proposals for revision of *AACR1,* and these involved its chapter 12. When these proposals opened so vital an area of Part III to reexamination, the lines of dispute were quickly drawn by those who may not previously have seen the rules as a potentially multimedia code. Whereas those who chose not to follow the earlier LC rules had previously drawn up their own rules (some of which gradually acquired regional or even national recognition in widespread use), the time suddenly seemed ripe to press for a standard more acceptable than *AACR1.*

This effort gradually focused on the four different publications which *AACR2* cites as the "primary sources for the development of rules for nonbook materials," as follows:

1. The committee responsible for the Library Association rules comprised members representing chiefly the interests of specialist, even

archival, collections of individual media. It was not committed to working from *AACR1* Part III as a point of departure, since the British text had specifically disclaimed British responsibility for that part.

2. The three authors of the so-called Canadian Manual set out to rework Part III of *AACR1* in a manner they felt to be more compatible with its Parts I and II, while specifically covering a much wider range of media.

3. The authors and author committees of the successive editions of the AECT rules in the United States were chiefly concerned with the media of school librarianship and the functions of school media centers. They did not view *AACR1* as the necessary departure point for their rules.

4. The North American members of the *AACR* revision committees eventually produced the revised chapter 12 explicitly as a stopgap to provide urgently needed standards for some newer media, while not tampering any more than absolutely necessary with Part III of *AACR1*. These committees included at times one or more members of the Canadian and the AECT groups mentioned just above, and benefited from the frequent presence of a member of the British committee mentioned above.

Correspondence among all these committees and persons was, as the diplomats say, "frank and thorough." There is no question that each group saw its method leading to the "final solution," though some saw it within the framework of *AACR* and others outside it. After 1967, each group published its work, rather than leave it as internal committee documentation. Publication was of course a means of exposing these various efforts to widespread testing and critique, and of course it gave each committee's work a firmer claim to be favorably considered by any future standard setting body. A measure of professional dispute—even acrimony—was inevitable, but to the credit of all concerned, communication and cooperation among the four groups increased markedly through the early 1970s. Perhaps because of this, the final published forms of all four documents are remarkably similar in their general outlines and in most, if not all, details. The political process of consultation, negotiation, evaluation, and compromise was alive and well, at least within the Anglo-American community.

We have already heard something of the development of the IFLA ISBD program. It was perhaps inevitable that an ISBD group for nonbook materials should have been established in 1975. Although only three of its nine members came from the Anglo-American community, the four continuing Anglo-American projects (described above) constituted an important contribution to its work, because of the thoroughness and recency they represented.

ISBD(NBM) and ISBD(G)

However, before the *ISBD(NBM)* was issued, events I've already described led to creation of the *ISBD(G)* as an umbrella structure within which each specialized *ISBD* could establish compatible provisions specific to its materials. In respect of the various nonbook materials, this event overtook in part the work of all previous groups involved in cataloging rules, since it established firmly that the "integration" philosophy would prevail, at least at the international level, over the "separate but equal" philosophy. It also overtook previous work in part in detail, inasmuch as certain definitions and practices were prescribed by *ISBD(G)*, leaving no choice to the discretion of those developing rules for particular media. On the other hand, it would be quite wrong to say that the interests and the needs of those concerned with nonbook materials had been overlooked or overridden. In fact, it was the establishment of an *ISBD(G)* which once and for all ensured that the printed book would no longer be the basis for the cataloging rules for all other materials. Rather, the book and each other type of material are equally subsumed within a standard which abstracts from them all. To the degree that this represents any departure from previous practice or theory, it represents an acknowledgment of the independent existence of the nonbook media in descriptive cataloging.

An immediate result of this new philosophy (and practice) of the position of the "nonbook" is that it is no longer relevant to speak of the nonbook media as a single concept. Items extremely diverse in their bibliographic and their physical format are treated together in *ISBD(NBM)*. In its final form, *AACR1* chapter 12 also covered a variety of media embodying quite different characteristics and problems. What should be identified within the scope of the term "nonbook materials" has never been successfully defined for cataloging purposes. Fortunately, this is now an irrelevant issue. We need not concern ourselves whether (for example) microforms are "books," "booklike materials," or "nonbook materials." In *AACR2* each medium, or each group of media forming a sufficiently unified and distinct unit to benefit from a common statement of a rule for description of the physical entity, is the subject of separate treatment in Part I, all under the general standards provided in chapter 1. There is no intermediate level of rules for the nonbook media as a whole.

If *ISBD(G)* in a single stroke settled some very basic issues of non-book cataloging, it also had to face some which remain, even now, unsettled. The choice and definition of terms to name the media remain the most troublesome. There are variations among commercial producers, manufacturers, salespersons, media specialists, and librarians, even within one country. While there is a central core of agreement, say, on what is a "kit" within North America, there is also plenty of disagreement around the fringes of that core. Often a different use of a type of material induces a different naming pattern. Certainly there are transatlantic differences within the English language which proved great enough that our ideal of a code, absolutely the same on both sides of the Atlantic, came to grief in the naming of the media themselves: rule 1.1C1 gives separate British and North American lists. In *ISBD(G)* there is *no* prescription of particular terms in any of its different language versions. Yet words had to be used, and inevitably it will be asked why a few terms appear in *AACR2* in apparent contradiction to those in *ISBD(G)* or *ISBD(NBM)*. This was surely the most frustrating of all the contentious issues in the development of *AACR2*: to have to settle on a particular word to use, knowing that there is no inherent logic in any particular decision, and that any decision would be roundly objected to by a vocal group somewhere.

Neither *ISBD(G)* nor *AACR2* could finally settle another difficulty which spans the entire field of nonbook cataloging: the "early warning" general material designation in the title and statement of responsibility area (or even earlier, following the uniform title in a heading). This is an area where logic and tradition seemed to clash most strongly, and where feelings ran as high as on any other issue. Whether or not this general material designation is or is not a desirable part of an entry also happened to divide the two sides of the Atlantic more deeply than any other issue, even the language one.

General Material Designation

Just as the language split resulted in two lists of terms, so was the "early warning" split resolved by a compromise. Inclusion of the general material designation is an option. The arguments for its inclusion, at least as an option, were successfully pressed in the development of the *ISBD(G)*, despite the fact that it appears at present the option will be exercized only within the North American cataloging community. But logic demanded that the use of the general material designation be equally optional for *all* types of material, despite the evidence that probably no library sees much virtue in applying it to everything. Certainly few will apply "text" to printed books. If the embarrassing proliferation of the symbol "GMD" in the 250 pages of *AACR2* Part I proves annoying, perhaps its very frequency will in time make it invisible.

The original purpose of the general material designation was not so much identification as file arrangement. It originated with early rules for the cataloging of sound recordings. Its position following the uniform title of a composition ensured that all entries for a recording would file in a group separate from the entries for the corresponding score or literary text. Arguments for its use to "identify" various media early in the entry came later, and were always on much weaker ground since the catalog entry inevitably provides an identification of the medium in the physical description area. In a fully automated environment, one might expect that a code in the leader or one of the control fields of the MARC record would more efficiently store the same information for use in a search and/or for output as a verbal designation.

The use of a general material designation as an early identification of the type of material may prove valuable in brief-entry indexes to fuller bibliographic records, where perhaps only the title and statement of responsibility area are given. There can be no doubt that after all the theory is laid forth, the only argument, and a totally convincing one, which sways many public service librarians toward insisting on use of the GMD, is the argument that few users of the catalog ever read down as far as the physical description area!

Sources of Information

The principal means of ensuring that the same printed book will be described in essentially the same way by various catalogers is the establishment of the title page as the principal source of bibliographic data. Similar expectations of uniformity in the description of a nonbook item are more or less unrealistic. The fault lies not in *AACR2* (or any other rules for description) but in the materials themselves. What every cataloging code attempts to respond to positively is the intelligent user's expectations in the identification of an item. When different "titles" can appear equally prominently on an item, on an accompanying leaflet, and on a container published as part of the item, can the user's expectations be anticipated except by an *ad hoc* cataloger's judgment? Can the expectations of any two users be equated, when we know that advertising and citation sources may report any (or even none!) of these titles?

What consideration do we give to a library's policy to abandon the containers in which items come, in favor of the use of sturdier but bibliographically unrevealing ones? Can we anticipate any name or title search for an item which bears no printed, or even no verbal, self-identification?

Like ISBD(G), *AACR2* prescribes for each separate type of material a "chief source of information," always by preference the one most closely associated with the physical nature of the item itself. The sources prescribed in chapters 7 through 11 range from the very precise and unequivocal ("adequate internal user label," 9.0B1) to the relatively diffuse ("the item itself including any labels . . . and a container," 8.0B1). Although one may readily interpret that the first-named source in such a combination should prevail when possible, even it may contain more than one "title" to choose from. A liberal use of notes and access points for variant titling is the only solution to a problem not of the cataloger's making.

What to Catalog?

All cataloging codes fail us at another point that is crucial to the identification of the same item in the same way by different catalogers, since no code prescribes *what* should be described in an entry, only *how* to format the description. Even in the world of printed books, libraries frequently differ in practice as to whether to catalog an item as a monograph or as part of a continuation, when both are possible in theory. In the world of nonprint, the definition and the practical uses of what are (in North America) commonly called "kits" give rise to numerous and widely divergent catalog entries for the same published item. Again, only the provision of access points for variant titles, titles cited in notes, and titles of the individual parts of a "kit" can ensure the identification of a given item. To date, few if any network data bases, whether manual or automated, provide such liberal access, since it is generally not essential to the adequate identification of books.

The definition of a "kit," and the rule governing its description (1.10), require that a judgment be made as to whether one class of material predominates within the item as published. If it does, the catalog entry describes the predominant material in areas 1 through 4, with the subordinate material(s) described in the same entry in one of the four ways prescribed as options to each other, in rules 1.5E and 1.9.

Two practical problems are evident here. First, the determination of whether or not there is a predominant material, and what it is, can be demonstrated to be highly subjective. In the case of a filmstrip/cassette combination, where the latter contains verbal recorded information about the content shown visually in the former, different catalogers feel quite strongly about which is "predominant." Tradition and background (verbal or visual orientation, etc.) and the specific use foreseen for the item(s) in the particular library (including even physical housing requirements) have much influence on the application of subjective inclinations. The rules deliberately avoid setting any priorities of one medium over another, and no body of cataloging practice which can be used as a national or international precedent for local practice has yet established itself.

The second practical problem lies in the rules' provision of options for four quite different methods of describing items "supplementary to" or "accompanying" the principal item that is being described. In fact, if treatment as a "kit" is possible, there are five methods. Again, the rules cannot suggest an order of priority since each method is based on a reasonable *ad hoc* judgment of the importance and/or degree of bibliographic independence of the supplementary item, a judgment no cataloger would like to give up since it is supposed to express commonsense values regarding how much time and effort is worth expending on an item. One of these four methods (the multilevel description) is virtually unknown in North American library practice and may or may not easily catch on here. Still, it is the only method which by definition ensures that the supplementary item is described fully (cf. rule 13.6). It would therefore have significant advantages in an automated system programmed to display bibliographic data at any "level" of description: that of the series, that of the monograph, or that of the supplementary or analyzed part. Alas, the present version of the MARC format does not provide for the realization of this potential.

Of the remaining methods of describing accompanying material, the "separate entry" method and the "notes" method are time honored, and the position at the end of the physical description area—introduced with the ISBD—appears to have been widely accepted. The situation could be worse: at least one method, previously used when applicable, the "dash entry," has been eliminated from *AACR2*. Still, entries prepared by different catalogers may appear widely different when so many options are provided.

It is precisely because of these difficulties, attending the description of a "predominant" component and its accompanying bits, that *AACR2* makes its only significant departure from ISBD(NBM) (section 1.2.3) and allows for the cataloging of any item comprising two or more different types of material as a "kit." (ISBD[G] does not prescribe on this matter.) However, a kit is not a separate type of material for purposes of the rules; hence it is not assigned a chief source of information, and rule 1.10C2 is but a brief summary of the possible complexities of its physical description. The cataloger may have to rely on a certain amount of extrapolation from rules in the various chapters of Part I, and on cataloging partly by analogy. There is no doubt that there is urgent need for a common stand on one principal issue: To use the example already given above, should that filmstrip/cassette combination be cataloged as (1) a filmstrip with accompanying cassette, (2) a cassette with accompanying filmstrip, or (3) a kit? Even if the title proper turned out to be the same, no matter which method is selected (and this is far from assured because of the almost whimsical packaging and titling practices of the producers), the three descriptions would be much different in detail. It should not be too surprising that, at the present, practice appears to follow whatever strong local or regional guidelines have been established in, say, state or provincial cataloging agencies, school district technical services departments, etc. One can actually detect a geography of the application of this judgment, and one awaits a national or international pattern to emerge, though without much hope at the moment.

Comprehensiveness and Balance

It was perhaps inevitable that the rules for nonbook materials in *AACR2* are less comprehensive than those for book and booklike (i.e. verbal) materials. We have been shaping and reshaping rules for the latter for centuries. Rules for the former have come piecemeal and (for the materials covered in this paper) largely since the Second World War. Through the final stages of amending *AACR1* there remained opposition to including rules for all existing media on the grounds that the code was designed for general research libraries. In *AACR2,* the only reasons for omitting any possible type of material preserved by any library were lack of acquaintance with the bibliographic nature of a new medium, or simply lack of committee time to discuss and formulate the relevant rules. Rules for holograms, sound pages, and flannelboards are lacking, and those for architectural renderings may be inadequate. But the dependence of all rules for description on those of the general chapter 1 means that the cataloger can create a reasonable entry for such materials with some confidence, even before specific rules are prescribed. We now have a cataloging code which can anticipate, and not merely follow, the bibliographic and physical specifications of a new medium.

The rules for nonbook materials are, however, less comprehensive than those for books in another, more serious way. For the latter, we have very complete rules dealing with both published and unpublished (i.e. unique item) examples. Chapter 4 is entirely integrated with chapters 2, 3, 5, and 11, so that, for example, both a published book reproduced as a manuscript and a published book consisting of a reproduction of a manuscript are equally dealt with in the rules.

Among the nonbook materials, sound recordings are the subject of a specific rule (6.11) for unpublished items. Other chapters deal with the obvious implications of formal publication or the lack thereof for the materials they cover, for example, in rules 9.4D1 and 10.4D2. After home-made sound recordings, however, the most frequently encountered unpublished materials in many libraries will be unique-copy unpublished films and videotapes, and microforms made singly to order from the original or from a master negative within the library's own photoduplication department. Such materials are not covered specifically in chapters 7 or 11, although provision of a rule like 6.11 in these chapters seems inevitable.

Problems of Interpretation

When these rules are written, it may be wise to reexamine the provision of date for unpublished materials. There is a clear logic to giving some such dates in notes (6.11C, 10.4F2) and others in the publication, distribution, etc. area (8.4F2), while provision is pointedly absent for giving the manufacturing date of a microform. Nevertheless, the present-day cataloger in many situations is required to consider not only the bibliographic entry but the coding in the fixed-field MARC tag. Even if it is not within the scope of *AACR2* to address this issue (whether or not it *should* have been is a much wider question, which Mr. Gorman has already raised at this conference), a reasonable interpretation of the use of these dates is needed.

In view of the extremely detailed and precise rules provided in chapter 2 for the physical description of printed books, it has seemed to some reviewers of *AACR2* drafts that the rules for this area of description for some materials in chapters 7 through 11 are rather skimpy. For example, no specific wording is given in rule 7.5B3 in the instance where the work that forms the basis of the description occupies only part of a single physical piece ("on 1 reel" would seem to me to be in keeping with the spirit of the rule). The indication of "color" and the description of a container are also treated in such a way as to leave some questions of detailed application. Inevitably, some arbitrary decisions have given rise to complaint, for example, the prescription of general reduction ratio statements rather than the specific multiplier factor for microforms (11.7B10) and the lack of specific ruling on the pagination of the micro-formed "original." If there are failings here in *AACR2's* provisions for nonbook materials, perhaps it is only because we have been led to ex-pect detailed case-by-case provisions. Even for printed materials, no rule has ever been able to prescribe absolutely for every possible variation of physical details of the item.

Since so many nonbook items are loosely associated with the name of a corporate body that is responsible for selecting, producing, author-izing, or initiating the content, and bear only a more distant, or no, association with a person who performs similar functions, the issue will frequently arise: whether or not to include the name of such a corporate body in a statement of responsibility. In the case of books, the location of a body's name on the title page is one of the means of determining whether it should appear in area 1, area 4, or area 7 of the bibliographic description. In the case of many nonbook items, there is no predictable location of information on the chief source (which is often the entire item). The examples in rules 7.1F and 7.4 deal only with their respective areas and thus do not clarify a common situation: If in the first example of 7.1F1 the Department of Botany clearly published the item, should its name appear in both areas 1 and 4, or only in area 4?

It cannot, of course, be the intention of the rules to prescribe speci-fically on this matter, since the problem is one of judging *ad hoc* the nature of the relationship between the body and the item's content. However, *AACR2* does represent a deliberate change from previous practice in this respect, because the previous concept of "authorship" has clearly been broadened to the present "responsibility" on the one hand, and on the other hand the scope of what is to be included in the publication, distribution, etc. area has also been expanded. Some over-lap in individual cases is inevitable, and a period of commonsense appli-cation will probably point to the best way to lean in what is, in effect, an "invisible option" in the rules.

Microforms

Early in the revision process there was much resistance to creating a material specific chapter in *AACR2* for microforms. It had been only in 1960 that the Library of Congress radically changed its cataloging rules for them. Previously, the description of a microform was a curious though perfectly intelligible mixture of the description of the micro-format and the identification of the work. Then the rules came to prescribe the description of a microform of previously unpublished material *as* a microform, but of previously published material *as* that material—an added note showing that the format in hand is not the original format.

The argument that what really matters to a user is not the format but the content is still a compelling one. Unfortunately for the proponents of this argument, modern cataloging rules have not pursued it to its logical conclusion elsewhere. Notably, and in a very similar context, a photographic book reprint by a new publisher has generally been cataloged as a new item even when the content remains the same and only the publication and format details differ. On the other side of the dispute, micropublishing generates new and different bibliographic identities in title frames and visible headers for much photographically reproduced material, particularly in the case of material newly collected for a microform publication from various original sources. It has also been increasingly difficult in practice to distinguish between microforms which reproduce previously published items and those which in themselves constitute original publication of the material, a distinction demanded for the application of the *AACR1* rules. The amount of original publication in microformat, including (notably) computer-output microform, where no "original" ever existed, is rapidly increasing. For all these reasons, the decision to catalog the format, not the content, is reflected clearly in *AACR2*.

The basic reason for this considerable change is, however, none of the above, but rather the *AACR2* philosophy that description, and access to the description, are two fundamentally separate problems in bibliographic control, a philosophy which has already generated considerable dispute at this conference.

Content vs. Format

The very replacement in *AACR2* of the term "heading" (implying something which is an essential part of a bibliographic record) with "access point" (implying no more than a filing position for a bibliographic record) is a subtle but important change. In the period of development of *AACR1*, Professor Lubetzky clarified the concept of the identifier of a *work*. This consists of a name heading (where the rules for choice of entry prescribe one) *plus* the title proper or uniform title as relevant. Only by searching such a work identification can we be assured that all versions of the work are located together: editions, translations and, in the present context, micro or macro reprints. Here—not in the function of description *per se*—is the key to locating the content of something, whether in its originally published format or in a later microformat; and *AACR2* does not alter this process of establishing such access points or filing locations for the description of a microform.

I suggest that the principal advantage of the *AACR1* method of microform description was not the accurate identification of the content of an item but rather the saving that was possible when a catalog record for an original publication could be used with minimal additions for a later microform of the same item. This was probably a significant advantage in the era of the card catalog, and when a high incidence of microforms were direct copies of earlier originals. Neither situation will be so predominant in the future.

Conclusion

In this paper I have attempted to present both the strengths and the weaknesses of *AACR2* in its treatment of the description of the types of material covered in its chapters 7 through 11, the chief "nonbook materials" of common parlance. If complete integration and balance have not been achieved uniformly, at least the major internal inconsistencies of Part III of *AACR1* have been resolved. If future practice shows that the provision of so many options was unwise, at least the options are consonant with *AACR2*'s general principles; and they have helped link future practice with some deeply embedded and very strongly urged previous practices. It may be expected that some options will be less and less used, and eventually slip into oblivion. The ideal of a single standard, uniformly applied, will not arrive on January 2, 1981, and the fault will rest as much with the vagaries of the materials themselves as with the rules' options and "soft spots."

The greatest hope for the improvement of bibliographic control for nonbook materials lies in *AACR2*'s potential for acceptance across a much wider spectrum of the library community than Part III of *AACR1* ever reached. Already, revisions are under way of two widely respected comprehensive manuals for the handling of nonbook materials in libraries: those of Jean Weihs in Canada, and the AECT in the United States. In following, as they have helped to formulate, the *AACR2* provisions for access points and description, these new editions should provide considerable impetus for greater standardization in all types of libraries.

Impact of *AACR2* on Serials and Analysis

NEAL L. EDGAR

I would like to set the stage with the observation that this conference strongly recognizes serials, and that this recognition should satisfy the feeling of serialists that they are "always" ignored. Serials *are* difficult to treat; and they will continue to be so. *AACR2* will make cataloging and bibliographic control easier for serials, but not all of the problems will be immediately solved.

The quotation below is from the minutes of the Joint Steering Committee for Revision of AACR. What more authoritative source can there be on the background and interpretation of *AACR2*? I refer to the October 1976 meeting in Toronto. Buried in a discussion of changing authorship, the following is reported on page 5:

P. Escreet suggested it would clarify the question if one got away from the concept that entering something under title means that one is treating something as a serial. M. Gorman said J. Byrum's point was that (the item under discussion) is not a monograph. Since the "universe" is divided into monographs and serials, if something is not a monograph, it must be a serial.[1]

I like that. The universe is divided into monographs and serials.

Recognition is woven into the text of *AACR2* in many ways. Descriptive rules identify seriality as a situation which may be found with any library material, regardless of the format. Rules of choice and form of access points do not separate serials for special treatment, any more than any other material is separated. The rules apply to items, in any format, which may be either monographic or serial.

What is a serial? One definition is found in the glossary of *AACR2*. Michael Gorman states in his Summer 1978 *LRTS* article that "seriality is a condition that may apply to any type of library material."[2] But he

---

1. *A National Periodicals Center: Technical Development Plan* (Washington: Council on Library Resources, 1978).

2. Michael Gorman, "The *Anglo-American Cataloguing Rules,* Second Edition," *Library Resources & Technical Services* 22 (Summer 1978): 214.

also states that "seriality is a publication pattern, not a bibliographic condition."[3] Which is it? I should not dispute the word of one of the joint editors, but I submit that seriality is both a condition and a publication pattern. Seriality is a publication pattern in that serials continue; and seriality is a condition in that serials change. These are the two major factors which differentiate serials from monographs, the only other possible publication pattern, according to the Joint Steering Committee.

Rules for Description

The first problem with serials cataloging is the implication that entry should be chosen before description is done. This follows from the organization of the present text, from the way many cataloging courses are taught, and from the physical appearance of catalog cards. It seems simplistic to say this, but catalogers have a tendency to hold that since the entry comes first, it must be chosen first. This is, of course, not the case, and this is one of the many reasons why the new rules are arranged the way they are—with description first.

A second problem is that the cataloger describes what is in hand, not what the cataloger does *not* have. With serial publications, there are things *not* in hand, namely the issues which have not yet been published —and sometimes some of the issues that have been published before a library becomes involved with the title. The question is, How to build a description of material in hand which will also cover material yet to be collected? Cataloging rules have to consider this anomaly, and *AACR2* is of considerable assistance in this.

A third problem is involved with making the description for serials look like the description for other materials. This aspect of cataloging is made easier by *AACR2* in that all materials gathered by libraries are described by a uniform set of principles, a technique not followed in all cases under present rules.

A fourth difficulty is related to one of the two most obvious ways in which serials differ from monographs: they continue—perhaps not always indefinitely, but they continue more often than not. This concept leads to open entry, and it leads to the indefiniteness of many cards or records for serials. With so many blank spots on cards, the information is often ambiguous, if not misleading.

---

3. Ibid., p.219.

A fifth difficulty is related to another way in which serials differ most obviously: they change. This change is almost human at times, with marriages, divorces, and offspring. And anyone who has tried his hand at serials cataloging knows there are far worse things. Examples are what happened to *Nature* and *Saturday Review* a few years back.

A sixth problem with serials is what might be called the nondistinctive title. There are of course the obvious examples, such as *Report* and *Bulletin,* but there are others also, such as *Momentum, Invention,* and *Focus.* For some reason, these titles cause more problems when they are associated with serials than when they are associated with monographs. I will have more to say about this in a few minutes.

All of these problems bring difficulties to description; and they bring problems to serial entry as well. Over the years, at least for periodicals, we have had earliest title under the 1908 rules, latest title under the 1949 rules, and successive title under the 1967 rules. Mixed with this has been the cloud of superimposition, that technique thought up in 1967 to avoid the work of applying the 1967 code, or *AACR1.* That decision, by the way, may well have been made in retrospect—the worst single decision in bibliographic control during this century. But we have made it, and we will have to live with it for a long time to come. In this paper I have serialists in mind because, for them, superimposition has been a far worse problem that it has been for the control of monographic publications.

Now I realize that I have suddenly started to talk about entry and not description, but this is with full intention. I want you to keep in mind that, for many serials, the description is the entry. And I want you to have in mind that, under the provisions of *AACR2,* this will be even more common. The pros and cons will be fought for some time to come, but you should understand, and at least intellectually accept, that this is the case under the provisions of *AACR2.*

The new rules bring to serials, as to other materials, a new standard for description, and I want to speak about this for a moment. The full story of the development of the *ISBD(S)* is beyond the scope of my presentation, but one or two aspects of the development for serials may be of interest. The basis probably is a 1967 study by Michael Gorman for IFLA, which supported the real need for universal bibliographic control. This landmark study led to the first of the *ISBD*s, the *ISBD(M),* issued in 1974. Also in 1974, the Joint Working Group of the IFLA Committees on Cataloguing and Serials used the *ISBD(M)* in formulating its "recommendations," which became the preliminary edition of the *ISBD(S).* Almost immediately, invitations for comment came from

IFLA, and the invitations could not have had better timing. It was in mid-1974 that the Catalog Code Revision Committee began its three years of ritualistic torture, as did similar committees in Canada and Great Britain (or, if you prefer, the United Kingdom).

Very quickly, it became apparent that the 1974 edition of the *ISBD(S)* simply would not be accepted as the basis for descriptive rules for serials. There are many reasons for this, perhaps the most important being the omission in the 1974 edition of what catalogers call a holdings area.

In an attempt to solve these problems, representatives from ALA, from Canada, and from LC (three of the five authors) drew up a common position paper on the *ISBD(S),* since a joint position was seen as stronger than three possibly differing positions from North America. This paper was presented to IFLA, with the endorsement of the Joint Steering Committee, as the North American position on the *ISBD(S).*

The impact of this position paper can be seen in the first standard edition of the *ISBD(S).*[4] Nearly every substantive recommendation in the paper was accepted and is now a part of the standard. The eight basic areas of the *ISBD(S)* are reflected in rules 1 through 8 of chapter 12. They are clear, logical, and consistent with the concept of the *ISBD* framework, and when applied correctly, will make a major contribution to universal bibliographic control.

Let me list six theoretical considerations in which this standard will help make cataloging of serials, or at least their description, a contribution to international efforts in cataloging.

1. To accommodate machine systems. The whole family of the *ISBD* is designed for this effort, and the *ISBD(S)* is a part of this contribution.
2. To approach uniformity of description. This is achieved in that the *ISBD(S)* is an international standard, and will help lessen deviations from country to country.
3. To clarify descriptive practice. The process of revising the *ISBD(S)* brought many countries closer to each other in theory; and the ease with which chapter 12 can be applied will bring practices even closer.
4. To maintain practices which are useful. Experience has shown that the *ISBD* system and its uniformity will tend to bring cataloging

---

4. International Federation of Library Associations and Institutions, *ISBD(S): International Standard Bibliographic Description for Serials* (London: IFLA International Office for UBC, 1977), 61p.

agencies closer to each other, even at the expense (in some cases) of difficult compromise.

5. To accommodate other international standards. This is most clearly seen in area 8 of chapter 12, which includes the ISSN and the key-title. The proven value of these devices and their use in *AACR2* is one of the demonstrations of international cooperation defined by *AACR2*.

6. To make serials as much like other materials as possible. This is of course achieved by accommodating all library materials in one common code, with one standard basis for description and one set of concepts for entry.

There is always a caveat of some sort. A number of recently published books concerned with the techniques of dealing with serials in one way or another discuss the *ISBD(S)*. But I want to point out that the ones I have seen and read, all published in 1978, discuss the wrong edition of the *ISBD(S)*. These books come from both America and the United Kingdom. I probably should not name names, but when you look at such books, please take care with the *ISBD(S)*. You must use the 1977 edition, called the "first standard edition." The edition published in 1974 is of academic and historic interest only.

Rules for Entry

The Paris Principles, upon which *AACR1* is supposed to be based, mention serials only three times: once in a footnote, defining the principle of entry under corporate body; once in section 11, which refers to works known primarily by title; and once in section 11.5, which calls for separate entry for serials issued under different titles. In none of these cases is the guidance particularly clear, and the guidance for serials by personal author is one of the cases where the Paris Principles are most vague.[5]

Perhaps no single rule in *AACR1* has received more comment, at least among serials librarians, than rule 6. The rule is worded in such a way that common interpretation places most serials under the provisions of an exception to a subsection of the rule. Rule 6 does not clearly dis-

---

5. International Conference on Cataloguing Principles (Paris, 1961), *Statement of Principles Adopted at the International Conference on Cataloguing Principles, Paris, October 1961*, edited and annotated by Eva Verona and others (London: International Federation of Library Associations, Committee on Cataloguing, 1971).

tinguish between, or give directions for, added entries and references. And the rule includes in 6B1 an exemplary list which has been taken as prescriptive. This may not be the fault of the rule itself, but this has been its common interpretation.

Rule 6 is also one of the points of departure between the American and British texts, since the rules in the two texts differ and thus generate varying practices among libraries. This is also one of the arguments for a single text, which has now been supplied.

Rule 6 also precipitated a large part of the practice of superimposition when LC chose not to follow its provisions in all cases and then continued its earlier practices.

Rule 6 is also the primary example in *AACR1* of the need to determine format or publication pattern as a basis for the selection of entry. It is now understood that format is not related to authorship, or responsibility, and that format is certainly not related to the principles of entry. But in *AACR1* there really is no escape, and catalogers must wait for *AACR2* for rational thinking on the matter.

During the discussions on rule 6, about two linear feet of comment came to CCRC's Team Two. Detailing the wide range of this opinion will have to wait for another time, but perhaps a brief summary is appropriate here. Five major positions on serials entry emerged during the debates:

1. Do not change the rule at all. Perhaps this is not a major position, but it had proponents. The principal argument is that the rule now differentiates sufficiently.
2. Enter all serials under "author." This is argued as one means of equal treatment for all materials, but it ignores the problem that authorship or responsibility of a continuing publication is apt to change. The position also ignores the fact that authorship or responsibility is sometimes multiple and sometimes almost impossible to determine. This principle also runs into problems of personal authorship for serials, which creates a number of contradictions just by itself. In addition, the problem of corporate authorship remains undefined in this configuration.
3. Enter all serials under title, even if generic. This position is close to supporting the concept of entry based on form. Also, this position cannot deal satisfactorily with the problems of nondistinctive titles. The position also runs into the problem of trying to define generic titles with a list. Such a list would quickly become prescriptive and would have defeated one of the purposes of rule revision.

4. Enter all serials with a distinctive title accordingly and those with a generic title under "issuing body." Here, all the problems exist side by side. What is generic and, therefore, what is distinctive? What about issuing bodies which change? In addition, this rule would generate inconsistencies based on what may well be temporary conditions.

5. The fifth position was to enter serials under the same provisions as all other materials are entered. The basic hurdle is the tradition that format dictates entry.

"No Special Rules for Entry of Serials" is a paper read by Michael A. Carpenter during the meeting on rules for serials entry on January 19, 1975. This concept dates back at least to the Paris Principles in 1961, since one of the purposes of the Principles is to create general guidelines for all materials collected by libraries, regardless of differences in format. But it seems to me that Michael Carpenter should, at the very least, share in the credit for shaping the rules in *AACR2* in such a way that they do not contain a separate rule of entry for serial publications.

As fate would have it, the solution was not as easy as this. The first position which CCRC took was to enter all serials under title. This would of course have been a separate rule for serials. Those who argued for this position wanted most of all to escape the traps of rule 6. The proponents, and I was one of them, could not see the simple truth of the Carpenter position. It took a year, but finally the recommendation was changed, so that all materials should be treated equally, regardless of format.

This position was not clarified until the issue of corporate authorship was finally settled. When the concept of "emanation" became clear, the concept of corporate responsibility for serials also became clear, and it became possible to settle on what presently exists in *AACR2* as the framework of entry for serials. Let me summarize this framework this way:

1. Personal authorship for a serial is permitted. In such cases, everything is done by one person, or possibly by clearly identified joint authors. If this cannot be shown, or if it is shown that multiple authorship is the case, or if the authorship is changing, or if none of the authors is specifically identified, entry will be under title.

2. A serial can fall into one of the categories defined in rule 21.1B2 as covering "a work emanating from one or more corporate bodies." The number of such works may very well be quite small

for most libraries, and thus many libraries should have relatively few problems with these publications.
3.   What is left? Title entry. And furthermore, according to rule 0.6 such records may consist of the description only. The title proper need not be repeated on a separate line above the description.

To some degree, this is an oversimplification, but I feel it safe and fair to state that, for most libraries, most serials will be entered under their descriptions in either manual or in machine-readable catalogs. The chief access point will be the title proper as defined in rules 12.1B and 1.1B.

In his review of *AACR2,* published in the February 15, 1979 *Library Journal,* Paul Fasana says, among other things, "The serial problem is exacerbated by the fact that no separate chapter on choice of entry for serials is included."[6] No separate chapter is needed, nor is one desirable. Rule 6 for serials has been banished, and good riddance.

Problems with Serials

In 1975 the Association of Research Libraries issued "The Future of Card Catalogs." In a presentation on difficult administrative problems for academic libraries, Joe Rosenthal says:

We recognize certain areas as being particularly difficult. These problem areas are not mutually exclusive; when you get them in combination, they are really bad news. One is serials. A second is one I talked a little about before, bibliographic communication and coordination . . .[7]

And so on for three more pages! Mr. Rosenthal tells us that serials are a problem! I would love to hear him define some of these problems, but meanwhile I will briefly mention twelve which I recognize in connection with *AACR2.*

Number 1: Which Chapters?
    Chapter 12 is one of three chapters in Part I of the code: chapter 11, "Microforms"; chapter 12, "Serials"; and chapter 13, "Analysis,"

6. Paul J. Fasana, "Review of *Anglo-American Cataloguing Rules,* Second Edition," *Library Journal* 104 (Feb. 15, 1979): 468.
    7. Association of Research Libraries, *The Future of Card Catalogs* (Washington: Association of Research Libraries, 1975), p.28.

which describe conditions which can exist in combination with any of the other conditions set forth in earlier chapters. For nonprint serials, the cataloger refers to the serials chapter and to the chapter for the appropriate format or medium.

However, for printed serials the cataloger cannot refer to the chapter for printed books. The cataloger will use the serials chapter and the general chapter for clarification of any of the rules. The only exceptions to this are references to 2.5C for illustrations and to 2.5D for the dimensions of an item.

Number 2: Statement of Responsibility

When an author is part of the title, the name is included in the transcription and may be given an added entry.

But the rules say that if no statement of responsibility actually exists, do not give one (see rule 1.1F2). This may create problems with some brief, nondistinctive serial titles. And indeed some unhappiness has already been expressed on this matter.

However, rule 1.1F1 says: "If a statement of responsibility is taken from a source other than the chief source of information, enclose it in square brackets." Perhaps if this provision can be applied, the problem will not really exist. I will have an additional comment on this when I mention another problem, differentiation of nondistinctive names.

Number 3: Changes in Title

For serials, the rule is simple and seems fairly clear. Rule 21.2C states, "If the title proper of a serial changes, make a separate main entry for each title."

Some confusion may arise with the term "main entry" in this context. This may be taken to mean those cases where the main entry is under title. This is not the intention of the rule. Clearly, when main entry *is* under title, there should be no question. But the change also applies to personal name entries and to titles under a corporate name. If the name for a main heading remains the same but the title proper changes, a new serial is the result, and, consequently, a new serial will be cataloged under a new heading.

Perhaps it would be clearer if the rule were to say something such as ". . . make a separate main entry for each title change." This is, however, the sense of the rule.

Number 4: Changes in Responsibility

Entry under personal author is allowed for serials in *AACR2*. If such an entry is selected, the serial would have to have been written entirely by one or more clearly identified persons—assuming that this can be determined. If this person changes, the rules indicate that the first entry would be closed and that a subsequent entry would be made for the name after the change. This should be nothing new or surprising.

If more than one person is responsible for a serial, the provisions of multiple or of unknown or uncertain authorship, or of mixed responsibility, or the rules applied to works produced under editorial direction will be considered. In almost every one of these cases, title entry will be the result. At least in the cases of editorial responsibility, these names may well not even be mentioned in the description, let alone be accorded added entries. Obvious examples are magazines and periodicals which undergo constant changes of staff. Surely, these changes would not lead to changes in entry.

The other possibility is corporate entry, and the rules clearly state that any change in the name of a corporate body generates a new entry (see 21.3B and 24.1B).

Number 5: ISDS/ISBD(S)/AACR2 Differences

The problem here is that these three standards do not agree on the basic treatment of title changes. This problem can be resolved, but it is a challenge yet to be met.

Guidelines for ISDS[8] defines a method for differentiating one title from another for the purposes of international control. The guidelines do this through the combination of key title and ISSN.

ISBD(S) is designed for bibliographic control, specifying content of a bibliographic description. *ISBD(S)* says nothing whatever about entry since the standard is not concerned with entry.[9]

It is to be hoped that neither of these standards will become a new cataloging code. Neither is intended for this purpose. This purpose is satisfied under the provisions of *AACR2*.

Number 6: ISBD(S) and Title Change

Another concern is that the *ISBD(S)* does not address the problem of title change. In my opinion the reason is quite simple. If the title of a serial changes, it is another serial and therefore will have another description under *ISBD(S)*. Since the *ISBD(S)* does not address the prob-

---

8. International Centre for the Registration of Serial Publications (Paris), *Guidelines for ISDS* (Paris: United Nations Educational, Scientific, and Cultural Organization, 1973).

9. International Federation of Library Associations and Institutions, op. cit.

lem of entry, there is no reason why the standard should deal with title changes.

Number 7: Problems with Key-Title

The National Library of Canada's paper, "A Possible Approach for Accommodating Key-Titles in Existing International Bibliographic Standards," defines several problems which relate directly to the control of serials through the application of international standards. The problems include:

1. In the *Guidelines for ISDS,* a monographic series is defined as a serial. The ISSN is a part of a series statement. Consequently, a serial element is injected on a monographic record.
2. Some confusion is created by the *ISBD(S)* in that the standard generates differentiation between bibliographic description and bibliographic identification. This becomes clearer if bibliographic description is defined as "the process of transcribing the title page information" and bibliographic identification as "the process of associating a unique name with each publication."[10]
3. The *Unisist Reference Manual* does not cover serials in themselves as they would appear in library catalogs. Coverage is limited to the description of parts of serials.

In addition to these problems, the paper recognizes and details several problems which exist with serials in more than one language. This problem is not limited to Canada; it is fairly common in government publications in Africa, Southeast Asia, in other parts of the world, and to some degree in the publications of international organizations.

The request is made that representatives from ISDS, IFLA, UNESCO, and ISO should meet and resolve at least three questions:

1. What represents a distinct serial?
2. How is the title proper to be determined for serials containing more than one language?
3. How is title proper to be determined when title page typography does not indicate a clear choice for the first word?

The point for discussion is that while *AACR2* and *ISBD(S)* are compatible, neither is wholly compatible with the ISDS Standard. The concepts of key-title and ISSN, and that they must be linked as a unity,

---

10. Edwin Buchinski, "A Possible Approach for Accommodating Key-Title in Existing International Bibliographic Standard," unpublished manuscript (1978).

are fine and are generally accepted. But when these standards clash with *AACR2* and *ISBD(S)*, some compromise is necessary.

Another focus here is on bilingual titles which create interesting problems for key-title and ISSN assignment since questions arise when one title changes and the other does not, and there are special cases with mergers and splits. These problems are generally not solved by *AACR2*'s provisions. Solutions are not suggested in the NLC paper, nor are they suggested here, but such definition will be needed in the next eighteen months.

NLC will suggest that separate bibliographic records will be made for each part of two-language publications. This procedure is outlined in a paper, prepared by LC and NLC, which was taken last week to Paris for a meeting on the revision of the ISDS guidelines. This solution will also be suggested as a revision to *AACR2*, so that such problems can be faced before the implementation of the new rules.

Number 8: Use of Key-Title and ISSN

Key-title is not intended as a catalog entry but as a unique identification when associated with an ISSN. Rule 21.29 permits making any added entry which would be useful, and thus an added entry for key-title may serve to separate bibliographic records which would otherwise seem to be the same. The same rule, 21.29, also permits an added entry for an ISSN. With these two approaches, any catalog could contain two different and at the same time unique entries for any given title which is close to, if not the same as, one or more other titles.

At least two hazards exist for this approach. These devices do not exist for all titles, and lack of them could open a library to the charge of inconsistent practice. Perhaps machinery could be established for adding key-titles and ISSNs when they finally are established, but this would introduce some clumsiness into local procedures.

Another hazard relates to the proposed National Periodicals Center. The technical development plan for the NPC states that if key-titles and ISSNs are not available at the time the Center processes an item, the Center will assign temporary key-titles and ISSNs.

If the National Periodicals Center is not authorized to issue key-titles and ISSNs, and I see no reason why it should be, the idea behind this international control device will be lost. What is to prevent conflict? How will these temporary titles and numbers be removed from the national records? And what about conflict between these titles and numbers and those later generated by NSDP and added to the national data base? These items are allowed in area 8 of chapter 12 in *AACR2*, but the NPC is not a cataloging agency. I can see there is room for discussion to avoid a number of possible problems in this matter.

Number 9: Differentiation of Nondistinctive Names

If nondistinctive names are personal, the rules contain adequate provisions for differentiation in all but a few cases. One example of a rule which does not require differentiation is 22.20. Only rarely will two or more individuals be responsible for works which cannot be told apart by any of their bibliographic characteristics. If all areas of identification are identical, might they not be copies 1 and 2? But seriously, how often will this occur? LC has stated that the overall average number of books by any one author is about 1.5. It has to be at least 1, but it isn't even 2! I don't know what will happen when such a situation arises, but I do not believe this to be a major concern.

In the case of corporate and geographic names, I submit that the rules will distinguish adequately among names.

The trouble seems to arise with nondistinctive titles, and I submit there is a solution. These titles can be differentiated by asking the Joint Steering Committee for a rule interpretation of 1.1F1 and 1.1F2, which can be read as contradicting one another. If, for serials, we could add a statement of responsibility, as allowed in 1.1F1, despite the statement's not being from the chief source of information, other preliminaries, or the colophon, in the case of nondistinctive titles, the titles would be differentiated. And this differentiation would be good enough in nearly all cases without further qualifications.

This interpretation could solve the problem of title added entries as well. It would also solve the problem of series added entries when the name of the series is a nondistinctive title.

Another part of this solution rests with the rules for added entries, 21.30J and 21.29D. The first of these deals with title added entries, and surely a series added entry is at least sometimes a title added entry. Rule 21.30J could also be interpreted by the Joint Steering Committee to include nondistinctive titles, differentiated, where necessary, by a supplied statement of responsibility and other qualifiers.

Should this be the case, or perhaps even if it isn't, rule 21.29D seems to allow about anything, including perhaps added entries not otherwise recognized or specifically constructed by the rules.

Number 10: National Level Bibliographic Record

The Library of Congress recently issued a document titled *The National Level Bibliographic Record—Books*. LC invited comment at a two-day meeting just before ALA's Midwinter 1979 meeting, which was cosponsored by the Association of Research Libraries, and the comments have been summarized in an article for the *Library of Congress Information Bulletin.* As a result, I assume at this time that the comments are aimed at the interests of the ARL group. The document may or may not be suitable for other libraries as well. Work is continuing, and seminars are planned for later this year on refining the document.

What is the problem here for serials, and how does this relate to the code? Two things. First, it will be interesting to see if the standard results in producing interpretations of *AACR2* without full communication and consultation with the Descriptive Cataloging Committee of ALA or with the Joint Steering Committee. If this consultation does not take place, I can see the beginnings of another set of cataloging rules.

The second aspect of the problem is to note that the standard is for books and not for serials. If the universe is divided into books and serials, a *National Level Bibliographic Record—Serials* will certainly be needed. I feel that the thrust for universal bibliographic control will be incomplete without such a standard.

Number 11: Identification of Options

AACR2 is part of a bigger picture—bibliographic control according to standards. Other parts of this picture are the definition and acceptance of international standards, and the identification of automation vehicles to control and transfer records created by the cataloging agencies. In this picture, the power and presence of OCLC cannot be denied. Nor can other vehicles such as RLIN and WLN be ignored. Efforts are now being made by OCLC to identify the options and alternatives in *AACR2* which will be followed by LC and OCLC in the production of MARC records and, consequently, a significant part of the national data base.

As part of this effort, modifications should be made to the MARC format so that it will appropriately handle the options chosen. In addition, modifications should be made to the MARC format which will eliminate the need for either "tolerable" or "compatible" headings, or any other forms of LC's "new superimposition."

Serials are reflected in this set of challenges in that their special problems must be considered if the programs for bibliographic control are to work. So far, at least, monographs have received the attention, and printed monographs at that. The work with the selection of options must at least ask if the selection will also work with, and be applicable to, the publication pattern and the bibliographic conditions which relate to serials.

Number 12: The Use of Uniform Title
to Differentiate Entries

The Library of Congress position paper, "Unique Identification of Serials under *AACR2*"[11] offers a solution to what is perceived as a major problem, and I would like to comment on both the problem and LC's suggested solution. First, let me quote from LC's paper:

Under *AACR2* the effect of the provisions for entering publications under corporate bodies is that access to series will be, for the most part, by title. Thus there will be an increasing need to distinguish between series having the same titles proper, although there are no directions in the rules stating specifically the manner in which series added entries consisting of the same titles are to be distinguished. This issue is directly related to the need for a unique identification for each serial and each of its manifestations.[12]

First, I am not, at this point, convinced that a need exists to distinguish between titles of series or serials which have the same titles proper. Many monographs have the same titles proper, and differentiation is not made between title added entries in these instances.

Second, the bibliographic description, taken as a whole, will differentiate among monographs or serials that have the same titles proper. The problem will not exist for most libraries, with very few exceptions.

The Library of Congress uses the journal *Realites* as an example of multiple manifestations of a serial with the same title proper. I suggest that few libraries, perhaps not even LC, have all twelve manifestations which LC seeks to differentiate. But this is quibbling. LC's suggestion is to use uniform title to differentiate. Let me quote just the basic suggested rule from the LC position paper:

If the title proper does not uniquely identify a serial, provide a unique identification in the form of a uniform title heading (for serials entered under title) or a uniform title (for serials entered under an entity).[13]

I suggest that this is not the solution. Again, let me quote—this time from *AACR2* chapter 25, "Uniform Titles," rule 25.1:

Uniform titles provide the means for bringing together all the catalogue entries for a work when various manifestations (e.g., editions, translations) of it have appeared under various titles.

---

11. "Unique Identification of Serials under *AACR2*" (photocopy) (Washington: Library of Congress, 1978[?]).
12. Ibid., p.1.
13. Ibid., p.5.

LC's suggestion appears to be the exact opposite of this direction for the use of a uniform title. Uniform titles are intended to draw manifestations of the same work together when their published titles differ. LC seeks to use "uniform titles" to differentiate manifestations of the same work when they have the same title.

Furthermore, LC's suggestion would create an entirely new set of rules for serials entry. This addition is not needed at this time.

I would further suggest that the paper on this point could well provide the thrust for a Joint Steering Committee rule interpretation which I suggested earlier: to differentiate titles proper by procedures already written into *AACR2*.

Major Decisions for Serials

As a brief summary, let me point to a few major changes that *AACR2* will bring to the treatment of serials:

1. The most apparent and obvious change is the new rules for description. These rules bring serials description into line with description of other library materials; they also present much-needed standardization.
2. The rules present a new view of entry for serials. Rule 6 is gone, and with some exceptions the large portion of serials will have title entry, consisting of the description standing alone.
3. New considerations of format clarify the concept that any material may be serial in nature and that the material in hand is considered first, with seriality taking second place, at least in the creation of bibliographic control.
4. Under the rules, separate items are cataloged separately. Indexes and supplements can be described as separate items. This change removes such horrors as dash entries and the "hiding" of some important publications in notes.
5. Serials in film format are now cataloged as film. Information about the original may be given in a note, but it is the film which is cataloged first. This brings American practice into line with international practice, and the change is needed and desired.

Implications

Implementation of *AACR2* is well beyond the scope of what I want to say concerning the impact of *AACR2* on serials; so I won't talk about it. The implications of *AACR2* do, however, bring a few things to mind, and I will tell you about three of them.

In my mind, the most important implication is the end of superimposition. For serials at least, this is one of the better aspects of *AACR2,* and this should go a long way toward ending some of the most difficult serial problems.

A second implication points to what will be done with catalogs. A large literature already exists on this, and one of the recent items appeared in the March 1979 *American Libraries.*[14] But I won't dwell on this problem because I believe that, while *AACR2 may* require changes in catalog structure, the literature of comment deals mostly with monographs, not with serials. What is forgotten here is that no matter what decision is made about the catalog structure, the bibliographic records for serials will have to be dealt with. How, for example, can a catalog be "closed," leaving serial entries behind, without transferring them to the new catalog structure? These problems have many variations. The point is that, for the most part, live serial records may have to be recataloged to conform to the provisions of *AACR2.* This will be needed to avoid committing the sins of superimposition and to avoid losing serials in a catalog structure that is being built on principles which differ from those that are used to structure the serial records in the first place.

The third implication is that serials cataloging will be easier and more consistent with cataloging for other materials. The provisions of *AACR2* will provide improved bibliographic control for serials. That is the impact of *AACR2* on serials.

Analysis

The "scope statement" for chapter 13 begins: "Analysis is the process of preparing a bibliographic record that describes a part or parts of a larger item."

Analysis also consists of relating the description of the smaller part to the larger part.

This description can be done in one of four ways, detailed in chapter 13:

1. The part can have an independent catalog entry.
2. The item can be described in a note, with a subsequent set of added entries.

---

14. Joe A. Hewitt and David E. Gleim, "Adopting *AACR2*: The Case for Not Closing the Catalog," *American Libraries* 10 (March 1979): 118–21.

3. The item can be treated under the "two-level concept" which is a part of *ISBD(M)*.
4. An analytical description may be made for the item. This may take the form of a general narrative card or record which would not be fully bibliographic in nature.

The analysis of some items provides for a fuller catalog, that is, one which is more intensive without necessarily being more extensive. The process requires additional steps for any cataloger, but it also provides fuller and more complete access to materials collected in libraries. There are three other characteristics of such records:

1. They are not required. This will mean that some libraries will make them and others will not.
2. Analysis is also subject to local agency rules. Thus while several agencies may make an analysis for the same items, the analyses may not follow the same patterns.
3. The rules apply to any library materials. As is the case with the chapters for microforms and serials, the chapter for analysis may be applied anywhere in Part I of *AACR2*.

Part 3

Access Points

Examining the "Main" in Main Entry Headings

ELIZABETH L. TATE

An idea that won't stay dead deserves careful examination. Just such an idea was considered by the Joint Steering Committee for Revision of AACR (JSC) at one of its early meetings, when fundamental decisions were being made. There was no time then for a careful examination of the idea; so I shall use the opportunity this conference affords to do so now. An idea that won't stay dead is likely to generate misunderstanding and heated argument. I intend to argue neither side of the question but, rather, to present all the objective evidence I can find on each side. Then you can decide whether I should have come to Tallahassee to praise Caesar or to bury him. I shall begin by defining the issue, then review the controversy historically, and, finally, present the data that research has provided on three facets of the question.

The ALA glossary defines "unit card" as "a basic catalog card, in the form of a main entry, which when duplicated may be used as a unit for all other entries for that work in the catalog by the addition of the appropriate heading." Since the Library of Congress began its printed card program, the most familiar unit card has begun with a heading, namely the main entry prescribed by the Anglo-American cataloging codes. One school of thought insists that a main entry heading is essential for the proper organization of catalogs. The other school of thought disagrees and proposes that the unit card consist only of a standard bibliographic description, which, of course, begins with the title. This proposal is the idea that won't stay dead. It has been called "unit entry," "unit cataloging," and "title main entry," but these terms are ambiguous. Therefore, I shall call the traditional unit card "author-unit-entry" and the other type 'title-unit-entry." Figure 1 illustrates "author-unit-entry" and figure 2 is a "title-unit-entry."

The issue of author-unit-entry versus title-unit-entry can easily be tangled with other issues, primarily those relating to form of entry. For purposes of this paper, let us accept the premise that one form of a name should be used without variation whenever it is used as a catalog entry. Then we can concentrate on whether the unit card must have a main entry heading or whether a standard bibliographic description could be an adequate unit card.

```
Bailey, Hamilton, 1894-1961.
    Bailey & Love's Short practice of surgery. —
16th ed. / revised by A. J. Harding Rains and H.
David Ritchie. — London : H. K. Lewis, 1975.

    xii, 1308 p. : ill. (some col.) ; 26 cm.

    Includes index.
    ISBN 0-7186-0403-2 : £10.00

    1. Surgery.  I. Love, Robert John McNeill,
1891-1974, joint author.  II. Rains, Anthony J.
Harding.  III. Ritchie, Horace David.  IV. Title.
V. Title: Short prac    tice of surgery.
RD31.B358  1975              617
```

Figure 1. Author-Unit-Entry

```
        Bailey & Love's Short practice of surgery. —
16th ed. / revised by A. J. Harding Rains and H.
David Ritchie. — London : H. K. Lewis, 1975.

    xii, 1308 p. : ill. (some col.) ; 26 cm.

    Includes index.
    ISBN 0-7186-0403-2 : £10.00

    1. Surgery.  I. Bailey, Hamilton, 1894-1961.
II. Love, Robert John McNeill, 1891-1974.  III. Rains,
Anthony J. Harding.  IV. Ritchie, Horace David.
V. Title: Short practice of surgery.
RD31.B358  1975              617
```

Figure 2. Title-Unit-Entry

Historical Background

The idea that won't stay dead was unrecognized on what was probably its first appearance. Its originator would have denied the idea, as can be seen from this comment:

The experience of all students, of all who use books, if carefully noted, will show that, in a vast majority of cases, whoever wishes to refer to books in a library, knows the names of their authors. It follows, that this form of arrangement must be, in the main, the most convenient; and if any other be pursued, it can but accommodate the minority, at the expense of the majority.[1]

For the union catalog he envisioned, Jewett favored author entry, but he was prepared to print classified or author catalogs for the libraries that were to participate in his venture. To streamline this operation he decided that all the headings, including the author main entry headings, should be stereotyped separately from the bibliographic descriptions, which he called "titles." The "titles," arranged alphabetically, could then easily be withdrawn and replaced as catalogs were assembled. Thus by a curious paradox, though Jewett was a staunch advocate of author entry, the working file he designed for his innovative scheme was essentially a title-unit-entry file.

Cutter substituted "main entry" for Jewett's term "principal entry" and defined it as "usually the author entry."[2] But the reasons he gave for the choice of an author entry could justify title-unit-entry just as well:

Among the several possible methods of attaining the OBJECTS, other things being equal, choose that entry

(1) That will probably be first looked under by the class of people who use the library;
(2) That is consistent with other entries, so that one principle can cover all;
(3) That will mass entries least in places where it is difficult to so arrange them that they can be readily found, as under names of nations and cities.[3]

---

1. Charles C. Jewett, *Smithsonian Report on the Construction of Catalogues of Libraries* . . . (Washington: Smithsonian Institution, 1852), p.12–13.

2. Charles A. Cutter, *"Rules for a Dictionary Catalog,"* Part II of U.S. Bureau of Education, *Special Report on Public Libraries* (4th ed., rewritten; Washington: GPO, 1904), p.21.

3. Ibid., p.12.

No one would seriously accuse Jewett or Cutter of advocating title-unit-entry. Rather, it was publication of the 1908 code that set the stage for the introduction of the idea. The successful cooperation that produced the 1908 code had encouraged hopes of an international code. J. C. M. Hanson, who had played a leading role in that cooperative effort, proposed an international code to the International Conference for Bibliography and Documentation in 1908. His proposal aroused considerable interest. Rudolf Kaiser assessed the possibilities in a paper he read to a meeting of German librarians in Hamburg in 1911. He saw little likelihood of international agreement on cataloging rules because of the fundamental differences between the Prussian Instructions and the Anglo-American code. He believed that catalog cards could be exchanged, nevertheless. So that national codes could be used to prepare the headings, Kaiser suggested that catalog cards be printed without headings.[4]

Though Kaiser's suggestion had no effect on cataloging practice, the idea was not completely forgotten. Almost two decades later, at the First World Congress of Libraries and Bibliography, a librarian from Prague reviewed the prospects for an international code and found them very discouraging. Nevertheless, he urged that the countries participating in the congress move in that direction by following four standards that he recommended. One of his suggestions was a standard entry that was to begin with the title, which he regarded as the most important element in the catalog entry.[5]

Again, no concrete action implemented the recommendation and nothing was heard of the idea of title-unit-entry for some time. Meanwhile, close encounters of the corporate kind had left doubts in Hanson's mind, which he voiced in an article entitled "Corporate Authorship versus Title Entry," published in *Library Quarterly* in October 1935.[6] Hanson did not see the Prussian Instructions as a viable alternative and merely hoped that the next edition of the 1908 code would bring an improvement in the rules for corporate entry.

Nevertheless, he was taken to task by Julia Pettee in an article in the July 1936 *Library Quarterly*. Her second paragraph reflects the long-

4. Rudolf Kaiser, "Vergleichung der englisch-amerikanischen Katalogregeln mit der presussischen Instruktion und die Frage einer internationalen Einigung," *Zentralblatt Für Bibliothekswesen*, 28, 9. u. 10. Heft (Sept./Okt. 1911): 426.

5. Zd. Tobolka, "Projet d'un code international de règles catalographiques" (First World Congress of Libraries and Bibliography, Rome and Venice, 1929), *ATTI* (Rome, 1931), 2: 130.

6. J. C. M. Hanson, "Corporate Authorship versus Title Entry," *Library Quarterly* 5, no. 4 (Oct. 1935): 457–466.

prevailing attitude of American catalogers, that a title main entry is a confession of failure.

The author is the first concern of the American cataloger. He searches for anonymous authors. If he is dealing with corporate bodies, he seeks to identify and name the society, institution, or governmental body responsible for the document. If he has an anonymous classic, the search goes back to the source of the classic, and in lieu of author he establishes a form of name under which this literary unit is most correctly known. Only in the case of hopelessly anonymous works or works of multiple authorship, where personal authors are too many to be serviceable as an entry form, does he resort to title entry.[7]

In her thoughtful, scholarly article, Pettee continues with a rationale for author-unit-entry:

The attribution of authorship is a first principle of American catalogers. But why this tireless search? A second principle, even more fundamental, which necessitates the search, emerges. The book in hand is considered not as a single item but as a representative of a literary unit. It is the province of the catalog to assemble these literary units, issued in various forms, under a single caption. . . . The attribution of authorship, or the substitution of a conventional form in lieu of author, is the quickest and surest way to assemble these units.[8]

In her view, the secondary entries suffice to fulfill the finding list function of the catalog if the main entry fails to do so.

The idea that the unit card might be other than an author entry surfaced again in 1945, when Boggs and Lewis published a code for cataloging maps and atlases.[9] They recommended that a unit card be prepared for each map, to which could be added the headings for the desired entries. The unit card *per se* would appear in the catalog only for those few maps that require a title entry. The appropriate heading for the main entry is geographical area, not author or title, so that their unit card is not the same as their main entry card. Buried in a brief footnote is the instruction that the main entry appear in the tracing as arabic

---

7. Julia Pettee, "The Development of Authorship Entry and the Formulation of Authorship Rules as Found in the Anglo-American Code," *Library Quarterly* 6, no. 3 (July 1936): 270.

8. Ibid., p.270–271.

9. Samuel W. Boggs and Dorothy Cornwell Lewis, *The Classification and Cataloging of Maps and Atlases* (New York: Special Libraries Assn., 1945).

numeral 1.[10] The title-unit-entry they devised was not merely a standard bibliographic description; instead it was a unit card for a catalog based on a principle of organization other than authorship.

A few years later, title-unit-entry was again suggested as a medium for the exchange of catalog data. In 1948 the assistant librarian at the Stockholm Stadtsbibliothek, Valter Ahlstedt, wrote a prize-winning essay called "Unit Cataloguing," later published in *Libri*.[11] He reviewed the history of the concept and pointed out the many variations that still were prevalent in cataloging rules and practices. He disagreed with American writers who considered the author entry the most important, and suggested that bibliographic descriptions be standardized and constitute the unit card, to which a library can add the call number and headings it prefers.

From the opposite corner of the world the suggestion came again. A public library assistant in Australia had read an invitation from the Librarian of Congress to send him ideas for attacking the problem of bibliographic control. Wilma Radford responded with an article proposing that each country be responsible for cataloging the books issued within its boundaries and for distributing the catalog record.[12] Recognizing the lack of an international code as a major obstacle, she saw a solution in the recommendations of Boggs and Lewis. She, too, suggested that the unit card be printed without headings and that the main entry appear as the first tracing. The idea, Radford reported, had been successfully adopted by the Library Board of New South Wales. Though she had no desire to abandon the principle of author entry, she believed that "the importance of the concept of main entry has been over-emphasized in our thinking about dictionary catalogs."[13]

By midcentury, then, three points of view had been expressed about unit cards and main entries. One is that unit cards without headings will facilitate the exchange of catalog data at the local, national, and international levels. Another is that unit cards without headings can continue to reflect the choice of main entry prescribed by any given code if the main entry appears as the first added entry in the tracing. The third is that author-unit-entries are more efficient for organizing a catalog and are essential for organizing the literary unit.

The best method of organizing the literary unit was on the agenda

---

10. Ibid., p.28.
11. Valter Ahlstedt, "Unit Cataloguing," *Libri* 1, no. 2 (1950): 113–170.
12. Wilma Radford, "Catalogs, Codes and Bibliographical Control," *College and Research Libraries* 10, no. 4 (Oct. 1949): 395–400, 428.
13. Ibid., p.398.

of the Paris Conference. Eva Verona, whose article in *Libri* precipitated the debate, expressed the opinion that the added entry can assemble the literary unit just as effectively as the main entry.[14] In her own words, "It should be the function of main entries in the alphabetical catalogue 1. to represent particular publications; 2. to bring together in the catalogue all publications by one author. . . . Added entries will link together all editions of a certain literary unit."[15] Lubetzky challenged Verona, maintaining that "the entry of editions and translations under their own titles as issued, with added entries to relate them, will encumber the catalogue with many useless entries, impair the systematic character of the structure of the catalogue and often confuse its users."[16] He illustrated his point of view with entries for the Bible.

Of course, much of the task of collocating entries is accomplished by using one form of a name or one form of a title without variation. But the question remains: Is the author-unit-entry the best method of assembling the literary unit? And this question dominates much of the discussion about author-unit-entry and title-unit-entry.

When the idea of the title-unit-entry popped up again, it had a new dimension. Librarians, such as Ralph Parker, intrigued with the prospects of computer-based catalogs, gave a different answer from Lubetzky's to the question "What price the main entry?"[17] At a conference on library automation in 1966, A. J. Wells threw down the gauntlet when he said:

In many ways it would be easier to plan a catalogue record which began with the title, for this would dispense with the notion of a main entry heading—a notion which has occupied more of our time to little purpose than everything else in librarianship except, perhaps, classification and subject indexing. There is little doubt in my mind that we could get international agreement on a standard format for a machine-readable catalogue record if we dispensed with the necessity for a main entry heading. In theory, it would be just as convenient, through the medium of the computer, to recall the whole

14. Eva Verona, "Literary Unit versus Bibliographical Unit," *Libri* 9, no. 2 (1959): 79–104.

15. Eva Verona, "The Function of the Main Entry in the Alphabetical Catalog—A Second Approach" (International Conference on Cataloguing Principles, Paris, 1961), *Report* (London, 1963), p.157.

16. Seymour Lubetzky, "The Function of the Main Entry in the Alphabetical Catalog—One Approach" (International Conference on Cataloguing Principles, Paris, 1961), *Report* (London, 1963), p.141.

17. Ralph H. Parker, "Book Catalogs," *Library Resources & Technical Services* 8, no. 4 (Fall 1964): 344–348.

catalogue record via any search factor, as it would be to recall part of it or to be referred to some other main entry heading for further search.[18]

In his "Main Entry: Principles and Counter-Principles," Spalding came to the defense of author-unit-entry.[19] Gorman also decided that, since the main entry concept is a useful principle for catalog design, author is as good a main entry as any, though not necessarily the "authors" conjured up by the 1967 *AACR*.[20]

A catalog that abandoned author-main-entry was actually published about this time. Massonneau examined Stanford University's computer-produced catalog and found it wanting, for a number of reasons that she explains in the Fall 1971 *Library Resources & Technical Services*.[21] At the University of Pittsburgh Graduate School of Library and Information Science, interest in the issue resulted in articles by Daily and others, and also in a doctoral dissertation by Hamdy. The title of the thesis edition indicates Hamdy's approach: "Title Unit Entry: An Argument for the Rejection of the Author Main Entry in Theory and Practice." Hamdy based his argument on three considerations. First, he examined the rules for choice of entry in the North American *AACR* and discovered that, at best, only 47 percent produce a true author main entry. Second, he found that relatively few rules assemble the literary unit by main entry alone, with added entries or subject headings being required in the other cases. Third, he cited examples of catalogers' inconsistencies in the choice of main entry and used decision making flowcharts to show that the selection of the main entry can be an inexact and time-consuming process. Hamdy, therefore, recommended a number of changes in *AACR1* to produce a code that would be based on the title-unit-entry principle.[22]

18. A. J. Wells, "The British National Bibliography" (Anglo-American Conference on the Mechanization of the Library Services, Brasenose College, Oxford University, 1966), *Proceedings of the Brasenose Conference on the Automation of Libraries,* ed. John Harrison and Peter Laslett (London: Mansell, c1967), p.24–25.

19. C. Sumner Spalding, "Main Entry: Principles and Counter Principles," *Library Resources & Technical Services* 11, no. 4 (Fall 1967): 389–396.

20. Michael Gorman, *A Study of the Rules for Entry and Heading in the Anglo-American Cataloguing Rules, 1967 (British Text)* (London: Library Assn., 1968), p.5–9.

21. Suzanne Massonneau, "The Main Entry and the Book Catalog," *Library Resources & Technical Services* 15, no. 4 (Fall 1971): 499–512.

22. M. Nabil Hamdy, *The Concept of Main Entry as Represented in the Anglo-American Cataloging Rules; A Critical Appraisal with Some Suggestions; Author Main Entry vs. Title Main Entry,* Research Studies in Library Science, no. 10 (Littleton, Colo.: Libraries Unlimited, 1973).

During the early 1970s, title-unit-entry promised a solution to a problem that was becoming increasingly troublesome. International Standard Serial Numbers, the International Standard Serials Data System, and CONSER directed attention to serials. The instability of the corporate author and the ambiguity of "nondistinctive" had made serials cataloging a major headache. Consistent interpretation of rules across national boundaries seemed an impossibility; yet it was necessary if these three programs were to succeed. Arbitrary entry of all serials under title looked like the answer, and it was seriously considered in the early stages of code revision.[23]

The concept of title-unit-entry has found adherents in other countries. Title-unit-entry is the underlying principle of the cataloging systems of Egypt and some other Arab countries.[24] In Japan, works were traditionally entered under title, until Western influence began to be felt in the library world. In 1952, after three abortive attempts to adopt an author-main-entry code, the first edition of *Nippon Catalogue Rules* appeared.[25] This code, based on the ALA rules, has subsequently been revised. *International Cataloguing* reports that the preliminary edition of the latest revision calls for unit cards without headings, which the Japanese call a "description unit card system." The basic entry is a standard bibliographic description; access points are provided, and one is designated an author main entry.[26]

Clearly, the idea that won't stay dead was very much alive when the LC representatives were meeting with some Processing Department officials to discuss the proposals before the Joint Steering Committee. As we grappled with such problems as the definition of corporate author, the artist as author, or the performer as main entry, time and again we were in agreement on the access points that were desirable. But time and again it was impossible to find an answer any of us liked to the question of which access point should be the main entry. More than once, as we agonized over these decisions, we said to each other, in effect, "With title-unit-entry this problem would be solved." The result was a recommendation that was presented to the JSC at the February

23. See Joseph H. Howard, "Main Entry for Serials," *Library of Congress Information Bulletin* 33, no. 47 (Nov. 22, 1974), A232–A236; C. Sumner Spalding, "*ISBD(S)* and Title Main Entry for Serials," *International Cataloging* 3, no. 3 (July/Sept. 1974): 4–5; and Fall 1975 issue of *Library Resources & Technical Services*.

24. Hamdy, op. cit.

25. Naro Okada, "Revision of Cataloging Rules in Japan," *UNESCO Bulletin for Libraries* 9, no. 10 (Oct. 1955): 212–213.

26. "UBC News," *International Cataloging* 6, no. 3 (July/Sept. 1977): 28–29.

1976 meetings. The recommendation proposed that the unit entry of *AACR2* be a standard bibliographic description, to which should be added a record of desirable access points. The code should provide instructions for recording an access point in a form suitable for collocating the works of an author or the representations of a work. In essence, this is the unit card without headings. JSC also explored the idea of designating one of the added entries a "focal access point" and recording it as the first added entry.

In March, however, LC withdrew its recommendation. A change as basic as this required detailed studies and, in this country particularly, discussion within the profession, for which there was no time because of JSC's commitments to its funding agencies. The title-unit-entry concept is not absent from the second edition, though. You can see it in the emphasis on access points, not main entries, and in this statement in the introduction:

The question of the use of *alternative heading* entries (i.e., sets of equal entries for each item described) was discussed but has not been embodied in the rules, largely because of the lack of time to explore the considerable implications of such a change. It is recognized, however, that many libraries do not distinguish between the main entry and other entries. It is recommended that such libraries use chapter 21 as guidance in determining all the entries required in particular instances.[27]

Perhaps this is the best of both worlds.

Comparison of Author-Unit-Entry with Title-Unit-Entry

In February 1976 there was no time to study or discuss title-unit-entry as a possible system of catalog organization. If there had been time for JSC to weigh the merits of author-unit-entry versus title-unit-entry, in my opinion, we should have examined the arguments pro and con in the light of relevant objective evidence. I have taken the time during the past few months to review a number of pertinent studies, and I should like to synthesize their findings for you now. Then I'll leave you to your own conclusions about future directions.

Research rarely provides unequivocal answers to questions, especially when the questions are broader in scope than the research and the research is uneven in quality. In spite of that fact, I shall focus the data

---

27. *Anglo-American Cataloguing Rules*, 2d ed., ed. Michael Gorman and Paul W. Winkler (Chicago: American Library Assn., 1978), p.2.

I've found on three questions. First, on the basis of the evidence at hand about catalog use and catalog users, can we compare the efficiency of the author-unit-entry catalog and the title-unit-entry catalog in fulfilling the users' needs? Second, is there any evidence on comparative costs of cataloging by these two methods? Third, is one type of entry likely to be more suitable than the other for the international exchange of catalog data?

Re: Catalog Design

Let's look first at the information that research has contributed about the characteristics of the catalog user, the information he or she seeks in the catalog, and the clues he or she brings to the search. In his article summarizing the catalog use studies that appeared from 1931 through 1970, Krikelas generalizes the findings about the catalog user as follows:

(1) At any given time, between 25 and 45 percent of the individuals entering a library will use the catalog; students comprise the largest single group of catalog users.
(2) The approaches taken to search the catalog vary and are related to the patron's educational status: the frequency of known-item (as opposed to subject) searches increases as the educational level of the patron increases.
(3) The majority of catalog inquiries are made to identify English language material, of relatively recent date, in order to complete classroom assignments.
(4) The most frequently used information on catalog cards is author, title, subject headings, call number and date of publication.[28]

Subsequently, a catalog-use survey in the United Kingdom found that more than one-third (41%) of a nonrandom sample of 3,252 interviewees said they never used the catalog (most of them were patrons of public libraries).[29] A study of a small public library in British Columbia discovered a clientele predominantly from the student-age group and the small number of senior citizens, and almost half of them never used the card catalog.[30] Students, then, are our best customers, but the subject

---

28. James Krikelas, "Catalog Use Studies and Their Implications," in *Advances in Librarianship,* ed. Melvin J. Voigt (New York: Seminar Press, 1972), 3: 210.

29. A. Maltby, *U.K. Catalogue Use Survey: A Report,* Library Association Research Publication, no. 12 (London: Library Assn., 1973), p.17.

30. Peter Simmons, "Studies in the Use of the Card Catalogue in a Public Library," *Canadian Library Journal* 31, no. 4 (Aug. 1974): 324.

catalog is their preferred tool. Those who use the author-title catalog are likely to have more formal education.

What is their purpose in using the catalog? The studies report consistently that the user of the author-title catalog is in search of a specific document. Few are interested in bibliographic data. Unfortunately, the studies have not been designed to find the number of patrons who deliberately seek all the works of an author or all the editions of a work. The one scrap of evidence I've found comes from the Lipetz study of Yale University catalog users:

At the instant of approach to the catalog, 73 percent of the users are attempting a search for a particular document (known item); 16 percent are attempting a subject search; 6 percent are attempting an author search (to find out what documents are on hand from a known author, publisher's series, or other source); and 5 percent are attempting a bibliographic search (to use the information provided by the catalog card for some document without any intention of locating or borrowing the document).[31]

There is little additional information about the 6 percent who attempt an author search. In the light of the data so far discovered, we have good reason to believe that the author-title catalog is used to locate the known item. We do not know how often the literary unit is the object of the search, or the purposes for which it might be sought. Nor do we know whether entries organized into a literary unit help or hinder the patron in his or her search for the known item.

What does the patron know about the known item he or she is seeking? Here is a brief summary of the evidence from four studies, described in detail in the literature of the past ten years. Ayres and three other investigators from a special library in England reported these results from their study of 450 requests: "The pattern which emerged showed that the title information was completely accurate for more than 90% of the sample, while the comparable figure for author information was under 75%."[32] Tagliacozzo and her colleagues, as part of their University of Michigan study, made a careful assessment of the correctness and completeness of users' information and concluded that "the chance that a user would approach the catalogue with perfect or nearly perfect

31. Ben-Ami Lipetz, *User Requirements in Identifying Desired Works in a Large Library: Final Report* (Washington: U.S. Dept. of Health, Education, and Welfare, Office of Education, Bureau of Research, 1970; ED 042 479), p.2.

32. F. H. Ayres and others, "Author versus Title: A Comparative Survey of the Accuracy of the Information which the User Brings to the Library Catalogue," *Journal of Documentation* 24, no. 4 (Dec. 1968): 268.

information is much higher in the case of titles than in the case of authors (70% v. 41.9%)."[33] Some of the patrons who were sampled in their study came to the catalog with written citations, while others relied on memory. The investigators were not surprised to find that a larger percentage of the written titles were complete and correct, but they had not expected to find that the slightly higher number of complete and correct written authors' names was not statistically significant. And the sample of authors' names, both written and memorized, was limited to personal authors only.[34]

The accuracy of memorized information about books was explored in an intriguing experiment conducted at the University of Chicago Graduate Library School in 1968. A number of volunteers (104), unaware of the real objective of the experiment, were asked to check ten titles of greatest potential interest out of a list of thirty. After finding the books in the stacks, the volunteer examined each, graded it in terms of interest, and prepared a brief comment for five of them, giving his or her reaction to the book. Two weeks later, the volunteers were asked to recall every detail they could about the five books upon which they had commented. The recall session involved both spontaneous and stimulated recall. Though the volunteers remembered a wide variety of details, recall of author and title was infrequent. Only personal authors or editors were included in this experiment. Analysis of the responses indicated that more of the volunteers remembered titles correctly and more were willing to make a stab at remembering a title. (Distribution of responses was as follows: for author, 15.9% = correct, 5.0% = incorrect, 79.1% = null ["don't know" or no answer]; for title, 22.7% = correct; 60.0% = incorrect, 17.3% = null.)[35] One of the investigators then searched the catalog with the bibliographic data as recalled by the volunteers. She was successful in finding entries for 71 percent. Because some of the recalled information was incomplete or incorrect, the search could entail examination of anywhere from one to more than 2,000 cards. A complete citation, with full author and title information, proved to be the most efficient approach. But the investigator discovered that "the next most expedient approach is title–no title searches involved consulting

33. Renata Tagliacozzo, Lawrence Rosenberg, and Manfred Kochen, "Access and Recognition: From Users' Data to Catalogue Entries," *Journal of Documentation* 26, no. 3 (Sept. 1970): 240.

34. Ibid., p.240–241.

35. Delores K. Vaughan, "Memorability of Book Characteristics: An Experimental Study," in *Requirements Study for Future Catalogs: Progress Report No. 2* (Chicago: University of Chicago Graduate Library School, 1968), p.18.

more than ten cards.[36] With defective author data, the length of the search depends upon the amount of information supplied, the number of possible candidates, and how prolific the candidates are. The investigator reported her success with the author approach as follows: "The probability of locating an object book through an author entry appears to decrease with increasing search length; no author entries were located beyond 100 cards."[37]

These three studies present evidence of the efficacy of the title as a finding device and suggest that even incorrect title information may be better than incorrect author information. Lipetz looked at the data from his study that in general favored title approach over author approach and reached a different conclusion: "The difference in usefulness between the two approaches does not appear to be large. Circumstances of catalog selectivity under particular entry terms can heavily favor the author approach for some searches and the title approach for others."[38]

How does the patron search for the known item? More than half (62%) of the catalog users at Yale University favored the author, though some used subject as an approach to an author, and vice versa.[39] Maltby detected a decided preference for the author approach in the United Kingdom.[40] In the University of Michigan study it was found that 85.2 percent of those who had a choice between author and title began with the author, even though in some cases their information about the title was more accurate.[41] However, the author that is preferred may very well be the personal author, not the corporate author.[42] Tagliacozzo and her colleagues unearthed some additional data about the behavior of the catalog user. Of those who failed on their first search, more than half looked no further, and few had either the information or the perseverance to continue beyond a third trial. These investigators observed that "the level of skill demonstrated even by senior scientists is generally rather low, rarely going beyond the rules of alphabetization. It seems that years of familiarity with library catalogs

36. Delores K. Vaughan, "Effectiveness of Book-Memory Data for Conventional Catalog Retrieval," *Requirements Study for Future Catalogs: Progress Report No. 2* (Chicago: University of Chicago Graduate Library School, 1968), p.48.

37. Ibid., p.50.

38. Lipetz, op. cit., p.4–5.

39. Ibid., p.47–49.

40. Maltby, op. cit., p.13.

41. Tagliacozzo, op. cit., p.244.

42. Elizabeth L. Tate, "Main Entries and Citations: One Test of the Revised Cataloging Code," *Library Quarterly* 33, no. 2 (Apr. 1963): 182–183.

have not induced a great sophistication in their use, which suggests that factors having to do with attitude, rather than skill, should be taken into consideration."[43] The library-school students who conducted the survey of the Burnaby Public Library in British Columbia saw a similar behavior pattern when searches failed, and noted a reluctance to ask for staff assistance; they, too, observed that patrons were unaware of filing conventions, lacked skill at alphabetization, and even had difficulty turning from one card to the next.[44]

The profile of the catalog user I've been able to draw from the information in these studies is, of necessity, unfinished. The investigations have varied in their use of scientific methods and in their objectives. One large and important part of the picture is missing—the library staff as catalog user. Nevertheless, the profile that emerges is more likely to be accurate than the portrait that is painted by imagination and wishful thinking. The user of the author-title catalog is a person with more formal education than his or her counterpart at the subject catalog. But the latter is not necessarily adept in using the catalog or particularly persevering. He or she is looking for the known item, using the author approach, even though the title approach offers greater promise of success.

Let us now compare the efficiency of the two principles of catalog organization in serving the reader just described. For that purpose, I have prepared some illustrations contrasting the author-unit-entry with title-unit-entry in three kinds of catalog: single entry, single entry with index, and the dictionary catalog. The entries you find in these illustrations have been plagiarized from LC galley proof issued between 1973 and 1976. The entries are not a random sample but have been chosen to show the strengths and weaknesses of each method. Insofar as can be done with seventeen entries, figure 3 illustrates the single entry catalog based on author-unit-entry. In figure 4, the same entries are presented as a single-entry catalog comprised of standard bibliographic descriptions. Figure 5 is a variant of no. 4, to show a single catalog based on a title-unit-entry principle which collocates a work that has been issued with variant titles. The customary notes, tracings, and cross-references would normally be included in each of these catalogs, and have been omitted from the illustrations only to save space. In the single entry catalog there would, of course, be no secondary entries. Our reader has one chance, and one chance only, to find the entry he or she wants, interfiled among several hundred thousand other entries.

---

43. R. Tagliacozzo and M. Kochen, "Information-seeking Behavior of Catalog Users," *Information Storage and Retrieval* 6, no. 5 (Dec. 1970): 365.
44. Simmons, op. cit., p.335.

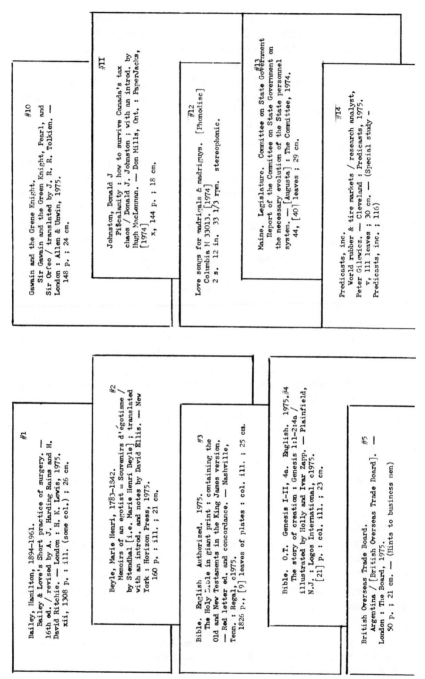

#10

Gawain and the Grene Knight.
    Sir Gawain and the Green Knight, Pearl, and
Sir Orfeo / translated by A. J. R. R. Tolkien. —
London : Allen & Unwin, 1975.
    148 p. ; 24 cm.

#11

Johnston, Donald J
    Fi$calamity : how to survive Canada's tax
chaos / Donald J. Johnston ; with an introd. by
Hugh MacLennan. — Don Mills, Ont. : PaperJacks,
[1974]
    x, 144 p. ; 18 cm.

#12

Love songs for madrigals & madriguys. [Phonodisc]
Columbia M 33013. [1974]
    2 s. 12 in. 33 1/3 rpm. stereophonic.

#13

Maine. Legislature. Committee on State Government
    Report of the Committee on State Government on
the necessary evolution of the State personnel
system. — [Augusta] : The Committee, 1974.
    44, [40] leaves ; 29 cm.

#14

Predicasts, inc.
    World rubber & tire markets / research analyst,
Peter Gilewicz. — Cleveland : Predicasts, 1975.
    v, 111 leaves ; 30 cm. — (Special study —
Predicasts, inc. ; 116)

#1

Bailey, Hamilton, 1894-1961.
    Bailey & Love's Short practice of surgery. —
16th ed. / revised by A. J. Harding Rains and H.
David Ritchie. — London : H. K. Lewis, 1975.
    xii, 1308 p. : ill. (some col.) ; 26 cm.

#2

Beyle, Marie Henri, 1783-1842.
    Memoirs of an egotist = Souvenirs d'égotisme /
by Stendhal [i.e. Marie Henri Beyle] ; translated
with an introd. and notes by David Ellis. — New
York : Horizon Press, 1975.
    160 p. : ill. ; 21 cm.

#3

Bible. English. Authorized. 1975.
    The Holy Bible in giant print : containing the
Old and New Testaments in the King James version.
— Red letter ed. and concordance. — Nashville,
Tenn. : Regal, c1975.
    1826 p., [9] leaves of plates : col. ill. ; 25 cm.

#4

Bible. O.T. Genesis I-II, 4a. English. 1975.
    The story of creation : Genesis 1:1-2:4a /
illustrated by Holly and Ivar Zapp. — Plainfield,
N.J. : Logos International, c1975.
    [21] p. : col. ill. ; 23 cm.

#5

British Overseas Trade Board.
    Argentina / [British Overseas Trade Board]. —
London : The Board, 1975.
    50 p. ; 21 cm. — (Hints to business men)

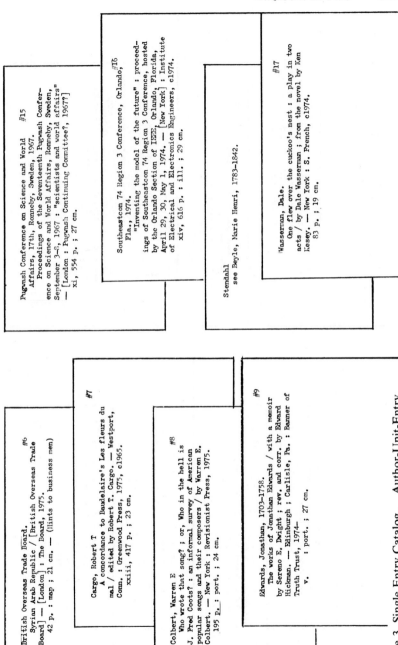

Pugwash Conference on Science and World   #15
   Affairs, 17th, Ronneby, Sweden, 1967.
   Proceedings of the Seventeenth Pugwash Confer-
ence on Science and World Affairs, Ronneby, Sweden,
September 3–8, 1967 : "scientists and world affairs"
— [London] : Pugwash Continuing Committee?, 1967?]
   xi, 554 p. ; 27 cm.

Southeastcon 74 Region 3 Conference, Orlando,   #16
   Fla., 1974.
   "Inventing the model of the future" : proceedings of Southeastcon 74 Region 3 Conference, hosted
by the Orlando Section of IEEE, Orlando, Florida,
April 29, 30, May 1, 1974. — [New York] : Institute
of Electrical and Electronics Engineers, c1974.
   xiv, 616 p. : ill. ; 29 cm.

Stendahl
   see Beyle, Marie Henri, 1783–1842.

Wasserman, Dale.   #17
   One flew over the cuckoo's nest : a play in two
acts / by Dale Wasserman ; from the novel by Ken
Kesey. — New York : S. French, c1974.
   83 p. ; 19 cm.

British Overseas Trade Board.   #6
   Syrian Arab Republic / [British Overseas Trade
Board] — [London] : The Board, 1975.
   42 p. : map ; 21 cm. — (Hints to business men)

Cargo, Robert T
   A concordance to Baudelaire's Les fleurs du
mal / edited by Robert T. Cargo. — Westport,
Conn. : Greenwood Press, 1975, c1965.   #7
   xxiii, 417 p. ; 23 cm.

Colbert, Warren E   #8
   Who wrote that song? ; or, Who in the hell is
J. Fred Coots? : an informal survey of American
popular songs and their composers / by Warren E.
Colbert. — New York : Revisionist Press, 1975.
   195 p. : port. ; 24 cm.

Edwards, Jonathan, 1703–1758.   #9
   The works of Jonathan Edwards / with a memoir
by Sereno E. Dwight ; rev. and corr. by Edvard
Hickman. — Edinburgh ; Carlisle, Pa. : Banner of
Truth Trust, 1974–
   v. : port. ; 27 cm.

Figure 3. Single Entry Catalog,   Author-Unit-Entry

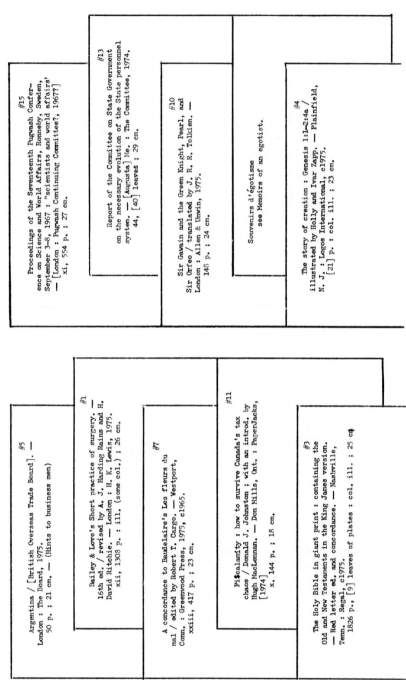

#15
Proceedings of the Seventeenth Pugwash Conference on Science and World Affairs, Ronneby, Sweden, September 3–8, 1967 : "scientists and world affairs" — [London : Pugwash Continuing Committee?, 1967?] — xi, 554 p. ; 27 cm.

#13
Report of the Committee on State Government on the necessary evolution of the State personnel system. — [Augusta] Me. : The Committee, 1974. 44, [40] leaves ; 29 cm.

#10
Sir Gawain and the Green Knight, Pearl, and Sir Orfeo / translated by J. R. R. Tolkien. — London : Allen & Unwin, 1975. 148 p. ; 24 cm.

Souvenirs d'égotisme
see Memoirs of an egotist.

#4
The story of creation : Genesis 1:1–2:4a / illustrated by Holly and Ivar Zapp. — Plainfield, N. J. : Logos International, c1975. [21] p. : col. ill. ; 23 cm.

#5
Argentina / [British Overseas Trade Board]. — London : The Board, 1975. — (Hints to business men) 50 p. ; 21 cm.

#1
Bailey & Love's Short practice of surgery. — 16th ed. / revised by A. J. Harding Rains and H. David Ritchie. — London : H. K. Lewis, 1975. xii, 1308 p. : ill. (some col.) ; 26 cm.

#7
A concordance to Baudelaire's Les fleurs du mal / edited by Robert T. Cargo. — Westport, Conn. : Greenwood Press, c1965. xxiii, 417 p. ; 23 cm.

#11
Fi$calamity : how to survive Canada's tax chaos / Donald J. Johnston ; with an introd. by Hugh MacLennan. — Don Mills, Ont. : PaperJacks, [1974] x, 144 p. ; 18 cm.

#3
The Holy Bible in giant print : containing the Old and New Testaments in the King James version. — Red letter ed. and concordance. — Nashville, Tenn. : Regal, c1975. 1826 p., [9] leaves of plates : col. ill. ; 25 cm.

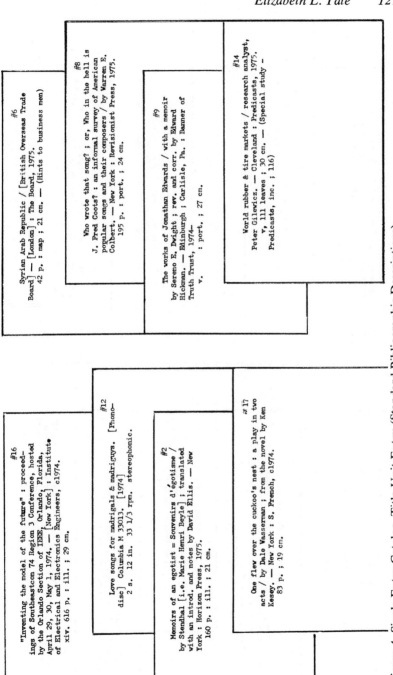

Figure 4. Single Entry Catalog, Title-Unit-Entry (Standard Bibliographic Descriptions)

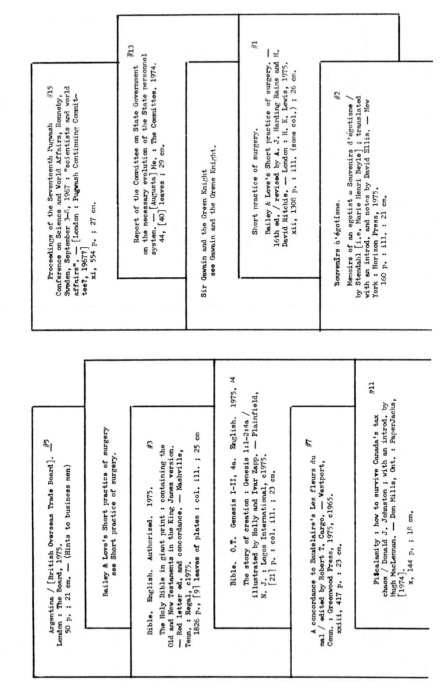

#15

Proceedings of the Seventeenth Pugwash Conference on Science and World Affairs, Ronneby, Sweden, September 3-9, 1967 : "scientists and world affairs". — [London : Pugwash Continuing Committee?, 1967?] xi, 554 p. ; 27 cm.

#13

Report of the Committee on State Government on the necessary evolution of the State personnel system. — [Augusta] Me. : The Committee, 1974. 44, [40] leaves ; 29 cm.

Sir Gawain and the Green Knight see Gawain and the Grene Knight.

#1

Short practice of surgery.

Bailey & Love's Short practice of surgery. — 16th ed. / revised by A. J. Harding Rains and H. David Ritchie. — London : H. K. Lewis, 1975. xii, 1308 p. ; ill. (some col.) ; 26 cm.

#2

Souvenirs à l'égotisme.

Memoirs of an egotist = Souvenirs d'égotisme / by Stendahl [i.e. Marie Henri Beyle] ; translated with an introd. and notes by David Ellis. — New York : Horizon Press, 1975. 160 p. : ill. ; 21 cm.

#5

Argentina / [British Overseas Trade Board]. London : The Board, 1975. 50 p. ; 21 cm. — (Hints to business men)

Bailey & Love's Short practice of surgery see Short practice of surgery.

#3

Bible. English. Authorized. 1975.

The Holy Bible in giant print : containing the Old and New Testaments in the King James version. — Red letter ed. and concordance. — Nashville, Tenn. : Regal, c1975. 1826 p., [9] leaves of plates : col. ill. ; 25 cm

#4

Bible. O.T. Genesis I-II, 4a. English. 1975.

The story of creation : Genesis 1:1-2:4a / illustrated by Holly and Ivar Zapp. — Plainfield, N. J. : Logos International, c1975. [21] p. : col. ill. ; 23 cm.

#7

A concordance to Baudelaire's Les fleurs du mal / edited by Robert T. Cargo. — Westport, Conn. : Greenwood Press, 1975, c1965. xxiii, 417 p. ; 23 cm.

#11

Fi$calanity : how to survive Canada's tax chaos / Donald J. Johnston ; with an introd. by Hugh MacLennan. — Don Mills, Ont. : PaperJacks, [1974], x, 144 p. ; 18 cm.

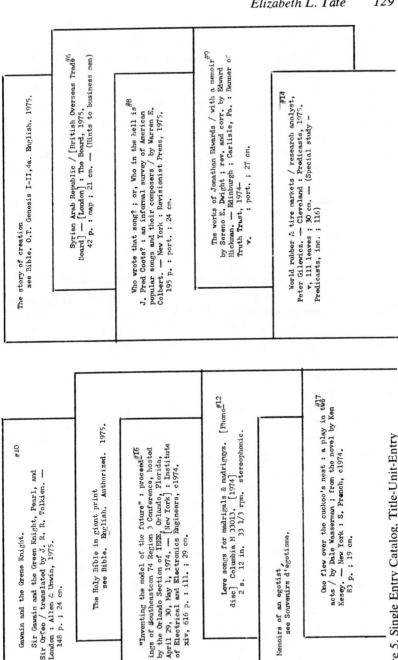

The story of creation
    see Bible. O.T. Genesis I-II,4a. English. 1975.

Syrian Arab Republic / [British Overseas Trade #6
Board] — [London] : The Board, 1975.
    42 p. : map ; 21 cm. — (Hints to business men)

Who wrote that song? ; or, Who in the hell is #8
J. Fred Coots? : an informal survey of American
popular songs and their composers / by Warren E.
Colbert. — New York : Revisionist Press, 1975.
    195 p. : port. ; 24 cm.

The works of Jonathan Edwards / with a memoir #9
by Sereno E, Dwight ; rev, and corr, by Edward
Hickman. — Edinburgh ; Carlisle, Pa. : Banner of
Truth Trust, 1974-
    v. : port. ; 27 cm.

World rubber & tire markets / research analyst, #14
Peter Gilewicz. — Cleveland : Predicasts, 1975.
    v, 111 leaves ; 30 cm. — (Special study -
Predicasts, inc. ; 116)

Gawain and the Grene Knight.   #10

    Sir Gawain and the Green Knight, Pearl, and
Sir Orfeo / translated by J. R. R. Tolkien. —
London : Allen & Unwin, 1975.
    148 p. ; 24 cm.

The Holy bible in giant print
    see Bible. English. Authorized. 1975.

"Inventing the model of the future" : proceed- #16
ings of Southeastcon 74 Region 3 Conference, hosted
by the Orlando Section of IEEE, Orlando, Florida,
April 29, 30, May 1, 1974. — [New York] : Institute
of Electrical and Electronics Engineers, c1974.
    xiv, 616 p. : ill. ; 29 cm.

Love songs for madrigals & madrigals.   [Phono- #12
disc] Columbia M 33013. [1974]
    2 s. 12 in. 33 1/3 rpm. stereophonic.

Memoirs of an egotist,
    see Souvenirs d'egotisme.

One flew over the cuckoo's nest : a play in two #17
acts / by Dale Wasserman ; from the novel by Ken
Kesey. — New York : S. French, c1974.
    83 p. ; 19 cm.

Figure 5. Single Entry Catalog, Title-Unit-Entry

If I were that reader, I would certainly prefer to search the author-unit-entry catalog for the work by Jonathan Edwards (item 9), the report issued by the Committee on State Government of the Maine Legislature (item 13), and the proceedings of the Pugwash Conference (item 15). Depending upon the information with which I began the search, I would not anticipate difficulties in finding the two works by the British Overseas Trade Board (items 5 and 6) or the survey prepared by Predicasts, Inc. (item 14). But with only one chance to win, I should be happier with the title-unit-entry catalog in figure 4 for item 1, because I can't remember the first name of the Bailey, who collaborated with Love; for "One Flew Over the Cuckoo's Nest" (item 17), because I saw the movie but haven't the foggiest notion who did the play; for "Fi$calamity" (item 11), because I can't recall whether Donald Johnston spells his surname with a *t*; for "Inventing the Model of the Future" (item 16), because I always have trouble finding author entries for IEEE conferences; for Sir Gawain and the Green Knight (item 10), because uniform titles baffle me; and for "Who Wrote That Song?" (item 8), because I don't know who wrote that book. It doesn't matter for "Love Songs for Madrigals & Madriguys" (item 12), which has a main entry under title according to *AACR*. For the rest, I suspect that my chances of success or failure are about equal in either catalog.

In contrasting these two catalogs I have intentionally cast myself into the role of reader to underline the fact that it would be difficult to evaluate objectively the efficiency of either single entry catalog because of all the variables that determine the reader's approach. Each work has two principal elements of identification: author and title. In some cases author is a strong clue; in other cases it is title. In still other cases, both are strong clues and sometimes both are weak. When both are weak, retrieval will be difficult in the single entry catalog, no matter what the principle of catalog organization may be. Our only objective evidence on the matter indicates that the reader's information about the title is likely to be more accurate than information about the author, but that he or she has been conditioned to search first under author.

In an author-unit-entry catalog, one form of the author's name serves to collocate the works of an author. The same logic can be applied to a title-unit-entry catalog, and one form of a title could be selected to collocate the various representations of a work. In figure 5, I have rearranged the seventeen entries to illustrate my concept of such a catalog. To evaluate its efficiency, we would certainly need a great deal more objective evidence about the utility of this type of organization for our reader. In a large, single entry catalog, it does offer a method of assembling the variants of a work which is consistent with the concept of title entry.

The single entry catalog affords its user only one chance to find a given entry. For the single entry catalog in book format, an index can provide additional approaches. Figures 6 and 7 illustrate my version of the indexes, complementary to the catalogs in figures 3 and 4. For the title-unit-entry catalog, the index serves to collocate the works of an author. For author-unit-entry book catalogs that are issued serially, the reader must consult several volumes to see all the entries for a given author, but all will be in the same part of the alphabet. To inspect all entries for one author in the title-unit-entry catalog, the reader would have to consult even more volumes, but the index does supply the guide-posts. Neither of these indexes in itself seems superior to the other, but to me it seems clear that each of these single entry catalogs becomes a more powerful tool with the addition of an index.

```
Argentina ...............................................# 5
Bailey & Love's Short practice of surgery ..............# 1
A concordance to Baudelaire's Les fleurs du mal ........# 7
Fi$calamity ...........................................#11
The Holy Bible in giant print .........................# 3
Inventing the model of the future .....................#16
Love songs for madrigals & madriguys ..................#12
Memoirs of an egotist .................................# 2
One flew over the cuckoo's nest .......................#17
Proceedings of the Seventeenth Pugwash Conference on
   Science and World Affairs...........................#15
Report of the Committee on State Government on the
   necessary evolution of the State personnel system
   [Maine]............................................#13
Short practice of surgery .............................# 1
Sir Gawain and the Green Knight .......................#10
   [etc., etc.]
```

Figure 6. Title Index to Author-Unit-Entry Catalog

```
Bailey, Hamilton ......................................# 1
Beyle, Marie Henri.....................................# 2
British Overseas Trade Board
   Argentina ..........................................# 5
   Syrian Arab Republic ...............................# 6
Cargo, Robert T........................................# 7
Colbert, Warren E .....................................# 8
Edwards, Jonathan .....................................# 9
Johnston, Donald J.....................................#11
Maine. Legislature. Committee on State Government .....#13
Predicasts, inc. ......................................#14
Pugwash Conference on Science and World Affairs, 17th,
   Ronneby, Sweden, 1967 ..............................#15
Southeastcon 74 Region 3 Conference, Orlando, Fla., 1974 #16
Stendahl...............................................# 2
Wasserman, Dale ... ...................................#17
```

Figure 7. Author Index to Title-Unit-Entry Catalog

For the dictionary catalog on cards, the format of the secondary entries constitutes the chief difference between the catalog based on author-unit-entry and one built from title-unit-entries. An author-unit-entry card set and a title-unit-entry card set for the publication from Predicasts Inc. can be seen in figure 8. The proponents of author-unit-entry claim that second-level organization by author is more desirable than second-level organization by title for all secondary entries. The proponents of title-unit-entry disagree and, in defense of their position, point to the success of subject files arranged chronologically and to the practice in some libraries of ignoring the second-level author heading in filing added entries.

When the dictionary catalog is on MARC tape, the format of the secondary entries is unimportant. The entry is approached by keyboarding at the terminal all or part of the access point the reader has selected. The access point is shown on the screen as an index term co-equal with other index terms, but with no corresponding entries. The entries in the file under the desired index term are shown on the screen as main entries only.

We have looked at a great deal of evidence, trying to find an answer to the first question I posed: Can we compare the efficiency of the author-unit-entry catalog and the title-unit-entry catalog in fulfilling the users' needs? I do not know your reaction, but for me there is no conclusive evidence in support of either principle.

Re: Cataloging Costs

Now for the second question: Is there any evidence on comparative costs of cataloging by these two methods? There is, unfortunately, little information on the cost of selecting author main entries. Hamdy prepared flowcharts of the possible steps in the process and concluded that

The selection of the main entry, as specified by the rules, requires a considerable amount of decision making and searching through reference sources, which is both time-consuming and costly. On the average, the selection of a main entry by a rule might require 42 steps of decisions and processes. According to the subrules this might require an average of 8 decisions and processes. Depending on the number of references given by a rule and the nature of the item being cataloged, the number of decisions required might double or triple.[45]

---

45. Hamdy, op. cit., p.129–130.

```
    Gilewicz, Peter.
Predicasts, inc.
    World rubber & tire markets / research analyst,

                MARKET SURVEYS.

            Predicasts, inc.
            World rubber & tire markets / research analyst,

Predicasts, inc.
    World rubber & tire markets / research analyst,

                Predicasts, inc.  Special study ; 116.

                Predicasts, inc.
                    World rubber & tire markets / research analyst,

    RUBBER INDUSTRY AND TRADE.
Predicasts, inc.
    World rubber & tire markets / research analyst,

                TIRE INDUSTRY.

                Predicasts, inc.
                    World rubber & tire markets / research analyst,

    World rubber & tire markets.
Predicasts, inc.
    World rubber & tire markets / research analyst,
Peter Gilewicz. — Cleveland : Predicasts, 1975.

    v, 111 leaves ; 30 cm. — (Special study -
Predicasts, inc. ; 116)




    1. Tire industry.  2. Rubber industry and trade.
3. Market surveys.  I. Gilewicz, Peter.  II. Title.
III. Series: Predicasts, inc.  Special study ; 116.
HD9161.A2P67  1975        338.4'7'6782
```

Figure 8. Author-Unit-Entry

Gilewicz, Peter.

World rubber & tire markets / research analyst,

MARKET SURVEYS.

World rubber & tire markets / research analyst,

Predicasts, inc.

World rubber & tire markets / research analyst,

RUBBER INDUSTRY AND TRADE.

World rubber & tire markets / research analyst,

Special study - Predicasts, inc. ; 116.

World rubber & tire markets / research analyst,

TIRE INDUSTRY.

World rubber & tire markets / research analyst,

    World rubber & tire markets / research analyst,
Peter Gilewicz. — Cleveland : Predicasts, 1975.

    v, 111 leaves ; 30 cm. — (Special study -
Predicasts, inc. ; 116)

    1. Tire industry. 2. Rubber industry and trade.
3. Market surveys. I. Gilewicz, Peter. 2. Predicasts, inc. III. Series: Special study - Predicasts,
inc. ; 116.
HD9161.A2P67 1975   338.4'7'6782

Figure 8 (*continued*) Title-Unit-Entry

Hamdy's flowcharts are, of course, based on the first edition of *AACR,* but even if similar charts were available for the second edition, it would be difficult to translate the process into dollars and cents. To determine the labor costs, the step of selecting the main entry would have to be isolated from the other steps in descriptive cataloging. Yet in actual practice the preparation of the bibliographic description and the determination of name forms yield valuable data on which to base the decision about main entry.

In the introduction to Hamdy's dissertation, Daily predicts that "the work of descriptive cataloging can be done by library technical assistants if a title unit entry method is employed."[46] Savings of this magnitude seem unlikely, however, for the skill of the trained cataloger will still be needed to determine the forms of personal and corporate names. Title-unit-entry as a principle of catalog organization need not dictate any particular policy regarding forms of entry. They are two distinct and separate issues.

The number of items that are likely to be affected by a proposed change is one indicator of possible savings. Only works that would require a choice of author main entry offer the possibility of savings with title-unit-entry. To get some idea of the number of cases in which title-unit-entry would decrease the cataloger's workload, I have spent quite a few hours poring over a random sample of main entries in LC's card catalog. I have not yet, alas, spent enough hours, so that I can report only preliminary results at this conference. The sample was limited to printed card main entries in the Cyrillic and Roman alphabets with imprint dates prior to 1960. It is very difficult to estimate accurately the number of main entries in this category, but the statistics in the LC annual reports suggest that it quite possibly is close to three million. A work was tallied as requiring a choice of main entry if (1) the tracing included added entries for personal or corporate names, (2) the tracing included added entries for works other than the one being cataloged, with the exception of series, or (3) in the absence of such added entries, the main entry was a uniform title or a form heading. Over the years the pattern of added entries has changed with changing rules and policies, but these criteria should provide a crude barometer, without requiring subjective judgment. As of March 2, I had inspected main entries for 1,344 works, of which 347, or 25.8 percent, required a choice of main entry, as defined.

A primary function of a main entry is to assemble the literary unit. To see how often a main entry might be needed for that purpose, I

---

46. Hamdy, op. cit., p.12.

reviewed each author file in its entirety for any scrap of evidence of an actual or potential need for assembling literary units. By limiting the sample to entries with imprint dates prior to 1960, a time span of a minimum of eighteen years had been allowed for the appearance of other editions or translations. The files provided evidence that 165, or 12.3 percent, of the 1,344 works either had or might someday require the assembling of a literary unit. Where no choice of main entry is required, however, a title-unit-entry provides the mechanism for assembling the literary unit just as well as the author-unit-entry. To illustrate with Fi$calamity as an example, the name of the author, Johnston, Donald J., appears on the top line of an author-unit-entry; it would appear as the only name in the tracing of a title-unit-entry. No decision making would be required to find the focal access point, if one were needed.

The subsample of 165 literary units was then further analyzed to see how many were among the works requiring a choice of main entry. Fifty-three of the literary units would have needed a focal access point. Of the 347 choices of main entry, only 15.3 percent were needed to assemble a literary unit. Or to calculate the percentages differently, of the 347 choices of main entry made by the cataloger, 294—or 84.7 percent —were not needed for the purpose of assembling a literary unit.

While I was writing this paper, I read a review of a recently published conference proceedings. The reviewer characterized the conference as the same old warhorses, saying the same old things. So in order to bring you something new, I continued my experiment a little further. Another function of the author-main-entry is to facilitate the formulation of secondary entries for a work. I looked at the 1,344 works to see how many had occasioned a secondary entry. Four had been the subject of another work, while twelve figured as added entries. Of these sixteen, only three would have needed a focal access point; the rest were for works that required no choice of main entry.

While counting the secondary entries for works, I noticed several for works that were not in the catalog; apparently the cataloger had been able to formulate these on the basis of information found someplace other than an author main entry in the catalog.

If we assume that further data support the hypotheses these statistics suggest, the results can be interpreted in different ways, depending upon whether for you the glass is half empty or half full. The future may very well bring an increase in the number of works requiring a choice of main entry as the cataloging of nonprint materials increases. It seems safe to hypothesize, though, that—quantitatively speaking—assembling the literary unit and providing secondary entries for works are not major functions of the catalog at present.

These data should have some relevance to the question of assigning book numbers, which the proponents of author-unit-entry regard as an important purpose of the main entry. One function of the book number is to create a unique identification number out of the class number. That function can be, and is now, fulfilled efficiently with a book number derived from either author or title. A second function is to bring together the works of an author on a given subject. I question the extent to which an author number accomplishes that function in a large library that uses close classification. A third function is that of assembling the literary unit on the shelves. It would be possible to assemble a literary unit on the shelves by title; but let's assume that we wish to continue to assemble certain literary units by author for our student patrons who must read a play by Shakespeare by the end of the week. It would be no problem for a shelflister to assign an author number on the basis of a title-unit-entry with only one name in the tracing. Only those that involve a choice present a problem; for these, a focal access point could be provided after the fact—that is, when a library actually has a literary unit to assemble. The number in this category would probably be small, if the 3.9 percent that I found at LC is indicative. In short, it would be possible to devise shelflisting procedures that would permit the use of title-unit-entry and eliminate the need for the preselection of a focal access point, if title-unit-entry is considered an economical method. But perhaps we need first to ask some hard questions about optimum collection organization in today's libraries.

I have presented my evidence on the second question regarding cataloging costs from which I have reached this conclusion. The Anglo-American cataloging codes have put a high price tag on descriptive cataloging, but there are insufficient data to predict the reduction in price that title-unit-entry might bring.

Re: International Exchange of Catalog Data

Let's hope for better luck with the last question: Is one type of entry likely to be more suitable than the other for international exchange? The idea of using the standard bibliographic description as the unit of exchange originally appeared when the possibilities of an international catalog code were explored. Then the differences between the Prussian Instructions and the 1908 Anglo-American code were so fundamental that an international code seemed an impossibility. Since then, the Prussian Instructions has been superseded by the *RAK* (*Regeln für die alphabetische Katalogisierung*) and the 1908 code by *AACR* (*Anglo-American Cataloguing Rules*). Both have been formulated with the Paris Principles in mind, and the Pàris Principles were hammered out primarily to serve as a foundation for national codes that would facilitate universal bibliographic control. With these developments, has the author-unit-entry become a satisfactory unit of exchange? A recent article by Rudolf Lais reports an investigation that throws some light on this question.[47]

At the suggestion of F. G. Kaltwasser, an inquiry was begun to determine the extent to which LC cataloging could be used without change in libraries that follow the *RAK*. The investigators examined 395 printed LC cards for monographs, of which 12 percent were corporate main entries, 8 percent title main entries, and the rest personal authors. They compared the LC cards with entries prepared according to *RAK* with regard to the choice and form of main and secondary entries. Of the 27.8 percent that were not in agreement, two-thirds differed in choice of main entry.[48] As you might guess, more than half of these were cases in which LC selected a corporate main entry, while *RAK,* with its narrower definition of *Urheber,* called for a title main entry. It will be interesting to see if the definition of corporate author in *AACR2* will result in more entries that correspond to the *RAK* entries, even though the two codes approach the problem from quite different points of view.

Additional data, relevant to the question of the author main entry as the unit of international exchange, can be found in a recent doctoral dissertation by C. Donald Cook. He compared LC cataloging, entries in the *British National Bibliography,* and entries in *Canadiana* for 515 titles. Only 16.1 percent were identical in choice and form of entry in all three sources. Choice of entry accounted for 3.3 percent of the differences, while variations in form were found in over 80 percent. He concluded that "the *Anglo-American Cataloging Rules* are effective in achieving standardization of choice and form of heading in the cataloging of the three national agencies only to the extent that the agencies are willing to apply the rules which have been mutually agreed upon."[49] It should be noted that changes made in *AACR1* subsequent to each of these investigations would have affected the results.

47. Rudolf Lais, "RAK und AACR: Gemeinsamkeiten, Unterschiede, Annäherungstendenzen," *Zeitschrift für Bibliothekswesen und Bibliographie* 23, no. 3 (1976): 141–150.

48. Ibid., p.142–143.

49. Charles Donald Cook, "The Effectiveness of the *Anglo-American Cataloging Rules* in Achieving Standardization of Choice and Form of Heading for Certain Library Materials Cataloged in Canada, Great Britain and the United States from 1968 through 1972" (unpublished DLS dissertation, School of Library Service, Columbia University, 1976), p.162.

There will need to be not only an international cataloging code but also uniform policies in application before the author-unit-entry becomes a completely satisfactory unit of exchange. With title-unit-entry there should be greater uniformity, because the sources of information are more obvious, the data elements are more easily recognized, and there are fewer applicable rules. But there is still scope for some differences in interpretation though I have no evidence to offer on that side of the coin.

Conclusion

I have now offered you all the evidence I've been able to find on each side of the main entry controversy. Author-unit-entry has emerged as the predominant system for organizing catalogs of library collections in the Western world. It has not always been the predominant system, and even after it was generally accepted by librarians, others have preferred different methods of organizing catalogs. Over the years, the author-unit-entry system has resulted in a multiplicity of rules, which have been variously interpreted to produce entries that are not free from inconsistencies. To overcome this obstacle to the international exchange of catalog data, the idea of the title-unit-entry was proposed. During the past six decades the idea has appeared, disappeared, and reappeared with variations; its appropriateness for the computer-based catalog has brought it to the fore recently. The idea that won't stay dead has been vigorously opposed. To help us weigh the merits of the case, I've combed through the relevant studies in search of objective evidence with which to compare the two systems in terms of their efficiency for the catalog user we actually know, possible cost differentials, and their suitability for international exchange. I wish there were more objective evidence to weigh. To reach a sound answer, we need to know more than we do about staff use of the catalog, the cost-benefits of the literary unit, and the optimum organization of the collections as well as the catalog. Meanwhile, I have decided on the basis of these five conclusions whether I wish to bury Caesar or to praise him, and I hope that this paper has thrown some light on the question for you.

1. Both author and title approaches are of vital importance in a catalog. Other features of a catalog should be sacrificed, if necessary, to provide both, and to provide the title approach in particular.
2. Neither author-unit-entry nor title-unit-entry provides easy retrieval of works with weak author and weak title clues.

3. If the only possibility is a single entry catalog, the title-unit-entry catalog will probably serve the patron better than the author-unit-entry catalog.
4. For multiple-entry catalogs, it's six of one and half a dozen of the other.
5. For the exchange of catalog data, title-unit-entry is probably more efficient than author-unit-entry.

Choice of Access Points: Personal Authors as Main and Added Entry Headings

GORDON STEVENSON

Introduction

Entry and Access

The first chapter of Part II of the second edition of *Anglo-American Cataloguing Rules* is entitled "Choice of Access Points." The terminology is somewhat new and the perspective from which the topic is approached is very new, but the topic itself has been with us as long as we have had cataloging codes. Long identified as the concept of "entry," it has been one of the less controversial aspects of code development and has been comparatively stable since the first Anglo-American code of 1908.[1]

The term "access point" and the terms it replaced, "entry" and "entry point," suggest that there are also cards in a manual file which are not access points. But it is obvious that every card in the file is a

---

1. *Catalog Rules: Author and Title Entries,* compiled by committees of the American Library Assn. and the (British) Library Assn. (American ed.; Boston: American Library Assn. Publishing Board, 1908).

potential access point. A potential access point, however, is not an access point for a specific user if that user cannot find it. And if the user cannot find it, more than likely the catalog malfunction is the result of the extremely complex system that is needed to structure headings for large files, rather than some cataloger's decision as to the choice of access points. In any case, as far as the catalog user is concerned, the whole system is a system of access. Thus decisions on access points are tied in with that crucial point at which the user begins to interact with the system.

The principles that were followed in developing practical rules of access in the new edition are based on traditions which, in fact, predate the code of 1908. Indeed, some of the principles were enumerated by Panizzi in the middle of the nineteenth century, and some of them go back into the eighteenth century. For this reason, those sections of the new edition with which I am concerned here will not cause changes of any great moment. Some music librarians may be upset if a cadenza to a concerto is entered under the name of the person who wrote the cadenza, rather than the name of the person who wrote the concerto. Those spirits from the other world who communicate through a medium may rejoice that they now get main entries. Ghost writers are assured of their continued anonymity.

A Historical Note

The most recent innovation in terms of access points, at least insofar as they relate to descriptive cataloging, occurred during the last quarter of the nineteenth century, when concepts of corporate entry and corporate authorship were developed. The concept of corporate entry surely emerged as a practical necessity, and only later was the concept of corporate authorship developed. Since then, the major issues have been the construction of appropriate and consistent headings to represent, interrelate, and arrange entries. As has been the convention, then, the chapter under discussion does not deal with the construction of headings, but with what have been known as "rules of entry." The issue is what entries are needed, not the methods of systematizing the headings which represent these entries.

My topic, then, is comparable to chapter 1 of the first edition of the code. The earlier first chapter was the cornerstone of all that followed. In looking for the origins of this tradition, I reread the rules which Panizzi published in 1841. Oddly enough, Panizzi took it for granted that works would be entered under the names of their authors and did not specifically say so. His first rule is a brief statement on how to organize a description: "Titles to be written on slips, uniform in size."[2] A decade later, Charles Coffin Jewett apparently assumed that everyone would use slips of uniform size. His first rule states that catalogers are to transcribe titles in full "as they stand upon the title-page."[3] It is interesting that the code we are considering today is reminiscent of these mid-nineteenth-century systems in beginning with the mechanics of physical description, a tradition which had ended with the publication of Cutter's rules in 1876. Since then, codes in the Anglo-American tradition have begun with essentially the same rule. Cutter wrote: "1. Make the author-entry under (A) the name of the author whether personal or corporate, or (B) some substitute for it."[4] In the code of 1908, this first rule was changed to "Enter a work under the name of its author whether individual or corporate."[5] With only relatively insignificant changes in wording, this rule is found as rule number one in the codes of 1941, 1949, and 1967.

The User's Perspective

The removal of discussions of rules of entry from their primary place at the start of the code, as has been noted, indicates the new emphasis on bibliographic description as the source of decisions on access points. This is the case because once a bibliographic data record has been constructed—that is, after we have extracted from the document those data elements which are to constitute its profile—and once this record is entered into an automated file, any item in that record may be used as an access point if the system is so programmed. I don't think we yet know the full implications of this in terms of providing new, more efficient, and unconventional access points for catalog users.

The slightly different terminology (i.e. the use of the term "access point" rather than "entry") is more than a relatively insignificant semantic difference. It clearly indicates a new perspective. The two terms, entry and access, reflect the respective points of view of catalogers and users of catalogs. We, the catalogers, decide what entries we will make.

2. British Museum, *The Catalogue of Printed Books in the British Museum* (London, 1841), 1:v. The rules are reprinted in Nancy Brault, *The Great Debate on Panizzi's Rules in 1847–1849: The Issues Discussed* (Los Angeles: School of Library and Information Science, University of California, 1972), p.85–89.

3. Charles C. Jewett, *Smithsonian Report on the Construction of Catalogues of Libraries . . . with Rules and Examples* (2d ed.; Washington: Smithsonian Institution, 1953).

4. Charles A. Cutter, *Rules for a Dictionary Catalog* (4th ed., rewritten; U.S. Bureau of Education, Special Report on Public Libraries, Part II; Washington: Government Printing Office, 1904), p.26.

5. *Catalog Rules* (1908), p.1.

The users of the catalog choose their own access points. If all goes well, the entries we have made will indeed provide the users with access to the references which they want. But generally speaking, if we are to believe the results of some catalog use studies, things do not go well in as much as 20 percent of known-item searches in large libraries.

It seems a safe assumption that users of catalogs, for the most part, do not set out to look for main entries or added entries (except in the case of added entries which are subject headings).

The user may have a number of bibliographic clues, but—one way or another—comes to some decision about which one will be used to enter the file. In a sense, whatever clue is used *is* the "main entry," as far as the specific user is concerned. The user probably does not care whether we call it a main entry or an added entry, and indeed may not even know the difference between the two forms. A good entry is one that works. How well do our entries work? How often do they work?

In his recent review of catalog use studies, F. W. Lancaster comments on the catalog use study sponsored by the American Library Association in 1958.[6] He noted that "in one case out of every five . . . the user was unable to locate an entry that was actually present in the catalog and [that] this 20% failure rate may be a low estimate."[7] He also noted that a sample of 203 searches was made by staff members of participating libraries and "16% produced failures to locate entries for items which were actually in the catalog."[8] This information is relevant to a consideration of access points only to the extent that failures were caused by the lack of an entry, rather than the complex structure of files and headings (i.e. the access point was there, but the user looked for it in the wrong place). In other words, given the typical user's expectations about the catalog in its traditional form, we have probably been making the right decisions about entries—it is the complex structure of headings which leads to user failure.

Potentials for Unconventional Access

Even though all bibliographic data elements could be structured into access points or fields, this is not to say that all of them would be used very much, or even at all. I suspect that in exploiting the potentials

6. American Library Association. *Catalog Use Study,* ed. V. Mostecky (Chicago: American Library Assn., 1958).

7. F. W. Lancaster, *The Measurement and Evaluation of Library Services* (Washington: Information Resources Press, 1977), p.24.

8. Ibid.

of online searching, we will find that subject and materials specialists may be of some help. Let me give you one example of this.

Researchers and scholars who work with recorded sound frequently want access to their sources by matrix numbers of disc recordings and sometimes by manufacturers' code names and label (or catalog) numbers.

Matrix numbers are those incised in the metal parts or matrices which are used in the manufacture of disc recordings. Every disc that is reproduced from a set of matrices will have the same number (it is part of the shellac or plastic of the disc). Manufacturers' label numbers are the code numbers, printed on disc labels. For most of us, these discographic data elements would be rather unconventional access points; but they may be more useful than one might think.

Consider, for example, the complexities of clarifying precisely what we mean by the term "work" when one of the physical manifestations of a work is a sound recording. If we are cataloging a work, obviously we must identify that work so it can be distinguished from all other works. Once recorded, that specific manifestation of the work must then be distinguished from other manifestations. In the case of works of composers, we frequently have opus numbers or thematic index numbers to provide unequivocal identification of specific works, all versions of which can be pulled together by means of these identifiers. But there are many cases in which specific manifestations of a work are issued under different labels and sometimes with different titles. For example, there is a recording made by Fletcher Henderson and his orchestra in 1924 which illustrates the need for using the matrix number as a discographic data element. The work, in this case, consists of a little less than three minutes of sound.

Actually, as a material object, the work is a metal disc, etched with grooves created by a vibrating stylus. These specific grooves were issued (i.e. reproduced and published) at least twenty-seven times. And in most of these issues, the information on their respective labels is different (titles are different, the name given the orchestra is different, etc.). Only by using matrice numbers can the many different issues of the work be identified.[9]

The numbers which discographers call "label numbers" serve a somewhat different purpose. For example, one might want to find out if a library has a very specific recording, say George Szell's recording of

---

9. Walter C. Allen, *Hendersonia: The Music of Fletcher Henderson and His Musicians, a Bio-Discography* (Highland Park, N.J.: Walter C. Allen, 1973), p.162.

Beethoven's *Fifth Symphony,* which he made with the Concertgebouw Orchestra of Amsterdam. In accessing a manual file, after having found "Beethoven," and then his *Fifth Symphony,* one still has to deal with the ten to thirty different recordings of this work, which one might find in a large collection, to find out if the specific Szell version is on hand. This could be done more expeditiously by entering the file under the manufacturer's number, which is "Col. MG 3031." Thus three steps could be reduced to one. The name "Beethoven" is bypassed, as is the title of the specific work, and one goes directly to the specific version one wants. Now the beauty of all this is that the manufacturer's abbreviated name and the number for the specific disc, "MG 3031," are used to identify the work not only in trade sources (such as the Schwann catalogs) but in most other citations, references, and discographies.

In fact, the quickest way to retrieve a bibliographic entry when making a known-item search in an online catalog system may be the International Standard Book or Serial Number. It is not at all beyond reason to expect that within a few years, style manuals for authors of journal articles and books may ask that these numbers be used in citations. Certainly, in the case of journals, such numbers would probably save massive amounts of time in locating titles in large local collections, union catalogs, and interlibrary loan systems.

The point is that there are possibilities, some of which we may not yet have thought of, for accessing online files. In any case, potential access points are enumerated in the bibliographic description. They are, however, not limited to those in the initial description, for other access points can be added if they are wanted.

People who know far more about the bibliographic potentials and limitations of the computer than I do, have indicated that this technology will not, indeed cannot, affect sound (i.e. traditional) bibliographic practice. I am going to have to think about that for this reason: Everything I know about technology indicates that it *does* have externalities. I should think that few people today would argue with the premise that the mechanical means by which messages are transmitted (and catalogers construct bibliographic message systems) has a profound impact on the nature of the content and structure of the message—which is to say that the entire system is affected by the new technology.

Some Rule Changes

In getting more specific about the new edition, I do not want to make a rule-by-rule comparison of the old and the new. Rather, I will comment on only a few changes which strike me as interesting.

At the start, two important points should be noted: "The rules in Part II apply to works and not generally to physical manifestations of those works," and the rules "apply to all library materials, irrespective of the medium in which they are published or of whether they are serial or nonserial in nature" (p.277). Thus in terms of entry there is indeed a considerable change in the conceptualization of principles from that in the first edition. This is *not* to say that the final result—that is, the outcome as to the choice of entry—is necessarily different.

As has been noted, most of the five chapters in Part III of the first edition contained rules of entry and rules for description. And some of us still think in terms of questions such as these: "What is the main entry for a filmstrip?" "What is the main entry for a sound recording?" Abandonment of this approach and an increasing generalization of basic principles is obviously a continuation of the progress made in the first edition. It seems to work most of the time. However, there are some cases where it is in the nature of the physical medium that some special problems emerge. A good example of this is sound recordings, where to catalog "works" would involve, in some cases, cataloging as many as sixteen or more compositions, found on one disc recording. So there are a number of cases in the new chapter where the general nature of the approach must be modified. Otherwise, the chapter roughly parallels chapter 1 of the first edition. It falls into two broad sections: general rules and special rules. The special rules (21.31 through 21.39) are comparable to the special rules in the first edition: certain legal publications, administrative regulations, court rules, sacred scriptures, etc.

The general nature of the first series of rules for access points may be illustrated by the treatment of maps. In the first edition, if one looks under the index term "Maps," one will indeed find a reference to the rule for entering maps. We are referred to rule 210. Turning to this rule in the first edition, we read: "A map, a series of maps, an atlas, a relief model, or a globe is entered under the person or corporate body responsible for its intellectual content." If we look under the index term "Maps" in the new edition, we will find twelve references, but none of them refers you to a rule for the entry of maps. The rule we want is the basic rule for making access points, rule 21.1.

Now despite all that has been said about the concept of main entry, we are still going to make main entries. In terms of personal authors, we do what we have always done and use the concept of intellectual responsibility. However, the concept of corporate authorship has changed in the new edition, and I will leave it to Åke Koel to comment on these changes. I will only note that corporate authorship has ostensibly been abandoned, but corporate entries have not. If we do not now have corporate authorship, we do have something called corporate "emanations," and these, in fact, are blocks of material which are indistinguishable from some types of material that formerly were entered under principles of corporate authorship.

Thus that classic rule, which has been rule number one for a century, has been rewritten. No longer do we read "Enter a work . . . by one author under the person or corporate body that is the author . . . ."

There is, however, a close parallel between the old edition and the new in dealing with a series of special problems: rules 21.5 through 21.15 are general (e.g. works of unknown or uncertain authorship, works of mixed responsibility, etc.) and rules 21.16 through 21.23 are specific in terms of types of material (e.g. art works, musical works, sound recordings, etc.).

21.28: Related Works

In the case of related works, the new edition does not make special cases based on titles of works. The old rule (19A) says that if the work's title is "indistinct and dependent on the title of another work" it should be entered under the heading used for the other work. Furthermore, "auxiliary works the use of which is dependent on one particular edition of the main work (e.g., certain indexes, manuals, etc.)" are entered under the same "author and/or title as the work to which it is related." The new rule (21.28B) is a general rule: "Enter a related work under its own heading (personal author, corporate body, or title) according to rules in chapter 21."

21.23: Entry of Sound Recordings

This rule contains a major innovation in the cataloging of sound recordings. The old rule (250) reads: "The entry for a work, recorded on a phonorecord or set of phonorecords, is the same as the entry for the same material in its visual form." The rules for books, booklike materials, and music were applied to sound recordings. Principles of main entry and principles of authorship were such that entries under names of performers as main entries was not possible. Especially in the case of much recent popular music, this led to title main entries which were logically consistent, but patently absurd from the user's point of view. There were also some strange title main entries in classical music. An LP recording with the title "Arturo Toscanini Conducts Favorite Overtures" would be cataloged with the title as the main entry, and filed under *A* for Arturo. The problem, then, is collections of works by different composers which either have no collective title or collective titles that consist of performers' names. There is, for example, an entry for a reissue of early country and western music under its title, "J. Minor Band," which is thus filed under *J*.

The new rule which solves this problem is 21.23C: "Enter a sound recording containing works by different persons under the heading for the person or body represented as principal performer. If there are two or three persons or bodies represented, enter under the heading for the first named and make added entries under the headings for the others." This rule applies not only to sound recording collections which lack a usable collective title, but to all collections that are so identified in the rule (there is an exception to this, which I will take note of in a moment). The example under this rule is an LP recording with the title "Great Tenor Arias," which is a fine title. However, it is entered under the name of the performer because there are works by different composers.

The material in Part I, chapter 6 ("Sound Recordings") has some impact on decisions about the choice of entry in these complex situations. The block of rules under 6.1G provides ways of laying out descriptions for "items without a collective title," which provide an alternative to rule 21.23. When dealing with a sound recording of works by different composers, one does not always have to follow 21.23C and enter the item under the heading for the name of the performer.

6.1G1 If a sound recording lacks a collective title, *either* describe the item as a unit (see 6.1G2 and 6.1G3) *or* make a separate description for each separately titled work (see 6.1G4).

6.1G2 In describing as a unit a sound recording lacking a collective title, record the titles of the individual works as instructed in 1.1G.

If one does not want to describe it as a unit, one can make "a separate description for each separately titled work" (see rule 6.1G4). It is obvious that how one decides to treat these items will result in two different main entries. If the item is described as a unit, then according to rule 21.23C it will be entered under "the heading for the name of the principal performer." But if one describes the separately titled works, each of these works will be entered under the name of its composer, if the name of the composer is known.

The new code has recognized that some sound recordings contain collections of different works which have as their unifying feature one specific composer. Other collections have as their unifying feature one specific performer. In the first instance, the composer is the obvious choice for the main entry; in the second, it is good that it is now recognized that the performer, the unifying element of the collection, is the logical main entry. Now, a problem which is not resolved (at least to my satisfaction) is the case where the collection is unified by neither composer nor performer. It seems to me that in such cases, if there is a good title (and there generally is, because these are albums based on some theme), the main entry should be under title, rather than under the first named of many performers or resorting to individual descriptions of many separate works.

21.29: Added Entries

In the first edition, the directions for added entries were brought together in rule 33, the last section of chapter 1, where they followed "Special Rules" of entry. In the new edition, they precede "Special Rules." The broad subdivisions are essentially the same in both editions. However, there are a few minor changes (e.g. the section on "initials and abbreviations" has been removed from this section and placed in a more appropriate rule). In both editions it is clearly stated, but in somewhat different wording, that local circumstances may be such as to require more added entries than are called for in the general rules. Similar options are found in the rules for analytical entries for parts of bibliographic units.

Because of the importance of added entries for titles, a word about them seems to be in order. The first mention of added entries for titles in the new edition is a bit deceptive and suggests they be used quite sparingly:

21.29B Make an added entry under the heading for a person or a corporate body or under a title if some catalogue users might suppose that the description of an item would be found under that heading or title rather than under the heading or title chosen for the main entry.

However, when we reach rule 21.30J it is clear that the change in practice is not to fewer titles but to more titles, for there are only four exceptions to this rule: "Make an added entry under the title proper of every work entered under a personal heading, a corporate heading, or a uniform title."

Access by Authors and by Titles

Lancaster's review of catalog use studies includes Alan Meyer's excellent summary of "Some Important Findings in Catalog Use Studies." Some of his findings are relevant to the issue at hand:

Searching under author requires an average of five times as many card examinations as searching under title. With inaccurate bibliographic information, which is very common, that ratio increases considerably.[10]

People generally use authors for entry to the catalog before they use titles. This is true in all libraries, not just academic ones. It is especially surprising, considering that it usually takes longer to find a book by author than by title.[11]

Most people do not persevere very long in catalog searches. More than 50% will look up only one entry and then stop, regardless of whether or not they have found what they are looking for . . . .[12]

The next three items indicate the relative importance of access by authors and access by titles:

Most people remember titles better than authors.[13]

People often remember key words in titles even when they do not remember exact titles.[14]

Permuted title indexes greatly raise the success rate of searching for incomplete and half-remembered titles.[15]

These selected excerpts from Meyer's summary, besides indicating the importance of title added entries, also remind us that the systems we construct are not complete until they are used—a communications system exists only when something is communicated to somebody—and using them is a surprisingly complex behavioral act, an act that we can describe to some extent but to which, to date, we have brought only the most elementary analytical tools. Thus, although one could say much more about this new chapter on access points, I prefer to turn to a brief consideration of issues related to the foundations of the code.

Principles, Theories, Models

Some questions have been raised about the theoretical foundations of the code and the possible lack of underlying principles. If a principle

---

10. Lancaster, op. cit., p.70.
11. Ibid.
12. Ibid.
13. Ibid, p.69.
14. Ibid.
15. Ibid., p.70.

is a working assumption that serves as a guideline that tells us what to do in a variety of situations, then the code is indeed based on principles, although they are not always explicitly stated. The absolute autonomy of the concept of main entry, which was a basic principle of the first edition, has been modified considerably. And the principle of corporate authorship has been replaced by what one of the code's editors describes as "a rigorous operational definition of corporate responsibility."[16] There are, clearly, underlying principles, but whether there is a theory is another question.

According to a typical definition, theory constitutes "systematically organized knowledge applicable in a relatively wide variety of circumstances, especially a system of assumptions, accepted principles, and rules of procedure devised to analyze, predict, or otherwise explain a specified set of phenomena."[17]

Theories *explain* phenomena. Thus they are useful in predicting the course of events, human behavior, or physical phenomena. What would a theory of cataloging explain or predict? I don't think it would explain anything particularly useful (I presume it would explain or predict the behavior of catalogers). However, a cataloging code can be based on theories, and that is something else altogether. Such theories might be similar to those which explain such phenomena as the creation and diffusion of bibliographic data.[18]

Another source for theory would be theories of human communications behavior. What phenomena are we interested in? We are interested in the interaction between users or information seekers and catalogs. I suspect that this is what Phyllis Richmond had in mind when she is reported to have said that "the cycle of cataloging rule revisions needs to be broken, and there needs to be serious research into the way library catalogs are approached and used."[19] This cyclic pattern has existed because the information environment within which we work has constantly changed. In a quixotic moment, it occurred to me that the cyclic return of cataloging code revision committees speeds up each time it occurs. It took forty-one years to replace the code of 1908, eighteen years to replace the code of 1949, and eleven years to replace the code of 1967.

---

16. Michael Gorman, "The Anglo-American Cataloguing Rules, Second Edition," *Library Resources & Technical Services* 22 (Summer 1978): 219.

17. *The American Heritage Dictionary of the English Language,* ed. Peter Davies (New York: Dell, 1970), p.718.

18. I am thinking here of the types of theories and laws which have been developed in the field of bibliometrics, such as Bradford's law of scatter and the Zipf distribution.

19. "Report," *Library Resources & Technical Services* 22 (Summer 1978): 227.

If this rate of change continues, we will have another new code in five or six years, then another one in three years, and probably a code a month by the year 2000. This is absurd, but let us hope that the new edition will serve us for at least a decade or more. In the meantime, some theory may not only lay the foundations for improvement of the present code, it may suggest ways of making better use of it, or at least of understanding some of its problems.

If we can "analyze, predict, or otherwise explain" what goes on in the communications behavior which leads people to approach catalogs the way they do, then these theories might have some influence on the types of access points we provide. For example, one hypothesis that might be part of a theoretical construct of catalog access might be based on the examination question, reported by B. C. Vickery from a British postgraduate diploma examination, which asked students to comment on the statement "The design of any information service should be predicated on the assumption that its customers will exert minimal effort to receive its benefits."[20]

Keep in mind that we are talking about the catalog functions in what are identified as "known-item searches." If a search is for a known item, what is known must be known from some source—from another person or from some sort of citation. Perhaps it is for this reason that we have not had, as far as I know, a behavioral theory of catalog use. I should imagine that cataloging codes of the past and the present are based largely on general principles arrived at pragmatically and then tempered by the requirements of internal consistency.

If there is not a theory to explain behavioral aspects of catalog use, we *do* have a model which will indicate the problems inherent in any cataloging system. I am referring to the classic model worked out thirty years ago by Shannon and Weaver.[21] In its simplest form, this can be used as an all-purpose model that will fit (to some extent, at least) any system of communicating messages. It is a linear model which tracks the progress of a message from its source to its final destination. The model has five functional elements:

1. A message source
2. A system of encoding that message into a form useful for its diffusion
3. The actual mechanism for diffusing the message (i.e. the signal)

20. B. C. Vickery, *Techniques of Information Retrieval* (London: Butterworths, 1970), p.235.

21. C. V. Shannon and W. Weaver, *The Mathematical Theory of Communication* (Urbana: University of Illinois Press, 1949).

4. A decoding system
5. A receiver (i.e. the destination of the message).

An unwanted element is "noise," which interferes with the signal, resulting in a distortion of the message.[22] In the context of the topic of this conference, the source in the model is a document or package that contains information (here we define "information" as any set of meaningful symbols, and thus we have a definition that includes music [which is not information in the ordinary meaning of the term, but *does* consist of aural and visual symbols which apparently mean something to some people]). The creation of such documentary sources is not our concern. In fact, in descriptive cataloging we are not even concerned with the content of these sources to any great extent. We deal in labels. For example, in the case of sound recordings we are cataloging labels which identify what is recorded. I realize that this seems to contradict the principle that we catalog "works," not manifestations of works. (Obviously, I have a few problems with this concept, which I find a bit amorphous, but this is not the time to go into them.)

In any case, we get involved at the second stage of the model: catalogers are "encoders." We take sets of symbols and recode them into a more limited system of symbols. These we assemble into what is the "signal" in the Shannon-Weaver model. Our catalogs are signals. But unlike other systems of communication, our manual systems are inert. They are interactive only to the extent that we provide cross-references or directional cards.

In using these signals, these catalogs, the user is clearly the ultimate destination of the message, but the user is also the decoder. I can imagine information indexing systems which are so complicated that we not only need catalogers to construct them but decoders (i.e. "decatalogers") to get the right information to the right users.

Now the value of this simplistic model is that it indicates the possible source of a theory of entry. When we analyze living communications systems in terms of the Shannon-Weaver model, we find that there are a number of additional features which modify the whole process and affect its efficiency. We find, for example, that a feature of some systems is feedback. Since the user of a manual card file cannot communicate to the file, feedback is not possible. Will it be possible with online sys-

---

22. Professor Hans Wellisch reminded me that one should not talk about the Shannon-Weaver model without saying something about "noise." The catalog can probably transmit a good-to-perfect "signal," but there may be psychological or cultural "noise" which prevents or distorts its reception in the mind of the catalog user.

tems? I think it will, once we learn more about the behavior of library users. But far more important than feedback is the environment in which the system must function—this, I suspect, is the source of most of our problems. In the end, we are talking about the transmission of symbols. With just a few exceptions, in cataloging all of our symbols are words. And words are not just words, they are the mechanisms for human thought. My point is that if we draw a circle around the first part of the model, a circle to encompass source, encoder, and signal, we have an environment of symbols. Now whether or not the system works depends on the extent to which our system of symbols matches the symbols— that is, the words—which the users of the system have in their heads. This is what the new edition of the code tries to do, and it is more evident in the structure of headings than in issues of access points.

Here is the most basic set of assumptions that underlie the code:

Information is distributed in the form of packages: books, journals, sound recordings, and the like.

These packages are labeled in various ways. The labels may be title pages in books; they may be pieces of paper pasted in the center of disc recordings; etc.

About the same time that we enter references to these packages in our catalogs, they are being diffused, listed, noted, and referred to by people to whom they are of some interest, for one reason or another.

Our assumption is that the clues which lead people to know of the existence of these packages are somehow, directly or indirectly, drawn from the same labels we find when we catalog them.

We thus provide entries in our catalogs which will supply the users with access points that match up with the clues they may have acquired. The process of preparing these entries begins with description, the systematic recording of all relevant data elements.

The above is based on only the most minimal knowledge of how people think about bibliographic data. As far as I can tell, this revised edition of the code is the latest in a long line of codes in which the basic structure is based on some inner logic, derived from a more or less common bibliographic language that is used in sources which transmit and channel bibliographic data through society. We have wanted to be structurally consistent, with the idea that consistency is an aid to the catalog user. We could argue that there is a common world of bibliographic discourse which is part of the informational environment of those of us who construct catalogs and those who use the catalogs we construct.

But is there such a language? Not if we consider all potential users of catalogs based on our code. The enormous problems that are faced in structuring a code which aims to be international are evident when we think of the diverse audiences it is intended to serve: elementary and secondary school students, junior college and university students, an endless stream of subject specialists and professional people, technical workers, and the millions of people who constitute the extremely diverse groups that are served by our vast system of public libraries. This is why, in the history of cataloging codes, the greatest emphasis has been placed on internal consistency. We don't have much else to use right now.

A word, then, on consistency and logic. When Jim Ranz studied the history of library catalogs in the United States, he noted that in the nineteenth century it was clear that librarians wanted to structure their catalogs on systems of entries which exhibited three characteristics. "It was," Ranz wrote, "of utmost importance that the entry words be determined logically, systematically, and in a manner predictable by the reader."[23] All well and good, but though we may be logical and consistent, our logic is not necessarily the logic of library users. We have constructed a code which can be used to catalog anything, in any discipline or subject area, in any physical form, published at any time, anywhere in the world—such a code is needed to deal with the enormous world output of information sources. But our catalogs are used by *individuals,* each of whom lives in an informational environment which is minuscule compared to the one with which the code must deal.

The new edition is a complicated tool, but I do not see how it could have been otherwise. However, I believe that the first edition was even more complicated. Whether one agrees with me or not, librarians should have no problems in dealing with the rules of the new edition. The issue in the case of access points will not be the type of access points as such, but the headings that are used to identify these access points. In evaluating these changes—and they can only be evaluated by working librarians, those who are daily involved with the catalog and with the public—I hope that the major criterion will be the extent to which there is a better match between the bibliographic data that people bring to the catalog and the structure of the new headings.

23. Jim Ranz, *The Printed Book Catalog in American Libraries: 1723–1900* (ACRL Monograph, 26) (Chicago: American Library Assn., 1964), p.30.

Form of Headings for Persons, Geographic Names, and References

BARBARA A. GATES

This paper will address three chapters in Part II of *AACR2*: chapter 22, "Headings for Persons"; chapter 23, "Geographic Names"; and chapter 26, "References."

Headings for Persons

As was stated earlier, each chapter in *AACR2* is arranged with general rules, followed by specific rules. In chapter 22 the rules have been developed to provide easier access for the catalog user.

The general rules for the name and form of name precede rules for special types of names, additions to names, and names in certain languages. The first three rules, 22.1–22.3, are the general rules for selecting the name for a person and the use of accents and other diacritical marks and hyphens; selecting the name for a person when that person has used different names; and selecting the name for a person when that person has used different forms of a name.

These rules deal entirely with selecting the personal name to be used and do not discuss the form the name will have as an entry. The examples in these rules are presented as they might appear on a title page, that is, John Smith, Robert Taylor.

Having selected the name to be used, we must determine the form of the name as an entry element. Rules 22.4–22.11 deal with these matters. The examples in these rules are presented in entry form.

Rules 22.12–22.20 set out the instructions for additions to names, and rules 22.21–22.28 cover the special rules for names in certain languages, with illustrative examples. Throughout the chapter, instructions for references to other names or forms of names are provided as they are appropriate.

The next step in cataloging an item, after the bibliographic description of the work is completed, is to select the access points. Using the chief sources of information in a person's works, we determine the form of name by which he or she is commonly known. It is important to stress this—the name by which he or she is commonly known—whether a full name, a name with initials, a name consisting only of initials, a name with a title of nobility, or a pseudonym. For example:

Jimmy Carter
H.D.
Sister Mary Joseph
Jean-Léon Juarès

Having done this, the cataloger may discover that the person uses different forms of a name. What is the common, or predominant, form of name the person uses? This is determined from the form most often used in the person's works, in reference sources, or, in instances of change of name, the latest form of the name.

If a person uses one pseudonym for all of his or her works, or if he or she is predominantly identified in reference sources by one pseudonym, select the pseudonym. For example:

Nevil Shute
not Nevil Shute Norway

Some people use more than one pseudonym, or a real name and one or more pseudonyms. Select one of the names if the person is identified predominantly by that name in later editions of his or her works, in critical works, or in reference sources. A footnote to this rule states that the cataloger should disregard reference sources that always list a person under his or her real name. For example:

Erle Stanley Gardner
not A.A. Fair
not Charles J. Kenny

However, if a person who uses pseudonyms is not predominantly known by one name, select for each item the name that appears in it and make references connecting the various names. For example:

John Creasey
(*real name used in some works*)
Gordon Ashe

Michael Halliday
J.J. Marric
Anthony Marton
Jeremy York
(*Pseudonyms used in some works*)
Make explanatory references to and from the various headings
   for Creasey *as required*

People often vary the form of the name they use in their works. This means the cataloger must determine the common or predominant form of the person's name. If no one form appears to be predominant, select the latest form, and if still in doubt use the fullest form of the name. For example:

Morris West
(*Most common form:* Morris West)
(*Occasional form:* Morris L. West)

When the name of a person is written in nonroman script and entered under surname, romanize the name according to the table of the language selected by the cataloging agency. There is an alternative to this rule that provides for use of a romanized form of names well established in English reference sources.

Once the cataloger has decided on the predominant name or names, and form of name or names to be used, the next step is to select the entry element of the name.

For a person entered under given name, include any words or phrases denoting origin, domicile, occupation, or any other characteristic. Precede the words by a comma, except Icelandic names, when the words denote a place. (In *AACR1,* if the words or phrases were an integral part of the name, no comma was used.) For example:

John, the Baptist

For persons commonly known by initials, such as H.D. for Hilda Doolittle, letters or numerals are entered, using the initials, letters, or numerals in direct order.

AACR1 called for the addition of titles of nobility and terms of honor for any person who bore a title. *AACR2,* on the other hand, states that titles of nobility and terms of honor or address are added only when they are commonly used by a person in his or her works or in reference works, thus following the general principle of using the predominant name and form of name used by a person. For example:

Byron, George Gordon Byron, *Baron*
Gordon, *Lord* George

Buchan, John
not Baron Tweedsmuir

Christie, Agatha
not Dame Agatha Christie

We have repeatedly stated that the rules for headings of persons call for the predominant name used by a person in his works, and is the name from which the entry is developed. In this context, names that contain initials or consist of initials were the source of lengthy discussions during the code revision process. Rule 22.16 discusses this matter:

If part or all of a name is represented by initials and the full form of the name is known, add the spelled out form of the name in parentheses if necessary to distinguish between names that are otherwise identical. Refer from the full form of name. If the initials occur in the inverted part of the name (forenames, etc.) or if the name consists entirely of initials, add the full form of the inverted part or of the whole name at the end of the name.

Smith, Russell E. (Russell Edgar)
H.D. (Hilda Doolittle)

If the initials occur in the entry element of the name(surnames, etc.) add the full form of the entry element at the end of the name.

Rodríguez H., Guadalupe (Rodríguez Hernández)

Optionally, make the above additions to other names containing initials.

This is a major departure from *AACR1,* which provided for filling out initials. It also has major implications for the arrangement of names in card catalogs and in established microform catalogs.

There are two other changes in this chapter. The first one (22.17A5) is a new provision, which states:

If a child or grandchild of a ruler is known as *Prince* or *Princess* (or their equivalents in other languages) without a territorial designation, add that title (in English if there is a satisfactory English equivalent). Add any other title associated with the name, or if there is no such title, add:

a) *daughter of, son of, granddaughter of,* or *grandson of*
and b) the name and title of the parent or grandparent. . . .

Anne, *Princess, daughter of Elizabeth II, Queen of the United
Kingdom* [. . .]

William, *Prince, grandson of George V, King of the United
Kingdom*

The final change in this chapter is in rule 22.18, which states that
"flourished" dates for the twentieth century are no longer used. Thus
there is no way to distinguish between identical names of two or more
people of the twentieth century when birth and/or death dates are not
known.

The changes in the rules in this chapter for selection of name, form
of name, and form of entry present many questions of how to integrate
these new entries in existing catalogs. Small libraries may be able to
change entries in their catalogs as necessary to conform to *AACR2,* but
most libraries will probably have to start new catalogs. Whatever form
the new catalog takes, instructions will have to be developed to link the
two catalogs in order to guide the user.

Geographic Names

Geographic or place names are used to distinguish between corporate
bodies with the same name, as additions to corporate names, such as
conferences, and as headings for governments. Although place names
are an integral part of corporate name headings, the rules for using
places have been assigned to a separate chapter (23) in *AACR2.*

The chapter is organized into four sections: general rules, changes
of name, additions to place names, and place names (which includes a
term indicating a type of jurisdiction).

The general rule calls for the use of the English form of the name
of a place if there is one in general use, as determined from gazeteers
and other reference sources in English-speaking countries. When no
English form of name is in general use, use the vernacular form of name.
If more than one official language is in use in a country, use the form
of the place name commonly found in English-language reference
sources.

Names of places change just as other names do. Since place names
are an integral part of corporate names, different place names are used,
as appropriate and as required by the relevant rules in chapter 24, such
as rule 24.3E for government names or rule 24.4C6 for additions to
corporate names.

The principal changes in the rules in this chapter are in rule 23.4, "Additions to Place Names":

1. All additions to place names are in parentheses, thus eliminating the confusion of some additions to place names in parentheses and some not in parentheses that existed in *AACR1*. The name of a larger place is preceded by a comma. For example:

Budapest (*Hungary*)
Magyar Nemzeti Galeria (*Budapest, Hungary*)

2. The general rule provides for additions to place names to distinguish between two or more places of the same name, or
   a. Optionally, to make additions, whether or not there is a need to distinguish between places of the same name, or
   b. Optionally, not to add the name of a larger geographic area to the names of a state, province, or territory in Australia, Canada, or the United States; of a British county; of a constituent state of Malaysia, the U.S.S.R. or Yugoslavia, or of an island used as an addition.
3. Add to a place name the state, province, or territory in Australia, as well as in Canada or the United States.
4. Three rules have been provided for places in the British Isles:
   a. For counties, regions, or islands, add *England, Ireland, Northern Ireland, Scotland,* or *Wales* as appropriate. Do not abbreviate *England, Ireland,* or *Scotland,* as has been done in the past.
   b. For other places, but not cities, add the name of the county in England, Wales, or the Republic of Ireland.
   c. In Scotland, add the name of the region or islands area.
   d. If the county or region is a phrase, also add *England* or *Scotland.*
   e. If the place is in Northern Ireland, add *Northern Ireland.*
   f. A new provision has been added for places, other than a county, in the United Kingdom which bear the name of a jurisdiction that has ceased to exist. Add the name of the geographic county in which the place was located when it was a jurisdiction.
   g. If the jurisdiction was not part of a county, add the name of the country.
5. For place in cities, this rule has not changed, but it now includes an administrative part of a city identified by a number, formerly treated as a subdivision of the city.

6. In rule 23.4J, when an addition to a place requires an additional word or phrase to distinguish two places, add it to the place, as in *Frankfurt-am-Main (Germany);* but if there is no word or phrase, add a narrower geographic qualification before the name of the larger place, for example: *Friedburg (Bavaria, Germany).*

In *AACR1,* the narrower geographic qualification followed the larger geographic area.

7. Reference is made to chapter 24, "Headings for Corporate Bodies," when a place name does not include a term that indicates a jurisdiction and such a term is needed to distinguish between two or more places of the same name (see rule 24.6).

Users of *AACR2* in this country will have greatest difficulty in learning the new rules for additions to place names in the British Isles.

References

This chapter remains much the same as in *AACR1,* chapter 5. The rules summarize, in general terms, the particular types of references noted in the earlier chapters of Part II.

Examples of the references have been expanded to reflect the changes in the rules for choice and form of entry.

New rules have been written for name-title references, references for initials, numbers, and abbreviations:

1. Name-title references
   a. Make a name-title reference when editions of a work of an author are entered under two or more different headings.
   b. Make a name-title reference from the inverted form of initials when the initials are entered in direct order, for example:

   D., H.
   Helidora and other poems
   see **H.D.**

   c. Make a name-title reference from the real name when a pseudonym consists of initials, a sequence of letters, or numerals. If the initials stand for a phrase, make a name-title reference from the phrase in direct order.
2. "See also" references
   Make "see also" references from each heading for works of one person entered under two different headings. For example:

Wright, Willard Huntington
  see also **Van Dine, S.S.**
Van Dine, S.S.
  see also **Wright, Willard Huntington**

3. Initials for corporate names
    If the filing system used in the catalog files initials with full stops
    differently from those without full stops, refer from the from with
    full stops to the form without full stops used as a heading. Also
    refer from a form without full stops to a form with full stops. For
    example:

U.N.E.S.C.O.
  see **Unesco**
NAAB
  see **N.A.A.B.**

Optionally, refer from initials without full stops, as well as
with full stops, to the name used as a heading.

4. Numbers
    If in the filing system numbers expressed in numerals file differ-
    ently from numbers expressed in words, refer from the form of the
    heading expressed in words. For example:

Drei October-Vereeniging
  see **3 October-Vereeniging**

On the other hand, if the numbers are expressed in words, refer from the form of the number in the heading expressed in numerals.

5. Abbreviations
    If in the filing system abbreviated words are filed differently from
    words written in full, and the position of the abbreviated words
    affects the filing, refer from the form of the abbreviated word writ-
    ten in full.

The final change in this chapter that we should note is the elimination of *AACR1* rule 122B, concerning "see also" references from names
of international and diplomatic conferences to uniform titles of international conventions and peace treaties (because it is no longer applicable).
The change is discussed in rule 21.35A2.

The Corporate Complex (Including Choice and Form of Entry)

ÅKE I. KOEL

The first thing one is tempted to say about the corporate complex is that corporate bodies are not always corporate, nor do corporate names always refer to groups of people. Thus we have two misnomers in our beloved librarianese that we are destined to continue to live with, even in the new era of the second edition of the *Anglo-American Cataloguing Rules,* to dawn upon us January 2, 1981, God and the Library of Congress willing.

This new code, *AACR2* for short, redefines the role of corporate bodies in bibliographic control. This shift in thinking is manifested both in theory and practice, being perhaps more drastic on the theoretical level and less so on the practical level.

The redefinition of the role of corporate bodies is one of the most important changes in *AACR2,* a thorough understanding of which is imperative for the proper application of the new rules.

I have divided my paper into two parts: theory and application. I shall proceed with a discussion of the changes in theory, then the changes in application.

Theoretical Problems

Background

The first major code to sanction the use of corporate bodies as main entry was published in 1841 as part of the *Catalogue of Printed Books in the British Museum.* It listed ninety-one cataloging rules under the heading "Rules for the Compilation of the Catalogue," and rule IX reads as follows:

Any act, resolution, or other document purporting to be agreed upon, authorized, or issued by assemblies, boards, or corporate bodies, (with the exception of academies, universities, learned societies, and religious orders, respecting which special rules are to be followed,) to be entered in distinct alphabetical series, under the name of the country or place from which they derive their denomination, or, for want of such denomination, under the name of the place whence their acts are issued.[1]

Note that this rule authorizes the use of a distinct type of main heading for corporate publications but does not mention corporate authorship in this connection.

Over the years, use of corporate main entries spread, especially in the English-speaking world; "corporate main entry" became "corporate authorship" and, as such, ultimately became part of our cataloging tradition. For instance, both Cutter's *Rules for a Dictionary Catalog* and the 1908 ALA rules treat of corporate authorship as an established fact.

Thus a concept was introduced that had little or no theoretical backing—a fact that was reflected in the lively controversy it fostered in the library profession at the time. Many European codes, notably German and Scandinavian codes, categorically refused to recognize corporate authorship on theoretical grounds and treated such works as being anonymous.

The Paris Conference, held in 1961, finally managed to reach an agreement on the use of corporate bodies as main entry, a notable achievement from an international point of view. The *Statement of Principles,* issued by the Paris Conference, however, carefully avoids the term "corporate authorship," although "personal authorship" is repeatedly used elsewhere in the Principles. For example:

9. Entry under Corporate Bodies
9.1. The main entry for a work should be made under the name of a corporate body (i.e. any institution, organized body or assembly of persons known by a corporate or collective name)
9.11. when the work is by its nature necessarily the expression of the collective thought or activity of the corporate body, even if signed by a person in the capacity of an officer or servant of the corporate body, or
9.12. when the wording of the title or title-page, taken in conjunction with the nature of the work, clearly implies that the corporate body is collectively responsible for the content of the work.[2]

---

1. British Museum, Dept. of Printed Books, *Catalogue of Printed Books in the British Museum* (London: The Trustees, 1841), 1:vii.
2. International Conference on Cataloging Principles (Paris, 1961), *Report* (London: Organizing Committee of the International Conference on Cataloguing Principles, 1963), p.48.

Anglo-American cataloging tradition, as I have mentioned, has recognized corporate authorship as such, treating it in much the same manner as individual authorship. This tradition continued even after the Paris Conference. For instance, *AACR1,* published in 1967, six years after the conference, still defines "author" as "the person or corporate body chiefly responsible for the creation of the intellectual or artistic content of a work."[3]

AACR2

All this has changed in *AACR2*. Rule 21.1 sets out the conditions for authorship; thus rule 21.1A1 reads:

A personal author is the person chiefly responsible for the creation of the intellectual or artistic content of a work.[4]

The next rule, 21.1B2, deals with entry under corporate body. Because of its importance to our discussion, this rule is presented here in its entirety:

Enter a work emanating from one or more corporate bodies under the heading for the appropriate body if it falls into one or more of the following categories:

a) those of an administrative nature dealing with the corporate body itself
   or its internal policies, procedures, and/or operations
   or its finances
   or its officers and/or staff
   or its resources (e.g. catalogues, inventories, membership directories)
b) some legal and governmental works of the following types: laws, decrees of the chief executive that have the force of law, administrative regulations, treaties, etc., court decisions, legislative hearings
c) those that record the collective thought of the body (e.g. reports of commissions, committees, etc.; official statements on external policies)
d) those that report the collective activity of a conference (proceedings, collected papers, etc.), of an expedition (results of exploration, investigation, etc.), or of an event (an exhibition, fair, festival, etc.) falling within the definition of a corporate body, provided that the conference, expedition, or event is prominently named in the item being catalogued
e) sound recordings, films, and videorecordings resulting from the collective activity of a performing group as a whole where the responsibility of the group goes beyond that of mere performance, execution, etc.[5]

3. *Anglo-American Cataloging Rules* (North American Text) (Chicago: American Library Assn., 1967), p.9, n.2.
4. *Anglo-American Cataloguing Rules* (2d ed.; Chicago: American Library Assn., 1978), p.284.
5. Ibid., p.285, n.2.

You will have noticed that corporate "authorship" has been replaced by "emanation," defined on the same page as "a work [considered] to have emanated from a corporate body if it is issued by that body or has been caused to be issued by that body or if it originated with that body.[6]

The abandonment of the concept of corporate authorship brings *AACR2* closer to the Paris Principles, as well as to other post–Paris Conference codes, such as the German *Regeln für die alphabetische Katalogisierung,* issued in 1977 and also known as *RAK.*

Returning to the five conditions under which corporate main entry is authorized in *AACR2,* you will have noticed that legal works and works created in connection with the administration of justice have been included—a classical example of a type of materials where the application of the concept of authorship has never worked well, be it personal or corporate.

You will also have noticed that the rule referring to corporate name main entry is operational: that is, it does not identify the principles upon which it is based but rather enumerates the cases to which it applies. I should like to add that the American Committee (*CCRC*) spent many hours trying to define corporate authorship, but had to give up as it was not possible to identify a principle or set of principles upon which such a definition could be formulated. This is clearly an area where research is badly needed, no matter how unglamorous or meager the rewards.

Special Types of Materials

Cartographic Materials

From what has already been said, it should be obvious that cartographic materials do not qualify for corporate main entry, even when the piece at hand would state unequivocally "prepared by Rand McNally & Company." Only the name of the personal "author," that is, the cartographer, can be used as main entry. I would like to add that this would apply also when the cartographer is to be entered under his or her corporate name. In this case, the heading may read: "Rand McNally & Company. Chief Cartographer." A somewhat odd conclusion, illustrating the problems that corporate names, used for individual persons, may create. I shall come back to this problem later in this presentation.

---

6. Ibid.

Serials

As you know, *AACR2* has no special rules for the entry of serials; they are treated in the same manner as monographs.

The general effect of *AACR2* on serials will be a reduction of the number of titles entered under corporate name as main entry and a corresponding increase of title entries.

This change will mostly be caused by rule 21.1B2 (already discussed in this paper). The old provision in *AACR1* (the exception under rule 6B1) that directed the cataloger to enter a serial under the corporate body if the title "includes the name or the abbreviation of the name of the body" is now abolished. We shall probably not miss this rule very much, based as it was on neither authorship nor title entry principle.

There was an additional category of serials by corporate bodies that were formerly entered under corporate main entry, namely, publications that described results of the collective activity of the body. I am referring to statistical reports issued by various corporate bodies, not dealing with the body itself, many of which were issued by bodies such as the Bureau of the Census or Statistics Canada. Into this category also fall publications reporting meteorological or celestial observations and the like. All such publications, unless presented as the work of an individual (in which case that individual would be treated as the author), will be entered under title according to the provisions of *AACR2,* except when they emanate from a conference, an expedition, or an event.

Sound Recordings

AACR1 prescribed for sound recordings the same main entry as "for the same material in visual form." *AACR2* allows, under certain circumstances, main entry under performing group if the sound recordings, films, or videorecordings have resulted from the "collective activity of a performing group as a whole where the responsibility of the group goes beyond that of mere performance."[7]

Thus a sound recording called *Bonaparte's Retreat,* featuring folk tunes and songs by various composers, performed by a band called "The Chieftains, will be entered under the corporate name for that group.

---

7. Ibid., p.285.

Application of *AACR2*

Here we have divided the problems of application into two categories:
(1) problems with the choice of entry and (2) problems with the form
of entry.

Problems with the Choice of Entry

Personal Names, Corporate Names, and Pseudonyms
    In order to deal adequately with this problem, I have to backtrack
a little and recapitulate the general conditions that determine the use of
names for individuals and corporate bodies in *AACR2*. As we have
seen, rule 21.1A dealt with personal authors and rule 21.1B2 with corporate bodies as main entry. In the former case, the main entry was
based on authorship, in the latter, on emanation and certain other conditions that had to be met simultaneously.
    Let us pursue this a little further. To start with the individual, or
"personal author," he may use either his own name or an invented
name. The latter case is known as a pseudonym, and *AACR2* says that
in the choice of name it does not matter whether the name used by the
author is his real name or a pseudonym: whichever occurs more frequently should be used. Furthermore, rule 21.6D recognizes an additional category of pseudonyms, referred to as "shared pseudonyms,"
where a group of people uses an invented name, and directs us to use
the shared pseudonym instead of the authors' real names.
    Elsewhere, *AACR2*, directs us to use corporate headings not only
for groups of persons (i.e. corporate bodies) but also for individuals who
act in some official capacity, such as government and religious officials,
heads of state, and the like. Thus the president of Yale University may
appear as "Yale University. President."
    Now it so happens that Mr. Giamatti is also an author of books,
and, acting in this case not as the president of the university but as an
individual, he will be entered as "Giamatti, A. Bartlett (Angelo Bartlett)."
    (All this is old hat, of course, a condition well known to you from
AACR1.)
    To sum up:

A *person* may be entered under:
    own name
    or pseudonym
    or corporate name

A *group of persons* may be entered under:
shared pseudonym
or corporate name

It should be stressed that in *AACR2,* corporate bodies and corporate names are not identical concepts, nor are personal names and pseudonyms. This condition begs the question: Which rule applies to a person who is to be entered under a corporate name? Rule 21.1A, "Works of Personal Authorship," or rule 21.1B2, "Entry under Corporate Body"? Or, similarly, which rule applies to shared pseudonyms, as the rules do not say that corporate names have to look like corporate names and that shared pseudonyms have to look like personal names?

The confusion is caused by a conceptual overlap: "Individual person" and "group of persons" are logically exclusive; corporate names and pseudonyms are not.

What does this confusion do to the cataloger who tries to apply *AACR2?* As the rule for corporate main entry applies to corporate bodies only, it follows that a person, entered under corporate name, must fall under the rule for works of personal authorship (rule 21.1A) and be entered according to the principle of authorship rather than "emanation." For instance, suppose we have a map that states that it has been prepared by the "Chief Cartographer" of a named corporate body. The heading would then read, say, "Rand McNally & Company. Chief Cartographer," and this heading would become the main entry for the map according to the principle of authorship. We will thus have a corporate name main entry in a case where it is clearly barred for corporate bodies.

It is, therefore, very important to understand the distinction between "corporate names" used for individuals or for corporate bodies. The definition in *AACR2* of a corporate body does not clearly exclude shared pseudonyms, although the latter have to be entered under the principle of authorship and not of emanation.

I should add that this is my interpretation of *AACR2.* I have not had the opportunity to discuss this with people from the Library of Congress, who may, for all I know, draw different conclusions. This area is a little tricky, and all I can really do here is warn you of the pitfalls that a somewhat casual reading of the new code may create. Logical clarity here does not quite match the verbal clarity of the new rules.

Problems with the Form of Entry

As a general principle, *AACR2* instructs us to add the name of the place, in brackets, to a corporate name to ensure uniqueness of heading.

This, however, is not always applied when one expects it. For instance, under the chapter heading "Government Bodies and Officials," the new code instructs us to "enter a body created or controlled by a government under its own name unless it belongs to one or more of the types in 24.18."[8]

This rule lists ten such types, one of which (type 3) reads: "An agency with a name that has been, or is likely to be, used as the name of another agency, providing the name of the government is required for the identification of the agency."[9]

One of the examples reads: "Béziers. Musée des beaux-arts." And, as an afterthought, we find: "but Musée de Poitiers."

It seems clear that "Musée des beaux-arts" needs further identification; why not "Musée des beaux-arts (Béziers)"? As the example shows, the cataloger has to use the name of the government for identification, which, in turn, means that he or she has to know that the museum in Béziers is municipally run. This provision will cause some difficulties, as it is not always clear whether a corporate body of this nature is controlled by a government or not.

Then there is the old issue of the lack of distinction between similarly named buildings and corporate bodies. Thus the heading "Yale University. Library" may stand for a corporate body or a building, notwithstanding the fact that at least one earlier librarian of Yale used to respond to sightseers' question "Is this the Library?" with "No, Madam/Sir, the Library is inside." Thus the heading could refer to a particular book collection as well. It does not create serious problems for the cataloger, but it will for filing subjects and added entries in dictionary catalogs.

Finally, I come to my old, personal bone of contention. *AACR2* continues to authorize bilingual headings—headings where the first element is in English, followed by subdivisions in another language. This, of course, is caused by the principle of using the best known form of name in the English language if there is one. Sidestepping its effect on personal names, I would like to limit it here to corporate names only. Let us take names of jurisdiction, such as Italy for Italia, Vienna for Wien. The result are such headings as:

Italy. Presidente del Consiglio dei ministri.
Vienna (Austria). Stadbauamt.

---

8. Ibid., p.424.
9. Ibid., p.425.

As if a person who knows what Stadbauamt means is not expected to know that "Vienna" is "Wien." A little odd, at least in a research library.

In this connection, I also notice with regret that the Library of Congress has announced its intention to continue to use "Great Britain" for "United Kingdom," a name that has been obsolete since January 1, 1801. An example of outdated terminology, if there ever was one—and, I should add, somewhat discourteous to our British colleagues. There is the added problem that the Library of Congress is obligated by law to follow the forms of names approved by the United States Board on Geographic Names, which are not always identical with those prescribed by the *AACR2*.

Effect of AACR2 on Bibliographic Files

What follows is, by necessity, interspersed with statistics—my apologies to those who dislike this kind of thing.

Distribution of the Choice of Entry

We ran a test sample at Yale of titles cataloged in the month of August 1978, which excluded nonroman alphabet titles and materials in law, music, and most of our government publications (we catalog only those that go to departmental libraries).

The size of this sample was 5,617 titles, 5,169 (or 92%) of which were monographs and 448 (or 8%) serials. This sample had the following distribution of main entries:

4,130 (or 73%) had personal name main entry.
552 (or 9%) had corporate name main entry.
935 (or 18%) had title main entry.

You will understand that these titles were cataloged according to the provisions of *AACR1*.

We asked ourselves: Suppose this sample had been cataloged according to *AACR2*; how would that had affected the distribution of main entries? We estimated that 5,398 titles (or 96%) of the choices of entry would remain the same and that 209 titles (or 3%) would change from corporate name main entry to title main entry. Thus the new distribution of entries would be:

4,130 (or 73%) by personal name main entry
343 (or 6%) by corporate name main entry
1,144 (or 21%) by title main entry.

That is, there would be an approximate 3 percent reduction of corporate name main entries and a corresponding increase of title main entries.

Next we asked ourselves: Is there a difference in the distribution of the choice of entry between monographs and serials? The statistics were:

Monographs (5,169 titles): same entry 5,014 (or 97%)
different entry 155 (3%)
Serials (448 titles): same entry 394 (or 88%)
different entry 54 (12%).

All changes referred to as "different entry" were caused by changes from corporate name main entry to title main entry. Why this difference? An analysis of the affected titles revealed that, for serials, two rules caused all the changes: *AACR1* rule 6B1 exception (which directs us to enter a serial under the name of a corporate body if the title "includes the name or the abbreviation of the name of the body" [this rule is abolished in *AACR2*]) and *AACR2* rule 21.1B2 (which limits the use of corporate name main entry to "emanation" and to certain other conditions that have to be met simultaneously). For monographs, only the latter rule is relevant.

These findings are largely in accordance with predictions and/or hunches expressed or made by various persons about the probable impact of the new rules.

Distribution of Changes of Form of Name

You will recall that LC has released data that suggest that 17 percent of all names have to be changed, 11 percent of which are caused by desuperimposition and 6 percent by *AACR2*—provided, of course, that one has the same mix of titles as the Library of Congress.

We postulated that, for Yale, the percentage of names to be changed was likely to be less because we cataloged fewer government publications than the Library of Congress.

Two small samples that I have analyzed indicate a range of name changes for Yale between 7 and 10 percent. However, I am not convinced that my data are definitive; at best, they are indicative only.

Conclusions and Recommendations

These data suggest that, under certain conditions, it is economically feasible to interfile pre-*AACR2* and *AACR1* entries, provided one is prepared to deal with a 3 percent change of choice of main entry and with name changes affecting 10 to 17 percent of all names on file.

It is clear that this may be feasible for smaller card catalogues; for larger ones, broken files will have to be considered—assuming that no attempt is made to provide ISBD punctuation where it is lacking in pre-*AACR2* entries.

Also, as changing the form of a name is relatively simple in automated files that have authority control capability, the main problem with computerized data bases is the 3 percent change in choice of entry, all of which are from corporate name main entry to title entry.

Here one can argue that in an online environment the concept of main entry is of lesser consequence than in page format or card files, except when the data base is used for the production of one-entry lists, such as bibliographies.

However, as the majority of larger libraries seem to plan to move from card catalogs to COM catalogs (i.e. to page-format catalogs), the differences in choice of main entry probably cannot be tolerated and will have to be corrected by human intervention. It would seem best, therefore, not to attempt to integrate *AACR1* and *AACR2* entries and to have in one's COM catalog display pristine *AACR2* entries only, which should also be remembered when using "old" LC entries, after January 1, 1981.

Finally, serials will have more changes than monographs.

File Structure

As we said, there will be three distinct types of main entry: personal name, corporate name, and title. For corporate names, while *AACR2* aims at direct entry under name proper, an exception is made for ten types of government agencies that are entered subordinately, under the name of government, and for legal material that is entered under jurisdiction governed. In *AACR2,* "government agencies" includes institutions that are not directly involved in governing proper but are owned and operated by it, such as museums. If such institutions have nondistinctive names, they have to be entered under the name of the government, as we have seen from the example for the museum in Béziers. This means that we will have two types of file sequences for such institutions: one under their own name, if distinctive, and another under the name of government, if nondistinctive.

This problem spills over to countries where governments literally run everything, such as the Soviet Union, China, etc. It seems that we will have to enter every institution in such a country, if its name is nondistinctive, under the name of the governing jurisdiction. I hope that LC will issue guidelines for handling such cases.

Now you should not get the idea from my presentation that *AACR2* is not good: it is. It is just that I have chosen to discuss diffi-

culties only, and in this sense I am no better than the average media re-
porter: Only bad news is news.

Conclusions

Finally, let us ask ourselves: Have we solved all the problems of the
corporate complex in *AACR2*? Because I am of a somewhat cautious
nature and somewhat given to skepticism, my answer will be "Of course
not." But after giving some further thought to it, I would like to finish
on a slightly more optimistic note.

Borderline cases aside—they will always be with us—*AACR2* has
formulated rules referring to corporate bodies in a manner that makes
greater uniformity and, hence, greater predictability of headings more
likely. It has also narrowed the gap between European and Anglo-
American practice, both in theory and in application.

This code, as indeed any code must be, is a child of its time: it reflects the state of the art, if you will, of the time in which it was prepared. Those of us who were involved in this process became painfully
aware of the fragile nature of our theoretical constructions and knowledge: research is badly needed, if we are to have better codes in the
future.

Uniform Titles

JOAN K. MARSHALL

In preparing this paper I discovered something which I find quite remarkable. Since Cutter's statement in his rules of the objects and means
of cataloging, none of our working cataloging codes, including the one
under discussion here, has included any rationale for all of the varied
and complex instructions to "enter under . . ." If this cataloging code
were to be placed in a time capsule, it would be necessary to include

some statement of what we were trying to accomplish through these rules, if we expect some far future generation to understand the "why" of the rules rather than merely "what" the rules were.

As stated by Cutter and restated by Lubetzky in 1960 in his *Code of Cataloging Rules,*[1] and in the Paris Principles[2] in 1961, cataloging has two basic objectives. The first is to identify a particular manifestation of a work which is in the library and to distinguish that manifestation from all others the library houses. The second objective is to collocate the various manifestations of a particular work and the works of a particular author which are in the library. The first objective is met primarily through the rules for description. The second is met through the general rules for entry and specifically through the rules for uniform title.

The concept of using a uniform title to collocate the various editions of a work has been around a long time; rules for their consistent use, however, were slow to develop. Jewett's rules in *Construction of Catalogues for Libraries,* published in 1853, prescribed entry of all editions of the Bible or any of its parts, in any language, under the word *Bible.*[3] He also prescribed entry of a translation of an anonymous work under the title of the original, "whether the original be or be not in the library to be catalogued."[4] In neither instance does he provide a rationale for these rules. Cutter also provides for entry under the title of the original.

Jewett does not, however, deal with the problem of collocating various editions of anonymous works in the original language. His rule calls for entry under the first word of the title which is not an article or a preposition.[5] Nor does he deal with the problem of collocating translations of works of known authorship. Such translations are to be entered under the heading for the original work: a translation of the *Odyssey* would be entered under the heading for Homer. But Jewett's rule does nothing to collocate various editions of the *Odyssey* in the language of the original and in translation, nor to collocate editions in the same

---

1. Seymour Lubetzky, *Code of Cataloging Rules . . . Prepared for the Catalog Code Revision Committee* (Chicago: American Library Assn., 1960).

2. International Federation of Library Associations, *Statement of Principles Adopted at the International Conference on Cataloguing Principles, Paris, October 1961* (annotated ed.; Paris: IFLA Committee on Cataloguing, 1971).

3. Charles C. Jewett, *Smithsonian Report on the Construction of Catalogues of Libraries* (2d ed.; Washington: Smithsonian Institution, 1853).

4. Ibid., p.53.

5. Ibid.

language which have various title-page titles, such as the *Odyssey* and *The Wanderings of Odysseus.*

The 1908 British and American Library Association rules and the American Library Association rules of 1941 and 1949 advanced little beyond Jewett. Although the number of rules governing entry of anonymous works grew considerably from 1908 to 1949, the theory of the use of uniform titles did not change. The rules throughout this forty-year period consistently made a distinction between the treatment of anonymous classics and sacred works and the treatment of modern anonymous works. *Beowulf, Chanson de Roland,* the Bible, and the Talmud, for example, were to be entered under uniform heading; modern anonymous works were to be entered under title-page title if the author could not be identified. During this period, the American, but not the British, rules for entry of translations of anonymous works retreated from Jewett's position on entry under the title of the original work and prescribed entry under the title of the translation, with added entry for the title of the original.

The problem of collocating the various editions and translations of a known author's works was not addressed, in any of our cataloging codes, until 1967, with the publication of the first edition of the *Anglo-American Cataloguing Rules.* Between the publication of the 1949 ALA rules and the publication of *AACR1,* the means of achieving the second objective of cataloging (the collocation of the various manifestations of a particular work and the works of a particular author) were examined, debated, and written about at length. The IFLA *Statement of Principles,* usually referred to as the Paris Principles, which are based to a large degree on Lubetzky's work, were the culmination of that activity.

Both *AACR1* and *AACR2* are based, though not without exception, on those principles. The use of uniform titles, since 1967, is no longer restricted to classic works and sacred scriptures, and the problem of collocation under author was finally addressed.

In comparing the *AACR1* and *AACR2* rules for uniform titles, and their impact on our catalogs, I will follow, as closely as practicable, the order of the rules in the text of *AACR2.* The use of uniform titles in areas of subject specialization, such as music and law, is very difficult for a nonspecialist to evaluate. In discussing uniform headings for these types of materials, I will most often describe the change and its effect on our catalogs, but I will not attempt to evaluate the merits of the change.

Before I get into an actual analysis of the text, however, I would like to extend my sincere compliments to the editors on the precise and clear wording, and the logical arrangement of the rules. I am also grateful to whoever was responsible for the design of the book and for the size of the type and the page; and the "white space" makes the rules much easier to follow and the task of following them somewhat less forbidding.

As a member of the ALA Catalog Code Revision Committee, I would also like to comment on the rule revision process that began in 1974. Michael Gorman remarked that he believed *AACR2 would* probably be the last code produced, in quite the same way, through the committee process. I concur. Also, there were references to the "theology" of cataloging. To continue in the same vein, I believe that the very existence of this document, known familiarly as *AACR2,* all its imperfections notwithstanding, is a minor, if not a full-fledged, miracle. As a member of CCRC, I often felt that I was doing penance for some unspecified bibliographic sin I had unknowingly committed.

The Catalog Code Revision Committee membership endured seemingly endless three- and four-day meetings that ran from eight in the morning to eleven (or later) in the evening. We were enveloped in mountains of documentation, much of which was only distributed at the meeting and had to be read at one in the morning (or, by morning persons, at six in the morning). Discussion of issues that were early agenda items at these meetings was lengthy; no detail was felt too minor for remark. But during these lengthy meetings, as time grew short, major considerations, or at least considerations some of us perceived as major, would be given short shrift, or at least what some of us considered short shrift.

Before the major code revision effort, the *ISBD(M)* was issued; subsequent to that, the draft *ISBD(S)* was published. Analysis of the two documents revealed that the two statements were at odds in some instances, and the need to formulate an *ISBD(G),* upon which all description could be based, was recognized. These developments in descriptive cataloging resulted in CCRC's spending much more of its efforts on the rules for description than on the rules for choice and form of entry. I do not know if the same was true of the Joint Steering Committee.

I think the code reflects the disproportionate attention given to one area of concern, description, at the expense of concern for rules that would govern choice and form of entry. The rules for entry, I believe, occasionally suffer from this lack of time for reflection.

For example, the rule for entry of adaptations in *AACR1* prescribes entry under the adaptor with added entry under the heading for the original work. *AACR1* includes an exception under the rule, however, which reads: "In the case of paraphrases of Biblical texts, however, the added entry [for the original work] is omitted; a form subject heading is provided instead" (p.24). This exception is not allowed in *AACR2*; adaptations of biblical texts require an added entry under the heading for the Bible.

The entry of paraphrases of biblical texts under the entry for the Bible is a practice that the American cataloging community, at least, has attempted to avoid for a long time. The 1949 ALA rules prescribed the use of "paraphrases" as a form subdivision under the entry for the Bible for such works. *AACR1* dropped the use of most form subdivisions, in accord with the recommendations of the Paris Principles, and substituted the subject entry.

It was the decision of the Catalog Code Revision Committee, and the Joint Steering Committee concurred, that reference to subject heading practice should not be made in a code for entry and description. That was a reasonable decision, but when CCRC came to consider the problem this reasonable decision presented in reference to the rule for entry of adaptations, and the problem of biblical paraphrases, our decision was made very hastily due to the pressure of time to conclude that particular meeting. (Decisions, once made, were not reviewed if the Joint Steering Committee concurred.)

The committee's decision was to prescribe an added entry under the heading for the Bible of biblical paraphrases. This decision was based upon the committee's immediate reaction to the problem; there was no time for reflection. In retrospect, I believe we should have at least considered the possibility of simply making an arbitrary statement under the rule for adaptations, such as: Do not make an added entry for paraphrases or adaptations of sacred books. That would have been, I will be the first to admit, a very arbitrary rule. But many of the rules are, and have been, arbitrary—and for a very long time. Why, one could reasonably ask, if only three authors are named on the title page, is each of them of equal importance, while if four authors are named, only the first is important and must be entered in the catalog?

If such an arbitrary rule had been introduced, it would have been up to the local library or cataloging agency to decide what to do about collocating paraphrases of the Bible. Local cataloging agencies *did* deal with the problem of collocating the various Arthurian romances and Grail legends (without, I might add, explicit instructions for how to do so in *AACR1*), when, for example, the pseudo-author headings *Arthur, King (Romances, etc.)* and *Grail. Legends* (ALA 1949 headings) were not authorized by *AACR1*.

The effect of this *AACR2* rule change on public and school libraries, which are likely to have many more editions of Bible stories than editions of the Bible, is potentially very great. If each edition of stories has an added entry under the heading for the Bible, the file under the Bible, which even in a small library is relatively complex, will be artificially swollen. The user who looks for editions of the Bible will be impeded. And the user who looks for editions of Bible stories will never consult the file; that user will look, as usual, under the standard subject heading for such works, Bible Stories.

I would not want anything I have just said to be construed as pointing to a major fault with the new rules; it certainly is *not* a major fault. Local libraries may simply opt not to trace the added entry when it is assigned to editions of Bible stories; I sincerely hope they adopt this option. In addition, I could find no stated rationale for not making an added entry under the heading for the Bible for paraphrases of that work, just as added entries are made for any other adaptation under the heading for the original work. I can only assume that it was felt by early rule writers that since the Bible is considered sacred by many, the catalog should distinguish editions of the scriptures from noneditions.

Finally, to address my assigned topic: uniform titles. According to the guidance in both *AACR1* and *AACR2,* uniform titles are used to "provide the means for bringing together all the catalogue entries for a work when various manifestations (e.g., editions, translations) of it have appeared under various titles. They also provide identification for a work when the title by which it is known differs from the title proper of the item being catalogued" (*AACR2,* p.441).

The basic rule for the formulation of uniform title entries has been restated and rearranged, and examples have been added of nonbook uniform titles, but the rule remains substantially the same. The new layout of the text and the early decision to use the imperative in stating the rules call attention, however, to the rules (25.2D1 and 25.2D2) requiring title added entry under the title proper of works entered under uniform title. *AACR1* instructions read "prefer added entries" (p.146) to references from the title proper. The practice of making an added entry for the title proper is long standing; but the practice violates, I believe, if not the principle, the purpose behind the principle of uniform title entry. Uniform title entry is designed to facilitate a library catalog user's ability to discern whether or not the library owns a particular work. Some users want a specific edition of a work, and these users will not be poorly served by the title added entry; they may even benefit from it.

A person who is interested only in the London edition of Emerson's *American Scholar,* which was published as *Man Thinking,* would be relieved of the chore of going through the lengthy and more complicated file under Emerson if the title of the London edition were traced. But this type of library user is rare. It is much more common for a user to want *any* edition of a work. If this user looks under title and finds an added entry for *The Life and Adventures of Martin Chuzzlewit* (to use an example from *AACR2*), the fact that the library has other editions of that work will be lost. The loss of this information could make a difference between the library patron's obtaining or not obtaining a copy of a title.

The uniform title rules for entry of works created after 1500 (the date of publication distinction was also made in *AACR1*) have been reworked, but the result of applying the rules is the same in both editions of *AACR*. *AACR1* gave preference to the title of the original edition, but made an exception for entry under later title if a later title had become better known. Emerson's *American Scholar* is an oft cited example of a work's becoming better known under a later title. *AACR2* gives preference to the title in the original language which has become best known.

The basic rules for entry of works created before 1501 also are substantially the same. The rules for the entry of classical Greek works have been expanded to cover both classical and Byzantine Greek works. *AACR1* prescribed entry of classical Greek works under an English-language title if one were well established; otherwise the title to be used was the romanized Greek title. The rule was not implemented by the Library of Congress, which continued to use the Latin form of the title of classical Greek works as the uniform title. The *AACR2* rule (25.4B) offers a compromise that fails, I believe, to serve the needs of anyone; it most particularly fails to serve the needs of the cataloger. The rule prescribes the use of a well-established English-language title if there is one; a Latin title is given second preference; and the Greek title, romanized, is the final choice.

The nonscholarly user will not understand the title any better in Latin than in Greek; the scholarly user may be puzzled, if not confused, by the use of titles in three languages under one author; and the cataloger will have the added burden of determining if there is a Latin title after having determined that there is no well-established English-language title.

The determination of whether there is, or is not, a well-established English title can be time consuming, particularly if an author's body of work is small and has not appeared in many translations. Menander of Athens' *Perikeiromene,* for instance, is one of the examples in the code of a uniform title which is to be established in romanized Greek. If this were not an example in the rules, and if I were cataloging a translation of this work, I would first search the *National Union Catalog* to determine if there were a well-established English title. There are many editions of the work listed in the *NUC* under the title *The Rape of the Lock,* but they are all by the same translator. A few editions are listed under the title *The Shearing of Glycera,* all by another translator. A reference source translates the title as *The Girl with the Shorn Locks.* At this point I would probably decide that there is no well-established English title. Following the rules, however, I would then have to go through the same procedure to determine if there were a well-established classical Latin title.

The Catalog Code Revision Committee discussed the use of a well-established English-language title as uniform title for classical and Byzantine Greek works and recommended their use to the Joint Steering Committee. I do not recall, however, that use of a Latin title was discussed as the first alternative to an English title.

The next significant change in the rules is for uniform title entry of parts of a work (25.6). *AACR1* permitted separately published parts of a work to be entered subordinately or independently, "depending on the general nature of the larger work, the closeness of the interconnection of its parts, and the nature of the part in question" (p.153). *AACR2* does not allow this option for parts with distinctive titles. This is in accordance with the principle of direct entry, but it is an instance, I believe, where Cutter's caveat of user's convenience sometimes having greater weight than bibliographic principles should have been considered.

The independent entry of the various titles in Proust's *A la Recherche du Temps Perdu* is reasonable; all of the parts were originally, and traditionally still are, published separately. But the entry of one separately published tale from Chaucer's *Canterbury Tales* is not reasonable. A library is likely to have many editions of the complete work, which traditionally is published as a whole, and only very few editions of a few of the tales published independently. The user who goes directly to the title for the tale will be deprived of information about the many editions of that tale that the library has as part of the larger work.

It has been argued that entry of the *Knight's Tale* under its title, without reference to the larger work, is analogous to entry of *The Canterbury Tales* under its title without reference to editions of the complete works of Chaucer which are in the library. The analogy is valid as an analogy; but the argument is, I believe, specious. It would certainly violate the principle of entering a work directly under its title to enter every title subordinately under "works," and, more importantly, it would not create a useful file arrangement. Subordinate entry of all titles under "works" is patently unreasonable, but it is reasonable, I believe, to enter a separately published part subordinately under the heading for the work as a whole, if the part is not traditionally published independently.

The rules for collective title entries (25.8–25.11) drop the distinction made in *AACR1* between "selections" (which was to be used for collections of extracts selected from an author's works) and "selected works" (which was to be used for collections of whole works but which did not include the author's entire output). The application of the *AACR1* rules occasionally presented some problems. Selected works often contain some of an author's whole works *and* bit and pieces from others. But apart from any problem the rule may have presented, the determination of whether a work required one or the other of the *AACR1* collective titles was generally a bother, and the fine distinction was lost on most users. *AACR2* prescribes the use of "selections" for both types of selected works.

The other change in the rules for collective title entry is the use of "selections" as a subordinate element under the collective title for works in a single form, such as "essays," "plays," "poems," etc. The new rule reads: "If the item consists of three or more but not all of the works of one person in a particular form, or of extracts, etc., from the works of one person in a particular form, add *Selections* to the collective title" (p.452). I think this is nitpicking. I also think it will be burdensome to the cataloger and of little value to the public.

The three examples in the rules are Somerset Maugham titles. One can safely assume that works titled *Selected Novels* and *The Best Short Stories of W. Somerset Maugham* are incomplete collections. Can that assumption be made with the same assurance when the title-page title is *Six Comedies?* If we had a Maugham collection with the title "The Best and Worst Short Stories," could one safely assume that Maugham must have written some mediocre short stories and, therefore, the collection cannot be complete. Editors' and publishers' practices in creating titles for selected, and complete, editions of an author's work are extremely varied. If the distinction between "Poems," for complete editions of an author's poetry, and "Poems. Selections," for incomplete editions, is to have any meaning, catalogers will, in many instances, have to go well beyond the title-page information to assign a uniform collective title correctly.

The rules for uniform title entry of stories in many versions and cycles, again, are substantially the same; they are, however, much less wordy. The rules for entry of composite manuscripts and manuscript groups are the same, except that it is no longer possible to enter an unnamed manuscript under the word "manuscript," followed by a "concise phrase descriptive of the content or nature of the work" (*AACR1*, p.152). Striking this provision from the rules is in accord with the attempt to eliminate subject substitute, or pseudo-author, headings from the rules for entry. This particular provision merely served to collocate unnamed manuscripts, under the word "manuscript," in the catalog. The rule for entering unnamed manuscripts under the name of the repository (which has been retained) will serve the same purpose, and serve it more effectively.

The rules for uniform title entry of editions of the Bible and its parts have not been changed. The shape of the file may be affected by the general rule change mentioned earlier, however. The rules for direct entry under uniform title of Jewish sacred scripture have not been changed. *AACR2*, however, prescribes the use of *Encyclopaedia Judaica* as the authority for the form of the names of Jewish scripture, rather than the *Jewish Encyclopedia* (which is almost 70 years old); this will result in a number of changes in entry.

The rule changes for entry of other sacred scriptures reflect, I assume, greater knowledge than was possessed by the committees and editors who worked on *AACR1*. However much these changes may disrupt our catalogs, they are obviously mandatory. The most startling change is in the entry of Buddhist scripture; works that were formerly entered independently are now entered subordinately. I should point out that some of the changes in these rules are not new. The changes in the rules for entry of the Koran, for instance, were adopted by the American Library Association, the Library of Congress, the Canadian Library Association, and the (British) Library Association, subsequent to the publication of *AACR1*, and were issued for use in 1970; they have been in effect since that time.

The changes in uniform title entry for music are considerable. Some of the changes are the result of CCRC's effort to regularize the application and wording of music and literary uniform titles. *AACR1* prescribed that the uniform title of musical works with a specific title, such as Cole Porter's "Night and Day" (as opposed to a title that consists solely of the type of composition, such as symphony), should be the original title only if the language of the original is English, French, German, Italian, Spanish, Portuguese, or Latin. If the original title of a work was in any other language, the title most commonly used in the United States was to be used as the uniform title, and preference was to be given to a title in English.

The *AACR1* rule reflects a rather extreme American/Western European orientation that was not reflected in the rules for uniform titles of literary works. There may have been some justification for the language restrictions that are based in traditional music publishing, but in

AACR2 the rule calls for entry under the "original title in the language in which it was formulated," unless a later title in the same language has become better known (p.474). The rule for musical works that have a specific title is now the same as the rule for literary works.

A rule change that puzzles me is 25.27B. This rule requires that the uniform title for single works with titles that consist solely of the name of one type of composition—a sonata, for example—be constructed in the plural unless (this is what puzzles me) the composer wrote only one work in that form. In other words, if a composer wrote only one sonata, and its title was "sonata," the uniform title would be in the singular. If the composer wrote more than one sonata, editions of one sonata and editions of collections of his or her sonatas would be uniformly entered under the plural form, "sonatas."

The (American) Music Library Association (I do not know how much, or if, input into the recommendation was made by British and Canadian music catalogers) advocated this change so that collections of works and single works in the same form, by the same composer, would interfile. But how, in the case of a composer who is alive and still composing, can the cataloger know that a first (to this date), published sonata is the only one that the composer is going to write? As the cataloger establishes the entry in the singular, the composer may be completing the second in a long series of sonatas. It would make more sense either to adopt both the singular and the plural forms (they would not have been separated by much in the catalog) or to adopt the plural without concern for the composer's entire body of work. As the rule stands now, we have built a need for recataloging into the rules.

Another major change in the rules for uniform title entry of musical works is in the entry of works in one broad or one specific medium. In *AACR1,* collections of chamber music, piano music, or choral music, for instance, were entered subordinately under "Works"; for example, "Works. Chamber music," "Works. Piano," etc. *AACR2* prescribes entry directly under the medium as uniform title, for example, "Chamber music," "Piano music," "Choral music," etc. The (American) Music Library Association's position on this rule change, as I understand it, is that by eliminating "Works" as the uniform title entry word, and using the medium of performance as the uniform title, this rule is in conflict with other music uniform title rules. In other music uniform titles, the medium of performance is the secondary, not the primary, element of the title.

The decision not to enter these collections under "Works" was influenced by the fact that "Works" as a uniform title for literary works is used only for complete collections. Perhaps "Selections" should have been used as a substitute for "Works" in music uniform titles. However,

I do not see the difference between using "Essays" directly for works in that form and using "Piano music" directly for works in that form.

There are a number of other minor changes in music uniform titles. For example, under the provisions of *AACR2,* language is to be added to the uniform title of liturgical and translated works in all cases; *AACR1* did not require this addition in the case of full scores. Under the provisions of *AACR2,* two consecutively numbered excerpts from a work, which are published together, are assigned one uniform title entry, for example, "Brahms *Ungarische Tanz, Nr. 5–6." AACR1* required an added uniform title entry for the second excerpt. This change brings the rules for uniform title entry of consecutively numbered parts of literary works and musical works into accord.

Finally, the change I would prefer not to have to talk about since it is a very controversial issue, particularly in law libraries: the abandonment, finally, of all form subdivisions. The use of form subdivision is a very old collocating device. Its use was endorsed by Panizzi's rules for certain classes of materials, such as periodicals, encyclopedias, liturgies, etc., and it has been a part of American cataloging practice from the beginning. The ALA 1908 rules defended the use of form subdivisions against the opposition—that they "introduce form or subject entries into the author catalog"—on the grounds that they made the catalog easier to use (p.19). Most form subdivisions were dropped in *AACR1,* but "Liturgy and ritual," "Laws, statutes, etc.," "Treaties, etc.," and a few others, primarily for entry of legal materials, were retained. *AACR2* does not sanction the use of any form subdivisions.

Dropping "Liturgy and ritual" as a subheading of the names of established religions or churches will have little effect that I can perceive. Uniform titles have been in use as an additional collocating device, when they were needed under these entries, since *AACR1* was published. If a work does not require a uniform title, it will still be entered under "Catholic Church," "Church of England," etc., as appropriate.

The collocation of Jewish liturgical works, however, is a problem. "Jews. Liturgy and ritual" was not authorized by *AACR1* (an excuse for using it as an arbitrary collocating device was even offered in the 1949 ALA rules), but the Library of Congress has continued to use it as, I assume, the traditional solution to the problem. I assume that with the implementation of *AACR2,* Jewish liturgical works, which do not have titles that can be used as uniform titles—words unlike the *Hagadah,* that is—will be collocated by means of a subject entry.

I do not see the substitution of the uniform heading "Laws, etc." for the form heading "Laws, statutes, etc." as causing a major dislocation of the file for compilations of complete or partial collections of general laws. Nor do I see the direct entry of subject compilations of laws or of single laws under their citation titles as uniform title creating a major problem; I would, I think, even look upon such entry as an improvement. If I wanted the "Internal Revenue Act," I would prefer to look under "United States. Internal Revenue Act," where the file would be shorter, than under "United States. Laws, statutes, etc.," where I would find both general and specific compilations of laws.

A collocation problem I *do* see is the entry of general subject compilations of laws under title. As I read the *AACR2* rules, a work such as the *Compilation of Selected Labor Law Pertaining to Labor Relations* (which could not be entered under the corporate body that acted as compiler) would be entered under title. This might be considered, at first blush, as a problem since works formerly collocated under "United States. Laws, statutes, etc." would now be scattered. But is it a true problem? Would a library user, interested in such a compilation, ever look under our artificial collocating heading? I do not believe that anyone ever believed so—or the uniformly applied collocating subject heading, "Labor Laws and Legislation—United States," would not have been assigned.

The publication of the 1941 preliminary edition of the ALA cataloging rules prompted Andrew Osborn to write an article which he titled "The Crisis in Cataloging." In the conclusion of that article he stated:

Cataloging policies and practices are about to be set for another generation. Whether the people of the 1980's will say librarians and catalogers of today had as much understanding and ability as can now be attested for the people of the early 1900's depends on the success of the deliberations of the 1940's.[6]

The deliberations of the 1940s and later, I suppose we must assume, were not successful because we have another crisis in cataloging. I sincerely hope we are meeting this one in a manner that will not have the effect of creating still another crisis for some future generation. But perhaps having crises every forty years or so is just part of the nature of the cataloging beast.

In conclusion, I would like to state that any criticism I have made of the new rules for uniform title entry should not be taken as pointing out major faults that should force a reconsideration of implementation of *AACR2*. I believe there are ways the code could have been better; I also believe it contains some provisions which are marked improvements.

---

6. Andrew D. Osborn, "The Crisis in Cataloging," *Library Quarterly* 11 (Oct. 1941): 393–411.

Part 4

Looking beyond the Rules

Implementation of *AACR2* at the Library of Congress

BEN TUCKER

Discussing the application of a code of rules before it is fully implemented necessarily partakes of both fact and fantasy. Already published are (1) the decisions of the national libraries of Australia, Canada, the United Kingdom, and the United States relating to options in *AACR2,* chapters 1–2, 12, and 21–26;[1] (2) *AACR2* rule interpretations arising from the Library of Congress's implementation of the rules for form of heading;[2] and (3) the Library's policy statement to lessen the impact of *AACR2* on the MARC data base.[3]

This paper will deal with these facts only briefly. Speculation, or fantasy if you will, starts when one looks ahead to the day-to-day application of the rules, beginning in 1981. The daily application of the rules by Library of Congress catalogers will give rise to interpretations of many kinds, and this will be the most extensively treated topic in my paper. Finally, the role of the Library of Congress name authority file in the implementation of *AACR2* will be described, with some concluding speculations.

Options

In 1977 the Library of Congress began to define positions on the optional rules in *AACR2*. Proposals relating to chapters 1–2, 12, and 21–26 were distributed to the Library's reference staff and to librarians attending the 1978 ALA Midwinter Conference, and were published in

---

This paper, originally prepared in January 1979, has been updated as of December 1979.

1. *Library of Congress Information Bulletin,* July 21, 1978, and *Cataloging Service Bulletin* 2 (Fall 1978).
2. *Cataloging Service Bulletin* 6 (Fall 1979).
3. *Cataloging Service Bulletin* 6 (Fall 1979).

the *Library of Congress Information Bulletin (LCIB)* (Feb. 3, 1978), with an invitation to all librarians to consider them and send their comments to the Library. When the national libraries of Australia, Canada, the United Kingdom, and the United States (later called the ABACUS group) met at the Library of Congress in March 1978, the options were an important item on the agenda. The Library of Congress also conferred with the Library of the Government Printing Office and GODORT (Government Documents Round Table of ALA) about these options. When the final decisions were announced by the Library of Congress, they were therefore derived from opinions expressed by reference and catalog librarians both in and outside the Library of Congress, by librarians from many types of institutions, by GPO, and by ABACUS.

The question of displaying general material designations (GMDs), which is an option in *AACR2,* rule 1.1C, was handled specially. The published decision on this option says that information from which GMDs can be formulated is to be stored in machine-readable form, but a decision still had to be made as to whether they will be displayed in any way, for example, on the Library's printed catalog records. In *Cataloging Service Bulletin* (no. 2 [Fall 1978]), the Library of Congress asked the opinion of librarians and announced final decisions, based on their responses in *Cataloging Service Bulletin* (no. 5–6 [Summer–Fall 1979]).

The published statements do not tell the whole story, however. Although no significant revisionist movement is likely, some matters will continue to be debated. An example is the problem of designations of function as optional additions to headings used in secondary entries. The decision not to apply this option did not receive unanimous support. Contrary opinions were expressed by librarians dealing with particular kinds of materials, such as children's materials and legal materials, and a strong case was made for the utility of added entry designations of function when collocating or retrieving headings that are used for various purposes in secondary entries. Another interesting aspect of this problem is the growing international interest in "relators," which, if fully developed, would mean that every personal or corporate heading appearing in access points would be related to the work being cataloged through machine-readable coding of a large number of well-differentiated bibliographic or intellectual activities. While the international movement favoring "relators" has a somewhat different emphasis than the optional added entry designations provided by *AACR2,* continuing discussions with specialized librarians at home and at the international level could affect the *AACR2* policy in some way. Because of the range of interests to be considered, the question of designations of function is a good illustration of the point that some matters will continue to be discussed and argued. And after arguing out the differences we can identify now, we must also keep in mind the strong likelihood that actual application of the options after 1980 is certain to bring to light points that we were not able to see in 1977–1978, when our decisions were being formulated. It is true that in a few cases the ABACUS group of representatives agreed to disagree; the international exchange of bibliographic records reflecting these differences may also present grounds for further discussion.

Decisions on the options in chapters 3–11 of *AACR2,* which deal with the bibliographic description of nonbook materials, remain. The Library of Congress published proposals in the *Library of Congress Information Bulletin* (Aug. 10, 1979).

Gradual Adoption of *AACR2*

The impact of *AACR2* on the Library of Congress catalogs will be considerably lessened by the freezing of the Library's card catalogs. The MARC data base, however, will be carried forward as the nucleus of the new post-1980 catalog; bibliographic records in the MARC data base will thus be affected by the creation of headings under *AACR2*. The publicity accorded the financial concerns of library administrators outside the Library of Congress during 1978 made it obvious that library catalogs other than those of the Library of Congress had to be considered when evaluating the impact of *AACR2*. It is primarily because of these concerns that the Library of Congress decided to consider the categories of "compatible" headings, that is, groups of non-*AACR2* headings that would continue unchanged after 1980.

Although some of our friends have chided us, suggesting that the idea of "compatible" headings is actually a new version of superimposition, we do not think that the 1981 policy is sufficiently like the 1967 policy to be called "superimposition." Among the significant differences we see between the two policies are these:

1. Rules 98 and 99 in the 1967 *AACR* extended the policy of superimposition to large classes of new headings (e.g. universities and churches) in addition to existing headings; there is no rule suggesting superimposition in *AACR2*.

2. The 1967 policy affected practically every type of heading that anyone either at the Library of Congress or at another library, might need when creating new bibliographic records. This usually made it diffi-

cult, and sometimes impossible, for anyone outside the Library of Congress to know whether a heading was *AACR* or superimposed. The 1981 policy will provide a high degree of predictability because it is limited to a few very definite categories. Furthermore, well over half the headings in the MARC data base do not fall in these categories; that is, the 1981 policy for compatible headings will not be applied to the great majority of headings that appear on new records after 1980.

In formulating the categories, we generally aimed for headings that (a) would be likely to appear less and less often in the future, (b) would not file too differently from the purely *AACR2* counterpart, and (c) would not, by the very way they were structured, clearly violate *AACR2* rules (e.g. we chose not to consider "Jackson, Miss." compatible, insisting that only the purely *AACR2* form, "Jackson (Miss.)," should be allowed). These guidelines suggest that the 1981 policy is less inimical to the goal of uniformity than it might seem at first glance.

Are the categories of compatible headings the thin edge of the wedge, leading to, at least, ever more categories of "compatible" headings, or, at worst, to a full-scale superimposition of the 1967 type? The answer is no, because the list of categories is a closed one. Indeed, we have inclined toward the precisely opposite tendency. For two of the "compatible" categories, important exceptions have been made:

1. When a heading includes a well-known acronym that should be written entirely in uppercase, according to *AACR2* (e.g. "Marc 2 Research Firm," in which "Marc" should be transcribed as "MARC"), the heading will be considered non-*AACR2* rather than "compatible."

2. When the heading for a famous writer includes the term "pseud." (e.g. "Queen, Ellery, pseud."), the heading will be considered non-*AACR2* rather than "compatible."

We have also come across two new categories of headings that show minor variance from *AACR2,* very similar to the "compatible" categories, but we have refused to add them to the list:

1. Retaining an ordinal in a title of nobility (e.g. "2d Viscount").
2. Retaining specific birth dates in either the form "Jan. 1, 1890– " or "1890 (Jan. 1)– ." (*AACR2* calls for "1890 Jan. 1– .")

Another hopeful, though necessarily speculative, note that should be sounded is the possibility that compatible headings might be abandoned, perhaps bit by bit, at some time after 1981. Corrections might be made in the new catalog so that, as far as form of heading goes, eventually this new catalog could be an almost purely *AACR2* data base. Whether the possibility of abandoning compatible headings is realized or not, we all must understand how much more practicable it will be to identify these "compatible headings," given the definite nature of the categories and the fact that individual cases of compatibility are so identified in the Library's automated name authority file, than to locate the non-*AACR1* headings under the 1967 policy. Of course, abandoning compatible headings in the future must depend on the continued development of automated programs, not only at the Library of Congress but also at the other institutions with which we share the same needs.

Since October 1978 we have been coding some existing headings according to *AACR2,* and in doing so have noted that 80–90 percent of them are personal names. At least 95 percent of those that fall in one or another of the categories of "compatible" headings involve the matter of fullness of name. It is well known that most new personal authors do not endure: people who write publish an average of 1.2 books, if our catalogs are any guide. We have already excepted famous people from the "compatible" categories that deal with fullness of name. If any personal name heading continues to be used frequently after 1981, the person will be considered "famous" and excepted from the "compatible" group. It follows that non-*AACR2* headings for persons will disappear rapidly.

While the policy of "compatible" headings was not invented by the Joint Steering Committee for Revision of AACR, it was certainly foreshadowed in remarks made by the committee's chairman, Peter R. Lewis, in his preface to *AACR2*:

JSCAACR therefore envisions libraries and bibliographic agencies adopting first those rules (principally in Part I) the application of which has no significant effect on the arrangement and collocation of existing bibliographic records, even though some differences of style and content may occur between one record and another. The remaining provisions, where they differ from *AACR1* or from previous local practice, may then be most easily adopted at the time when newly designed cataloguing and bibliographic systems allow earlier records to be converted or reconciled; or when a new sequence or catalogue is to come into being.

So instead of tagging our policy with such an ugly word as "superimposition," we feel that it should be named according to its real nature, "gradual adoption of *AACR2*."

AACR2 Documentation

The Library of Congress will prepare various documents for its catalogers to ensure a proper application of *AACR2*. The statement describing which options will be followed is an obvious example. In some cases it may not be enough to say simply that an option will be applied; clarification may be needed, especially during the first few days or weeks of application. For example, we have chosen to apply the rule that is an alternative to 22.3C2. This means that for a person whose nonroman name is well established in an English-language form (nonstandard romanization), we shall prefer this form over the systematically romanized form. This alternative rule, which is for persons entered under surname, may need the help provided in 22.3C1 for the comparable rule dealing with persons entered under given name: "If no English romanization is found, or if no one romanization predominates, romanize the name according to the table for the language adopted by the cataloguing agency." An example of an option that needs specific direction to apply can also be found in the chapters on bibliographic description. We have chosen to apply 1.4C7, which permits adding the full address of the publisher to that area called the publication, distribution, etc., area, provided the publisher is not a "major trade publisher." We shall probably tell our catalogers to assume the addition of the full address is warranted when there is no ISBN for the item, provided the address appears in the item being cataloged or is otherwise easily available.

These statements that will direct our catalogers to apply some of the options in a particular way suggest rule interpretation. We already perceive the need for some genuine rule interpretation, but we wish to give the matter serious study between now and 1981.

Consider the rules for bibliographic description. Unlike Britain, for example, this country has had a long tradition of very detailed rules for bibliographic description. *AACR2*, Part I, is not nearly so detailed as our previous rules. Below the general provisions, there are far fewer specific rules to cover special situations. This is true not only of the general chapter but also of each of the special chapters, including the one for books. The premise is that a lot of precise guidance is not necessary if catalogers are trained in the general principles and allowed to follow their common sense. This is obviously the best approach when one is faced by a very unusual item that is similar to but not exactly like another peculiar item, already cataloged, on which a specific rule might have been based; as every cataloger knows, there is never an end to peculiar cases. Of course, such factors as an aesthetic predeliction for consistency, the machine requirements for proper formating, and other constraints to produce uniformity will in part continue. If uniformity is really needed, then specific written guidance will be unavoidable—provided there is not so much of this as in the end to contravene *AACR2*. It will be a nice dilemma for us, creating perhaps the most interesting problem in our initial day-to-day application of the new rules. The following points are a sample of the sort of ideas one may gather from reading *AACR2*, Part I; these ideas seem worth considering, even if they do not ultimately result in rule interpretation.

1. Several of the rules (e.g. 1.1F1) use the word "prominently." Provision 0.8 in the general introduction defines a "prominent" statement as a formal statement that appears in one of the prescribed sources of information for areas 1 and 2 of the description. The prescribed sources for the first two areas for books (chapter 2) are title page, other preliminaries, and colophon. "Preliminaries" is defined in the glossary, and after reading that definition one finally has a correct understanding of "prominently" as applied to books. Would it not be useful, at least at the beginning, to pull all of this information together into one statement for each type of material?

2. Under the revised chapter 6 of *AACR1* we experienced considerable difficulty in sorting out statements of responsibility and other title information. When we read 1.1F12, would it not be helpful to bear the importance of the last sentence of 1.1F15 in mind, which says: "Statements of responsibility may include words or phrases which are neither names nor linking words (e.g., 'written by Jobe Hill in 1812')"? The combination of the two rules means, among other things, that a single statement, combining other title information and a statement of responsibility, should usually be punctuated as a statement of responsibility.

3. When 1.4C7 is applied, so that a publisher's full address is transcribed, may words such as "Street" and "Avenue" be abbreviated to the forms normally used ("St." and "Ave."), even though appendix B does not list abbreviations for these words? If so, will common sense provide the guidance, or will this guidance have to be stated in so many words?

4. Rule 1.5B3 provides for a mention of the number of components that make up parts of an item, for example, the number of pages in the volumes of a multivolume work, by saying "as detailed in the following chapters." Chapter 2 takes care of this matter only for multivolume publications where pagination is added to volume numbers. Single-part publications obviously need the same provision when a designation such as "portfolio" is used instead of "volume," for example, "1

portfolio (8 sheets)." Will an interpretation be necessary to let all catalogers know that they may apply the provision to single-part items?

5. The general chapter provides for a "with" note (1.7B21), but no text prescribes the form of this note. Rule 2.7B21 gives *some* text, but it is chiefly from the examples that one derives the following ideas:

  a. Transcribe the title proper, the statement of responsibility, and the imprint, omitting other title information and the edition area.
  b. Use ISBD punctuation throughout the note, omitting only the area divider (period-space-dash-space) before the imprint (use a "normal" period and spacing instead). The area divider must be omitted because the whole note is within a single area (cf. 1.7A3).

Will it be worthwhile to give catalogers advice like this as a guide to the application of the chapter 2 provision? If so, attention should also be called to paragraph 0.14 in the general introduction: "Neither the examples nor the form in which they are presented should be taken as instructions unless the accompanying text specifically states that they should." Thus, if the Library of Congress makes a rule interpretation of the type described here, it will be the Library of Congress that lays down the law, not the examples in rule 2.7B21.

6. In rule 2.0B1, two important points are made rather clearly: (a) a substitute for the chief source (title page) is treated exactly like the chief source, and (b) a note is made whenever a substitute for the chief source is used. In the chapters on nonbook materials, however, the concept of a chief source substitute is less clearly presented. For example, it does not seem sufficiently clear, in cataloging under chapter 8, that a title taken from accompanying text (as the substitute for the chief source) should be transcribed without brackets. Also, a note about the source of the title seems even more necessary for some of the nonbook materials than for books. Is a rule interpretation of this type needed?

The ideas presented above, and similar notions that others might have, must be balanced against the recognition, already mentioned, that strict legislation on every point of description is undesirable. *AACR2* itself speaks to this issue (somewhat) in the general introduction, which says (0.9): "The necessity for judgement and interpretation by the cataloguer is recognized in these rules. Such judgement and interpretation may be based on the requirements of a particular catalogue or upon the use of the items being catalogued. . . . Uniform legislation for all types and sizes of catalogues is neither possible nor desirable."

Part II of *AACR2* will need some of the same kind of attention, possibly resulting in directives or explanatory documents that we call rule interpretations. Chapter 21, the first chapter of Part II, immediately raises various ideas or questions, of which the following are examples:

1. Under rule 21.1B2, one of the categories of items that may be entered under corporate body comprises "those that record the collective thought of the body (e.g., reports of commissions, committees, etc.; official statements of position on external policies)." Some catalogers may view this as a very restrictive category, thinking, for example, that the body must be a committee-type entity with a limited scope to its charge, and that the item must be a report that deals with this specific charge. Other catalogers may go to the opposite extreme and believe that "collective thought," considered loosely, is the key, so that any type of item, issued by any type of body, would fit, provided the item is not specifically and prominently attributed to individuals.

Is there a middle-of-the-road policy that suggests itself? What main entry should one select for the following item?

ALA rules for filing catalog cards, prepared by the ALA Editorial Committee's Subcommittee on the ALA Rules for Filing Catalog Cards, Pauline A. Seely, chairman and editor.

2. Rule 21.23B says for sound recordings that added entries should be made for the principal performers, unless there are more than three, in which case added entries are made only for the first. Large-scale productions, such as operatic recordings, as well as smaller-scale ones such as jazz ensemble recordings, commonly involve more than three principal performers. Will the cataloger be able to make added entries for more than one principal performer in these cases, appealing to 21.29D as the authority? (Note, however, that this rule only authorizes added entries "other than those prescribed in rule 21.30." What is needed is authority for exceeding 21.23B.)

3. Some of our ideas about interpretation as a means of clarifying a rule's intention might lead to rule revision after 1981; but it would be unwise to come to such a conclusion in 1979. For example, rule 21.33A, which concerns the entry of constitutions, includes the provision: "If the document is issued by any jurisdiction other than the one governed by it, make an added entry under the heading for the jurisdiction issuing it. Add the appropriate uniform title to the added entry if the document is a law." This type of added entry is even more necessary for the jurisdiction that promulgates the law—that is, the one from which the law emanates—whenever this jurisdiction is not the same as the one gov-

erned by the law, and is also not the one that issues the law. (The entity that issues the document might easily be a commercial publisher, and frequently is.) It would be altogether better if the text quoted above said: "If the document emanates from any jurisdiction other than the one governed by it."

In chapter 22 are other ideas or questions, for example:

1. In rule 22.1D2, the provision for the retention of hyphens between forenames obviously needs to be extended to surnames.

2. In the case of many famous nonwriters (e.g. artists), the Library of Congress catalogers will need to be cautioned that the form found in reference sources of the person's country really is the *AACR2* form. This is what the rule requires, and those of us who monitor the *AACR2* evaluation of existing headings at the Library have been surprised how often such correct *AACR2* forms are the same as the headings established in our catalogs under ALA and earlier rules. For example, Goya is entered under "Goya y Lucientes, Francisco de" in the *Enciclopedia Universal Ilustrada,* and this is exactly our "ALA" heading.

It seems clear that reference books have followed and, to a certain extent still follow, the same principles expressed by the ALA rules. In such cases, the Library's catalogers also may need to be warned against setting too much store by the rhetoric about "sought" forms, for they probably cannot base the heading on such sought forms as

> Michelangelo
> J.M.W. Turner
> Velázquez
> Rembrandt
> Théodore Géricault
> Caravaggio

but rather must use

> Michelangelo Buonarroti
> Joseph Mallord William Turner
> Diego Rodríguez de Silva Velázquez
> Rembrandt Harmenszoon van Rijn
> Jean-Louis-André-Théodore Géricault
> Michelangelo Merisi da Caravaggio

as *AACR2* requires by stating that reference works should decide the issue.

In considering chapter 24, it is useful to be aware of the work of the IFLA Working Group on Corporate Headings. Its final recommendations were issued separately in the summer of 1978 and were also published in *Cataloging Service Bulletin* (no. 2, Fall 1978), with a request for comments from the library community. Frances Hinton, in a memorandum of September 18, 1978, to the IFLA UBC Office, remarked on the surprising agreement between *AACR2* and the IFLA recommendations. Her excellent comparison of the two texts, however, pointed to gaps in both texts, where each contains the instruction or clarification that is missing in the other. For example, IFLA recommendation 7A says: "When the name of a corporate body appears in grammatical conjunction with other elements, use the form in which it can stand alone. Deutscher Verein für Orientforschung (*In source of information*: Bericht des Deutschen Vereins für Orientforschung)." Although this is accepted cataloging practice, it is not stated in *AACR2*. Further study of the IFLA recommendations is likely to suggest other needed rule interpretations.

The best example of a gap in *AACR2*, however, is represented by the following case, taken from a perusal of chapter 25: the need to differentiate multiple monographic series entered under the same title proper, for example, "Geological series." There is no rule in *AACR2* that tells how these works should be differentiated, particularly when they are used as secondary entries in other records. An instruction for catalogers must be supplied here, probably borrowing techniques from chapter 25. It might be argued that key-titles adequately differentiate identical serial titles. For a very cogent statement of the reasons why we cannot turn automatically to the key-title, one could not do better than consult Ronald Hagler's *Where's That Rule?* (Ottawa: Canadian Library Assn., 1979). He says:

Already, agencies involved in CONSER (and no doubt others) are considering the problems of the unique identification of serials in a way which can be fully linked to ISBD(G) and AACR2 practices of description. The "key-title," which is certainly valuable for other purposes, is not at the moment acceptable for this one, largely because the key-title is so far from a bibliographic title: it is an artificial construct—more so than the distinctive title of the preliminary ISBD(S)—authorized by an ISDS centre and not entirely predictable by a cataloguer with the serial in hand. It is also, of course, lacking for most serial titles in large library collections. Its purpose is simply unique identification, in conjunction with its inseparable partner, the ISSN. Both have a place in the description in the standard number and terms of availability area. Although the Library of Congress has been using the key-title as a means of referring among serial titles in the notes area (*Cataloging Service Bulletins* 117, 119), AACR2 does not refer to this possibility in the options offered in rule 1.7A4.

This is a very complex subject, which the National Library of Canada and the Library of Congress have studied at length. The basis for a solution of the problem was published in *Cataloging Service Bulletin* (no. 5, Summer 1979).

Other rule interpretations will be needed for much less earth-shaking reasons. We may have to issue temporary documents to our catalogers calling attention to the cases where our past practice must be abandoned. For example, Appendix A.7B of *AACR2* says that "s." in "s.l." should be capitalized, a change from our practice under the revised chapter 6 of *AACR1*. We shall also make a number of statements in our documentation to clarify minor points relating to the display of catalog records in card and cardlike formats. These statements typically will call for a continuation of past practice. Some examples are:

1.   Place a period at the end of the "publication, distribution, etc." area, unless the area ends with a bracket or parentheses.
2.   Omit a comma between the parts of the place statement in the "publication, distribution, etc." area when a bracket appears where the comma would be placed:

> London [Ont.]
> *not* London, [Ont.]

3.   For the physical description area and each note in the note area, start a new paragraph.

The published decisions relating to chapters 22–25 have arisen because we have been providing *AACR2* headings for informational purposes. As we continue to use *AACR2* in this way, and look to 1981, when we will fully implement *AACR2*, other decisions about rule interpretations will have to be made so that items that are to be cataloged are not held up while we consult widely. The documents produced as instructions to our catalogers will be published in *Cataloging Service Bulletin* and, at the same time, distributed to the reconstituted Joint Steering Committee for Revision of *AACR*, the ABACUS group, and certain others. Depending on the reactions of these bodies, our decisions may be condoned or reversed. Throughout, we intend to keep the library community completely informed on developments. We are, of course, looking forward to reviewing comparable contributions to a successful application of *AACR2* from the other national libraries.

Is rule interpretation always so serious? No, some of our statements for *AACR1* have been amusing or even hilarious. None of them, however, can begin to approach the bantering and felicitous wit of a rule interpretation dated May 11, 1927, and written by the Library's great Charles Martel:

The rule (A.L.A. 138) is optional. Either "sic" or "!" may be used; cataloguers ordinarily should use "!". In case of a very slight coquille (like that comma in "Sans, Souci") the reaction on the reader hardly rises to the explosive intensity of an exclamation, and the heavier but quieter "sic" seems less emphatic, while, on the other hand, in a frivolous title the scholarly "sic" would look pedantic and the "!" more natural.

Name Authorities

The heart of a descriptive cataloger's work at the Library of Congress is the bibliographic description of an item, the choice of access points, and the formulation of headings to be used in these access points. Describing an item and choosing the access points (main and added entries) take less time than formulating the authority records for the headings. To many of our catalogers, formulating headings is our most important activity and it is, consequently, the one that attracts them most. It continues to have much human, personal interest, a quality increasingly absent from many other aspects of our work. There is even humor in it; the day is brightened a little when one encounters titles such as "The Nuclear Components of the Sex Cells of Four Species of Cockroaches" or "A Literature Review on Mourning Dove Song as Related to the Coo-Count Census," but most refreshing of all are such wonderful, all-American headings as

> Slagboom, Teco
> Fox, Chattie Foster
> Toogood, Annie Coxe
> Looney, Lillie Littrell

At the Library of Congress we have a vast card catalog, called the Official Catalog, adjacent to the cataloging divisions. Each file of entries, either under a main or added entry or under a subject, is preceded by a card containing the authority record for the particular heading. This record contains the established heading, tracings for cross-references leading to the heading, and the information taken from any source to justify the heading and cross-references. Name authority records cover headings for persons, corporate bodies, geographic names representing jurisdictions, uniform titles, and series.[4] Such records have been created since about 1898 and now number approximately three million. The Official Catalog also contains all necessary cross-references leading to these headings. Behind the authority records are filed bibliographic records comprising main, added, and subject entries concerning name headings. This immense card catalog is the only place where a cataloger can find in one alphabet all of the name headings and the cross-reference structure that searching for the headings requires.

Since the Library of Congress will retain the present MARC data base as the basis of the new catalog after 1980, against which we will be searching and cataloging, it will still be necessary to maintain an Official Catalog for the Library's catalogers. As explained earlier, the reference structure for any heading created by the Library, including the headings used in the MARC data base, is available only in the Official Catalog. For two or three years after 1980, consequently, the Library's catalogers will continue to search headings in the Official Catalog. Headings found there will be re-created, as necessary, according to *AACR2*. If the heading does not appear under any form in the Official Catalog, or if it appears there and agrees in every way with *AACR2*, it will be input to the automated name authority system in its *AACR2* form. If the heading is already in the Official Catalog in a form at variance with *AACR2*, it will also be input in the automated name authority system, but in its *AACR2* form. In this case, the old non-*AACR2* form of the heading will be included in the name authority record as information, affording a link with the past.

The automated aspect of our name authority file began in April 1977, when the first records for new headings were converted to machine-readable form. This program was started with only a few catalogers. Other catalogers were brought into the program gradually. By April 1978 the last section of catalogers had been phased in, so that from that time all Library of Congress catalogers have been creating new headings in accordance with the automated procedures developed. We began adding earlier name authority records to the automated name authority system in October 1978. In a few of our cataloging sections, when the authority record for a heading being used in current cataloging exists only in manual form, it is re-created in machine-readable form. We hope that by 1980 all current authority work with either new or existing headings will contribute to the automated data base.

---

4. The *AACR* does not cover topical subject authorities or authorities for geographic names that do not represent jurisdictions; hence subject authorities are not within the scope of this paper.

Approximately one million headings are used in the MARC data base of bibliographic records, only some of which have records representing them in the automated name authority file. To enrich this file, we are working on a special project which, when successfully concluded, will mean—at a minimum—that every heading which appears in twenty-five or more MARC bibliographic records will have its authority record converted for input to the automated name authority file. We are listing separately the old and new forms for this special groups of headings. *Cataloging Service Bulletin* carries the list, beginning with the Fall 1979 number.

The automated name authority file will increasingly become our means of communication with other libraries that are also creating headings. When it is adequately developed, the file will enable other libraries to act independently with far greater confidence than is possible when deriving headings from our published bibliographic records. A machine-readable version of the automated name authority file is already available on tape, and beginning in 1980 we shall begin to issue it in a COM catalog form that will be cumulated.

The past, present, and future of authority work, as described here, is very much related to the adoption of *AACR2*. When we started the work on existing headings in October 1978, we began to evaluate these earlier headings in the light of *AACR2*. To most headings a code is assigned that indicates whether it is "pure" *AACR2*, merely compatible with *AACR2*, or completely at variance with *AACR2*. In this last case, the *AACR2* form is created and added to the record as information.

Coding for the *AACR2* form has run into one quite serious snag: cross-references. Some cross-references that have already been made under previous or current rules, or are being made under current rules, are required also by *AACR2* chapter 26. Of this group, however, the form of the heading referred *from* may or may not be valid under *AACR2*. Another group of these cross-references that already exists or is being formulated is invalid under *AACR2*. A third category of references comprises those that are required by *AACR2* but cannot be made today because of discrepancies between *AACR2* and previous rules. We have been forced to postpone any application of *AACR2* to cross-references until full adoption in 1981.

We view the addition of *AACR2* coding to current authority work as a most salutary exercise. It gives us the means of helping ourselves and others to understand what *AACR2* is all about. The problems, strategems, and solutions we come up with before 1981 will be communicated to others in a timely way. We shall have been forced to examine, evaluate, and question ideas and assumptions; the judgments we make and the procedures we adopt will be firmly grounded in practical experience. The decisions on the options, rule interpretations, or any other thought expressed before 1981 will have been tested. Since no bibliographic records will be changed or newly created as a result of our *AACR2* coding, there will be no inconvenience to users of existing catalogs. Much of the training of the Library's catalogers in applying *AACR2* chapters 22–25 will automatically be accomplished, and it is likely that, to a considerable extent, *AACR2* training can start in other libraries, depending on how they are able to use the information we publish before 1981.

International Implications of *AACR2*

J. C. DOWNING

It would seem very reasonable in presenting this paper to examine the international elements of the precursors of *AACR2*, to assess the influence of those codes, and to determine how they have affected international input into *AACR2* and what effect such input may have in the international appreciation of this latest set of Anglo-American cataloging rules.

For the purposes of this paper, I propose to exclude the North American continent from consideration, as I assume that earlier papers in the seminar will have fully represented the views of catalogers of Canada and the United States. Though the United Kingdom has been well represented in the authorship of *AACR2*, and its Library Association is one of the three publishers of the rules, I shall include in my paper references to implications within the United Kingdom, for a number of significant factors have changed the climate of bibliographic control in our country since the publication of *AACR1*.

I propose to divide my paper into the following major sections:

1. The international objectives of Anglo-American cataloging and that element that is apparent in *AACR1*, together with some indication

of the acceptance of that code beyond the immediate environment
of its authors

2.   The international constitution and input into *AACR2*, together with
a review of the potential constituency of the rules

3.   The role of national bibliographies in implementation of *AACR2*
and the prospects of adoption

4.   General conclusions

International Objectives of
Anglo-American Cataloging

It is fair to say that, other than in personal aspirations, Anglo-American
cataloging did not take shape until the early years of this century. To
one who has benefited in his visits to the North American continent from
the generosity of the publishers of the Dewey Decimal Classification it
is pleasing to repeat in this paper the motion approved at the annual
meeting of the (British) Library Association in Newcastle in 1904, that
"this meeting cordially approves Mr. Dewey's suggestion in favour of a
common code of cataloguing rules for England [!] and the United States,
and thereby instructs the Council to take the necessary steps to attain
this object."[1]

As you all know, the result was the ALA code of 1908, formally
known as *Cataloguing Rules—Author and Title Entries*. The preface of
that work indicated that those rules were "produced with a view to establishing uniformity of practice throughout the English-speaking race"—
a most laudable objective, in spite of the fact that it is now impossible
to identify the English-speaking race, though we are conscious univer-
sally of an English-speaking community, whether the language is the
mother tongue or that used to communicate in an interlingual or international situation.

I will spare you an account of the reception AA 1908 received,
though I cannot refrain from quoting from two reviews. The first is by
W. C. Berwick Sayers, a noted English librarian who lived well into the
second half of this century. Perhaps with his tongue in cheek, he wrote
in *The Library World* (June 1909) "that had the [cataloging] committees
been in nearer proximity [they were 3,000 miles apart] the four years
would have at least doubled, for the genus librarian has an inhuman love

---

1. J. Minto, "The Anglo-American Cataloguing Rules," *Library Association
Record*, 11 (July 25, 1909).

of argument."[2] It is interesting to contrast those four years with the time it took to produce *AACR1* and *AACR2*, though the latter benefited enormously from the fact that from the outset it was controlled entirely by a mutually appointed international body.

My second quote from the reviews of AA 1908 is a most perceptive one, from the pen of G. R. Bolton, which appeared in *The Library World* in April 1910. He wrote:

This Code of Catalogue Rules may serve as a formulation for an international system, although at present continental [i.e. European] practice differs very considerably from Anglo-American methods. It is a code likely to exercise a great influence on the profession. The time when each library is an individual unit, each having its own pet scheme, and differing from other libraries in some respects, is slowly, but nevertheless surely, passing into the limbo of forgotten things. The day of standardization, of centralization, and of co-operation is rapidly dawning, and with these, conformity to prescribed rules and professional methods—probably in all the ramifications of library work—will become all but compulsory.[3]

We are still pursuing, seventy years later, the objectives so clearly expressed by Bolton in 1910, but when one considers differences in magnitude of library services between now and then, it says something for our profession that at least some of us still hold those objectives dear.

It was that increase in magnitude which made the achievement of a single text in 1967 an impossible aim. There seemed to be, during the preparation of *AACR1*, a greater disagreement between the various elements within the American profession than between the thinkers and analysts on the two sides of the Atlantic. Nonetheless, the two principal national participants agreed on much, but time and compromise defeated any possibility of producing an integrated and coordinated set of rules. This was in spite of mutual visits between both parties, the labors of Lubetzky and Spalding, and the inspiration of the Paris Conference of 1961. The latter, ironically, preferring a common set of principles which could be applied to newly created rules in all languages, in place of a true international code of rules, led to the separate appearance of the North American and British texts of *AACR1*.

---

2. W. C. Berwick Sayers, "The Anglo-American Cataloguing Code," *Library World*, 11 (June 1909).

3. George R. Bolton, "Anglo-American Joint Code of Cataloguing Rules, 1908," *Library World*, 12 (April 1910).

It is sometimes forgotten that only Part I, the rules for entry and heading, were the result of Anglo-American cooperation. Parts II and III are very different in the two texts. In the North American text, Part II stemmed entirely from Library of Congress practice—the Canadians taking no part in its preparation, while the British text of that part recognized for the first time that current publishing conventions had extended the area of bibliographic information well beyond the title page.

We may, in the light of recent experience, bemoan the weaknesses of *AACR1*, but at the time of its publication we, in the United Kingdom, were only too anxious for its implementation. The *British National Bibliography* introduced it immediately in 1968. It is fair to record that the experience gained there by Michael Gorman and others has led to—what is expected will be—the improvements of *AACR2*. Many British libraries followed the example, in some way or other, of the national bibliography; even our former national library began to consider its advantages.

Since publication, libraries in upwards of forty countries have adopted or adapted *AACR1* for their own use, led in many instances by the example of their national bibliographies. It is true that the areas of adoption are largely English-speaking communities—many in Africa and Asia, where disciplines in librarianship had been absorbed from professional education in Britain or in the United States. Curiously, the practice of adopting a particular text did not always follow rational arguments, but was occasioned by the earlier appearance of the North American text, which preceded the British text by almost twelve months. This situation would not have existed had there been simultaneous publication of the two texts.

Dorothy Anderson, the director of IFLA's UBC office, in a review of the use made of *AACR1* found differing patterns of implementation. "In those countries where English is the only language, AACR can be considered as the national cataloguing code, accepted in its entirety," giving Australia and New Zealand as examples. "In other countries, where one of the languages of the country is English and there is a heavy concentration of English language publications appearing on the shelves of libraries, it is used for English language material, but with local adaptations for publications in other languages."[4] Singapore, Malaysia, and Hong Kong are given as examples in this category. Some countries have

---

4. Dorothy Anderson, "The Future of the Anglo-American Cataloguing Rules (AACR) in the Light of Universal Bibliographic Control (UBC)," *Library Resources & Technical Services* 20 (Winter 1976): 3–15.

a national cataloging code for their own-language publications, but use *AACR* for foreign-language imprints, especially those in romanized scripts. This is particularly true of Asian countries, such as Japan and Thailand.

A further category of use is those countries, principally European, that do not have a dominant language, and this group finds *AACR1* useful as a reference tool to aid catalogers. Such countries are Belgium, the Netherlands, Switzerland, and Yugoslavia. Libraries in Poland and Rumania consult *AACR1* as a guide to practice.

All the aforementioned use is confined to the English-text versions, either North American or British.

Such a categorization suggests a diminishing involvement in *AACR*, but we have now to look at a further category, one which is possibly much more influential—that of translation. Translations of one or the other text have been made in French, Persian, Spanish, and Portuguese, the latter versions being of particular importance in South America. Partial translations have also been made in Arabic, Greek, Japanese, Korean, and Urdu. The most ambitious project in this direction was made, however, by a group of Scandinavian libraries, anxious to improve and standardize their bibliographic disciplines. After close study of the British text, each agreed to prepare its own national rules in Danish, Finnish, Norwegian, and Swedish, to reach the closest approximation to *AACR1* and to introduce improvements and international standards. Conferences of these Scandinavian pioneers in 1970 and 1972 led them to record their impression that "the belief that a change in cataloguing rules reduces the value of an existing catalogue was often proved exaggerated and sometimes distinctly untenable."[5] They concluded that approximation to *AACR*, MARC, and the *ISBD*s appeared absolutely necessary in order to realize the project of organizing national data banks.

The implied significance of *AACR1* as a base for a universal code was countered by many criticisms, founded on experience in practice as well as comparison with the established principles of descriptive cataloging. Catalogers in non-English-speaking communities found difficulty in translating the text, due to their misunderstanding of the definitions and the lack of a comprehensive glossary. They found it impossible, from their experience, to translate with any exactitude such phrases as "primarily responsible for," which had been used freely by the editor in order to find reasonable solutions for intractable cases. Additionally, the preponderance of British and American examples in the rules created

5. "Cataloguing in Scandinavia," *International Cataloguing* 2 (Jan./Mar. 1973): 2–4.

problems for translators and those catalogers who rarely saw such material, but who had to apply the intent of the rules to publications produced domestically.

If *AACR1* cannot be regarded as a truly international code, in the universal sense, there is no denying that it has come to be accepted in its eleven years of existence as an international manual of cataloging practice.

International Constitution and Constituency of *AACR2*

As I hinted earlier in this paper, *AACR2* has been controlled in its preparation and production by a mutually appointed international body, representing equitably the three national elements which have contributed to it. The operation of preparing *AACR2* has therefore been conducted more practically than was possible in either AA 1908 or *AACR1*. Besides the three areas of input, we were able to secure editors representing the opposing shores of the Atlantic. The funds that were available permitted mutual discussion in each of the three arenas. Though I use "opposing shores," I mean this only in a geographical sense, for it was clear in the preliminary discussions that a primary objective was the production of a single text, thus avoiding the confusion and embarrassment initiated in the implementation of *AACR1*.

Happily, in the United Kingdom we were fortunate in having by 1974 some resolution of our earlier difficulties. We possessed, although in an embryonic state, a library that could truly be called national. Though many at this seminar will have regarded for years the Library of the British Museum as the national library of Great Britain, this was only partially true. Senior members of its staff had given much time and effort to the preparation of *AACR1*, but the service generally remained aloof from the broader sweep of library practice in the country.

The coincidence of the development of the British Library at the time we were considering the revision of *AACR* was too good an opportunity to miss. Those of us who were concerned for the unity of the profession in Britain were anxious to utilize the potentiality of that unity by harnessing the new institution to the common task of producing and implementing a new edition of *AACR*. We therefore had a base in Britain that, for the first time, was equal to those existing separately in the United States and in Canada.

The way in which the Joint Steering Committee went about its task of revising *AACR2* has already been described by previous speakers. I need only repeat the obligations it had to international objectives. The outstanding item here was the reconciliation of the two texts of *AACR1* into one, finally agreed upon text. Despite a number of optional alternatives, introduced to satisfy different aims not based essentially on national differences, this is the greatest single international factor in the appearance of *AACR2*.

Furthermore, an essential element in JSC objectives was the conscious attempt to take note of international interest, beyond the Anglo-American constituency, obtained from those areas which had had experience in the application of *AACR1*. Sumner Spalding, in his introduction to the first edition, expressed the relation between the rules and the principles enunciated at the Paris Conference of 1961. It was not the intent of JSC to move further from those principles but, if possible, to move closer to them—a movement already initiated by the committees responsible for the day-to-day amendment of *AACR1*.

Since the publication of *AACR1* in 1967, there had been developments in the international sphere which had been initially outlined in the recommendations of the Paris Conference. No discussion had been provided in 1961 for the international regulation of the elements of descriptive cataloging, as distinct from author and title cataloging. The International Meeting of Cataloguing Experts in Copenhagen in 1969 remedied this defect. As a result, the first "standard bibliographical description" was developed, which eventually led to a series of "international bibliographical descriptions." As you have learned from earlier contributions to this seminar, two *ISBDs* were by 1975 in a sufficiently advanced state to be regarded as essential elements in a revision of *AACR*. The problems created in the absorption of those international standards into *AACR2* has already been rehearsed. What *does* require repetition for the purposes of emphasis is JSC's determination not to reject, because of internal conflict, the principle that *AACR2* must be firmly based on international standards. To JSC must be paid firm credit for the development of the *International Standard Bibliographical Description (General),* which from now on should determine the shape of all future standards in this field.

In this portion of my paper it is important to note the decisions of JSC that have a significance beyond the immediate Anglo-American environment. These should lead to a ready understanding of the rules themselves and their acceptance as a consolidated base for comprehensive international use—a concern expressed by the Council on Library Resources when it generously decided to meet the greatest proportion of the expenses incurred in the revision. Besides conformity to international standards and the Paris Principles, JSC expressed a concern to introduce a wider use of European languages into the examples. The problem of translation was kept continuously in mind. To ensure this, the text has been expressed as simply as possible, in short sentences and paragraphs of limited extent. All statements of policy cited in the introductions have been numbered for easy reference from a comprehensive index. This should ensure that users, whatever their experience, should have little difficulty in finding their way through what, at first sight, may be regarded as a forbidding document.

Through the agency of Canadian representation, JSC was assured an immediate interest in the translation of the text into the French language, for prepublication rights were given to the Association pour l'Avancement des Sciences et des Techniques de la Documentation (ASTED) so as to permit the bilingual community of Canada the opportunity of using *AACR2* without any diminution of privilege to either community.

It was also agreed in general terms by JSC that it would recommend to the publishers that translation rights be granted to any organization of repute prepared to provide a text of *AACR2* in its own language.

As a further feature in the international role of the rules, JSC circulated the first draft, prepared at the conclusion of the editorial task, to communities outside the Anglo-American triangle. These were situated in Australia, Denmark, Kenya, Malaysia, New Zealand, and South Africa.

I mentioned earlier the interest shown by the Scandinavian countries in *AACR1* and the contribution it made to the harmonization of cataloging rules in the four northern European countries. We in Britain were happy to welcome representatives of those countries to an Anglo-Nordic Seminar held by the British Library Association's Cataloguing and Indexing Group at York in 1975,[6] when the prospect of a general *ISBD* was initially discussed. The views expressed on this occasion agreed, in most elements, with those generally voiced in responses to the invitation to comment on *AACR*, sent out late in 1974 to non-JSC countries by IFLA's Office of Universal Bibliographic Control.

It is worthwhile enumerating these points, which were précised for JSC by Elizabeth Tate, then Library of Congress representative.[7] Obstacles to total international acceptance were likely to be

6. "Anglo-Nordic Seminar on the Revision and International Use of *AACR*, York, 1975," *Catalogue & Index* 37 (Summer 1975): 1–2, 8–9.

7. Elizabeth Tate, "Comments and Suggestions from the International Cataloguing Community," JSC/LC Papers, 135 (Dec. 1975).

1. The definition of corporate authorship in *AACR1* that would result in a choice of main entry heading under corporate body for too many categories of material
2. Corporate headings which would be too complex
3. Multiplicity of form subheadings
4. A definition of personal authorship which would be far too broad for acceptance on the continent of Europe. (This definition was reduced, however, in a late revision of *AACR1*.)
5. Preference for the English form for certain personal and geographic names, contrary to the recommendation of the meeting in Paris in 1961 and in Copenhagen in 1969
6. Failure to use internationally accepted romanization systems
7. Orientation of *AACR1* toward publishing practices in Anglo-American countries, there being little consideration of the different practices in developing countries
8. Need for participation of other countries in the development of an international code

Additionally, there was reaction to the deviations which were not in harmony with the Paris Principles. *AACR1,* too, in its approach to serials, was difficult to follow, and did not fit current trends.

It would seem appropriate at this point to examine how far these criticisms may have been met in *AACR2,* though I do not propose to examine them in detail, for this will have already been accomplished by earlier speakers.

Certainly the definition of both corporate and personal authorship has been modified, not so much to bring either closer in line with European practice but, rather, to make the rules easier to use in any community. These modifications have been based upon experience gained in applying *AACR1.* The areas which led to ambiguous application in *AACR1,* let us hope, are reduced in *AACR2.* Similar comment applies to the creation of a multiplicity of subheadings, either in corporate authorship or in specialist areas such as religious and legal material.

Though full consideration was given to use of the vernacular for all forms of name, whether personal or geographic, it was finally decided by JSC that the dominant constituency implementing *AACR* would prefer to use the English form for certain names, such as "Saint Francis of Assisi," "Horace," "Florence," and "Venice."

The problem of romanization was a thorny one, which led to repeated discussion in JSC. There was great sympathy for the use of internationally prepared romanization tables. It was regretted, however, that such tables as yet covered only a limited number of languages; consequently the systems established in the areas contributing to *AACR2* would continue to be used for some time. In view of these facts, it was reasonable for JSC not to recommend any particular set of tables, but it did have responsibility for selecting one broadly accepted set for use in the examples to the rules. For this reason it chose the ALA/LC romanization tables.

It will be accepted that the range of examples in *AACR2* is more representative of material drawn from outside Anglo-American countries than was possible in *AACR1*. It was impossible to include examples of all cultures that were likely to be reflected in all the libraries that use it. Within the period allowed for preparation, *AACR2* is as catholic as it was humanly possible to make it. It is not generally appreciated that the time consumed in locating and quoting appropriate examples in many languages for the total range of documentation—monographs, maps, music, recordings, films, graphic material—was as long, if not longer, than that spent in determining the text, once policy had been confirmed by JSC.

When such a discipline as *AACR,* or an internationally used classification, is prepared, it is natural to expect claims from many sources for participation in the preparatory discussion. Regrettably, however, as noted by Berwick Sayers (earlier in this paper), the genus librarian has an inhuman love of argument. Should we ever achieve, rather than aspire to, a universal code of rules for cataloging, it will demand a far greater period of preparation, and consequently financial support, than was allowed for *AACR2*. Certainly JSC does not claim that its work can be regarded as more than a step in the direction of a universal code; let us hope that it will prove later to have been in the right direction.

You will have gathered that the constituency of *AACR* spreads from a central core of use in North America and Britain to those countries very close to us in culture and race. From this trunk the roots penetrate to communities that use English as a language of internal as well as international communication. Further channels develop a decreasing dimension, in areas where English becomes essentially an international language, until finally we reach communities with strong linguistic cultures of their own that have already-established effective disciplines in our area of activity.

It is obvious that the closer *AACR* moves toward totally accepted international principles, whether those of Paris, or any prospective revision of that text, such as is required by Michael Gorman in his article "Changes in Cataloging Codes,"[8] the closer it comes to serving as a uni-

8. Michael Gorman, "Changes in Cataloging Codes," *Library Trends* 25 (Jan. 1977): 587–601.

versal code. We must nonetheless concede that the reasoning for this arises not so much from our contribution to the enunciation of principles but from the acceptance of English as an international language.

The Role of National Bibliographies and the Prospects of Adoption

The development of national data bases through the medium of machine-readable cataloging processes has led to a change of role in the services of national bibliographic agencies. In pre-MARC days the only form of ready communication was the catalog card. Now, however, we can exchange bibliographic records by dispatching tapes or discs from one community to another. Indeed, we can go further and connect our data bases by means of online facilities which can be readily interrogated and just as readily absorb material. Because of this revolutionary change, national bibliographic agencies have to identify their operations against the needs of two opposing areas. First they have to satisfy the demands of their own domestic markets, but there is increasing significance in the potentiality of international exchange of bibliographic records.

Dorothy Anderson, addressing the British Library Association's Centenary Conference in 1977, identified the responsibility of a national bibliographic agency as follows:

The role of the national bibliographic agency has been described as the "nexus" of the national library system: the link, the channel of communication between the national and international library communities. . . . International communication may conflict with national demands at any time and in any context, and the agency must, therefore, keep balance between national users and their needs and the country's contribution to international exchange. As the international communications systems develop, the functions of the national bibliographic agency are likely to expand: exporting national records, receiving tapes on exchange from other agencies, maintaining authority control systems. It can only perform these functions successfully if there is constant and constructive co-operation and communication at national level.[9]

It follows clearly from this reasoning that if such services are valuable to an international community, it is essential that each member of such a community conform to requirements accepted internationally. Though

9. Dorothy Anderson, "Universal Bibliographic Control: The Implications," in *Proceedings of the Library Association Centenary Conference, 1977*, p.58–62.

it is accepted that *AACR* is not yet a code of rules that may be regarded as universal, it goes a long way toward that goal. The more bibliographic agencies that can be persuaded to adopt its practice, the nearer we are to improving the potentiality of international exchange.

With the onset of machine-readable cataloging, we have tended to overlook some of the ancillary uses of national bibliographies. Those that are produced at frequent intervals serve other purposes than that of providing centralized cataloging. They are used as book selection sources and, if cumulated regularly and consistently, as reference tools. They cannot, therefore, be influenced by the idiosyncracies employed in particular libraries, however great or significant those libraries may be. In seeking to serve a wide variety of users in place and time, national bibliographies cannot afford to be accused of favoring the whims of any particular category of user. It is essential, therefore, that they adopt a neutral mode. A code of cataloging rules, prepared internationally through cooperative machinery, is an attractive medium by which to present records nationally. We must expect some use of our tools by nonprofessionals. The more that we can encourage that use by consistent practice within our various reference sources, the greater will be the eventual appreciation by users in libraries.

Naturally, we are all embarrassed by the growth, during the lifetime of *AACR1,* of the machine-readable data bases. We know what they have cost to produce, and whatever our personal aspirations, we must be sympathetic toward the problems of modifying the records contained in those data bases—problems which are not essentially mechanical, but fiscal. However, it must be emphasized that the benefits which could accrue from a widespread acceptance of *AACR2* are likely to be most appreciated at the point the record is used, not necessarily where the record is created. Total effectiveness of *AACR2* is a cumulative experience, gained by many persons with differing needs in many places over extended periods of time. As Ron Hagler has so pithily said, "The future is longer than the past."[10]

I find it difficult to believe that anyone, operating a cooperative network center, will have the facility to evaluate the positive values of *AACR2.* Even with the interposition of machine records in our processes, we cannot ignore the fact that the development of traditionally printed national bibliographies since the conclusion of the Second World War has done much to develop the need for consistently constructed access points in the catalogs of libraries and in bibliographic services.

---

10. Ronald Hagler's comments in a talk on *AACR* to Canadian librarians, Ottawa, Summer 1978.

Whatever the opposition to the introduction of improvements in our practice, I cannot believe that such progress will not continue in the years to come.

Of course it is easy to counter this by observing that, in comparison with data bases, national or otherwise, traditional national bibliographies are not affected by the problems of locating books on shelves, nor by the limitations imposed in the provision of guides to comprehensive collections.

Nonetheless, the more widespread the adoption of *AACR2* by national data bases and national bibliographies, the easier it will be for consumers of those services to accept without modification records imported into their own systems.

A major criticism, which is voiced regularly concerning the preparation of national records, is that of currency. The introduction of MARC has led to an increase in the quantity of data included in any record. Though this may be considered essential in order to satisfy the wide range of consumer needs, it is difficult to find any compensation, other than increased labor costs, for the delay incurred in the preparation of the records. Here *AACR2* makes a positive contribution. It requires that access points for personal authors, indeed all authors, be given in the form of name used in authorship. This eliminates unnecessary research, permitting entries to be prepared with minimum effort.

The dominant philosophy of the new rules encourages economy and utility in the production of records. This philosophy must be adopted by all the principal bibliographic agencies—not because they will continue to serve as the sole bibliographic authority in each country, but because they are likely to become centers for the coordination of regional and specialized networks.

You will see that I have a firm belief that the way to effect widespread acceptance of *AACR2,* beyond its national constituency, is by encouraging adoption of the rules in national bibliographic agencies. We know that many communities have already adopted the International Standard Bibliographic Descriptions. As those standards have been implemented in Part I of *AACR2,* it is natural that much thought will be applied by those communities to the utilization of Part II.

Though only three Anglo-American countries have contributed to the preparation of *AACR2,* the three national libraries were happy to invite the Washington representative of the National Library of Australia to discussions concerning implementation. The wish to standardize the bibliographic processes of the English-speaking communities has been growing during the last decade. The first step in this direction was development of the National Program for Acquisition and Cataloging of the Library of Congress. Subsequent steps led to adoption by the national bibliographies of Australia, Canada, and the United Kingdom of the standard application of the eighteenth edition of the Decimal Classification—a step encouraged by the appointment of a British representative to its Editorial Policy Committee. A natural outcome of the meetings of the Joint Steering Committee for Revision of AACR was discussion among these national libraries of a mutual date for implementation.

Representatives of the four national libraries have met on two occasions since 1976, and will be meeting in Ottawa immediately after this seminar. In order to identify themselves distinctively, they have chosen to name themselves ABACUS—Association of Bibliographic Agencies of Britain, Australia, Canada, and the United States. They agreed, as you know, mutually to adopt *AACR2* and DC19 at the beginning of 1980, a date subsequently modified, for a variety of reasons, to January 1981. This agreement, though tempered somewhat by limitations imposed upon the Library of Congress, is still a sure base for dissemination of practice drawn from the new rules.

It has been possible for specialists from the four national libraries to discuss the possibility of a mutual attitude to all the options which occur throughout the code and, subsequently, to determine those areas of rules which may be difficult to interpret in each particular environment. Such an operation is, admittedly, difficult. It emphasizes only too clearly the confrontation that may develop between national and international needs—and how to determine which sphere should take priority in finalizing policy. Should one agree, first, at an international level, and apply those arguments to the national product for local consumption? Or should one first establish local needs through democratic process and then proceed to international discussion, perhaps with the prospect of arriving at solutions not compatible with international requirements? It would seem, from all experience gained during recent years in the production of international bibliographic disciplines, that the extreme arguments on either side are unlikely to produce effective results. Consequently, we must be prepared to accept machinery that is developed empirically.

I do not consider it my brief to speak for the ABACUS libraries generally, except to say that each has found the discussions stimulating. I trust that the association will continue to flourish and that it may eventually be possible to introduce additional members.

I am, however, prepared to say something of the attitude of the British Library to *AACR*. Before doing so, I must make it clear that the constitution of the British Library is unlike those of many other national libraries. It has been composed of a number of national institutions, each with a different history and a different set of obligations to its users. In 1974, at the time the Library was incorporated, the principal constituents deferred to no single code of cataloging, though *AACR1* was a strong contender for mutual acceptance. The acceptance of the role of joint author by the Library, on an equal footing with our Library Association, naturally implied acceptance of the rules as part of its general policy for the production of catalogs. Nonetheless, it could not be assumed that the constituent elements of the British Library would automatically accept the provisions of *AACR2*.

With this in mind, it was decided to set up a British Library Cataloguing Policy Discussion Group which would examine the text of the rules with the intention of identifying, in particular, those optional rules to be preferred, and indicating those areas of interpretative difficulty encountered. This group is now completing its task. It has already provided the British representative at ABACUS with positive papers from which it was possible to determine the range of our agreement with the other participants.

We are heartened by the general agreement this discussion group has achieved. It leads us to announce, quite categorically, that the British Library will adopt *AACR2* in full, without any unofficial modifications. Such a position was declared officially by Richard Coward, director-general of the Bibliographical Services Division at the Library Association's conference in Brighton in September 1978. He said:

Our straightforward gut reaction is that the British Library will adopt *AACR2*—and nothing but *AACR2*—as previously planned and announced in 1976. The great virtue of *AACR2* is that it will provide long term benefits of a catalogue based on a single, consistent set of principles. Adopting the code in 1981 instead of 1980 is an administrative adjustment, but in my view it is imperative that whatever the date, we must adopt the code, the whole code and nothing but the code.[11]

He went on to identify some of the problems which exist independently of *AACR2*:

The British Library started a new machine-readable catalogue in 1974. It is in the middle of a complex automation programme and is half-way between off-line and on-line systems. It is developing at least two major services in CIP and *Serials in the British Library* and its cataloguing activities are at

---

11. Richard Coward, "The British Library and *AACR2*," in *Proceedings of the Library Association Study School and National Conference, Brighton, 1978* (London: The Library Assn., 1979).

an all-time high. The time is never opportune for a change in cataloguing or a change in classification, but some times are certainly less opportune than others.

Somewhat similar sentiments were expressed, perhaps more formally, at the Standing Conference of African University Libraries, Eastern Area, in Nairobi, in 1977.[12] It recognized

the significance for international standardization of cataloguing practices of the new edition of *AACR* and recommends that consideration be given to:
  i) the adoption by university libraries of the new code . . .
  ii) the adoption by other libraries in each country of the new code . . .
  iii) the encouragement of library associations in each country to examine and discuss the new code . . .
  iv) the holding of seminars and workshops. . . .
In recommending the above, SCAULEA suggested that UNESCO and other agencies be approached for financial support.

The latter suggestion has already been passed on to the Cataloguing and Indexing Group of the British Library Association by IFLA's Office for UBC, in the expectancy that the group may be able to provide specialists willing to serve in seminars overseas. Such a measure of support from countries that are rapidly developing in bibliographic resources is a great encouragement to all of us who have worked on *AACR2*.

At this point it is worth summarizing the general characteristics of *AACR2* which will contribute to its consideration, if not total acceptance, in the library services of the world.

First, it has gained in logical structure over *AACR1*. The gathering together of the rules for descriptive cataloging of all media into one part, organized mnemonically according to primary concepts, will assist the integration of all kinds of materials into single catalogs. The organization of the rules for access points in Part II more clearly demonstrates the consistency with which JSC and the editors resolved the difficulties associated with the practice of *AACR1*.

Second, though still retaining rules for the choice of principal access points, *AACR2* has appreciated the neutrality of all access points affected by development of computer-generated catalogs. The retention of chapter 21 will assist those areas not yet provided with automated services.

---

12. Third Standing Conference of African University Libraries, Eastern Area, 1977, Nairobi, reported in *IFLA Journal* 4 (1978): 2.

Third, *AACR2* has respected the need for different levels of cataloging in varying circumstances, though it has provided exhaustive directions for the creation of the fullest type of record required in general use.

Fourth, it is not so inflexible as to cause the development of a multitude of local variations, or its complete rejection by library services. The equitable treatment of all kinds of material should lead to the acceptance of *AACR2* in the production of both general and specialized catalogs.

Fifth, its directions are expressed simply. Concepts have been enunciated with the object of easing translation.

Sixth, it respects forms of name used in authorship—a moral learned by the Library of Congress in providing headings in its CIP program that are acceptable to authors and publishers.

Incidentally, JSC, aware of the nonavailability of IFLA's publication *Names of Persons: National Usages for Entry in Catalogs,* requested that the UBC Office seek a revision, which appeared as the third edition in 1977. It is referred to in *AACR2* as a reference source for names in certain nonroman alphabets and names in non-European languages written in the roman alphabet.

Though such an aggregation of positive factors in favor of *AACR2* must appear convincing, it must be understood that there will be areas of the world which cannot or will not adopt *AACR* in practice. Such an area is the USSR and the Eastern bloc of nations, who, not solely because of political differences, but because of the nature of their culture and information systems, find it impossible to adopt *AACR,* but nevertheless may use, in their own codes, principles that are compatible with those we use.

General Conclusions

It is useful, finally, to reiterate specific points made in the *AACR2* general introduction.

0.9. The necessity for judgment and interpretation by the cataloguer is recognized in these rules. Such judgment and interpretation may be based on the requirements of a particular catalogue or upon the use of the items being catalogued. The need for judgment is indicated in these rules by words and phrases such as *if appropriate, important,* and *if necessary.* These indicate the recognition of the fact that uniform legislation for all types and sizes of catalogues is neither possible nor desirable, and encourages the application of individual judgment based on specific local knowledge. This in no way contradicts the value of standardization. Such judgments must be applied consistently within a particular context and must be recorded by the cataloguing agency.

0.12. . . . It is expected that users of the rules who do not use English as their working language will replace the specified preference for English by a preference for their working language. Authorized translations will be allowed to do the same.

0.13. . . . It is expected that authorized translations will, in examples, substitute romanizations derived from standard romanization tables prevailing in libraries in the countries or areas for which the translation is intended.

In view of the effort and expense incurred in the preparation and production of *AACR2,* in view of all the criticism that was incurred in the use of *AACR1,* in view of the constant growth of our catalogs and data banks, there is an urgent need for us to improve the methods by which we cumulate and exploit that data. Ron Hagler has earlier been quoted, saying "The future is longer than the past." Though we cannot ignore the past, we should never allow it to cripple the prospects for improving the future of our service.

Should we deny *AACR2* the chance to prove itself fully in the immediate Anglo-American context, the confusion and divergence incurred worldwide will prove more expensive in the long term than will the saving in the short term.

It is disappointing, in this context, that the American constituency has again, as it did in 1967, imposed limitations upon the Library of Congress so that it finds it impossible to accept some of the major provisions of the new rules. Incidentally, I do not regard modifications such as "House" and the abbreviation for "Department" as major. But I do consider the Library's limitation to apply *AACR2* rules for personal authors only to those new to LC's catalogs as a practice which will create untold confusion and uncertainty. Librarians and catalogers in many countries have seen LC's participation in *AACR2* as acceptance that its experience in applying superimposition upon *AACR1* was a practice to be regretted.

Such policies, either superimposition or tolerable headings, appear to ignore the fact that a catalog, whether automated or not, is a living organism. It is never perfect, yet it seeks perfection. To restrain its ability to modify itself—the essential element in evolution—because of administrative constraints, is a denial of a catalog's true purpose. It is now possible, with the marvels of automation, to provide alternative access points or references, and for the cost to be jointly shared by all who contribute to a cooperative data bank.

Whatever strictures we may apply to the Library of Congress in this respect, we must be heartened by its decision to provide *AACR2* data in its retrospective authority records. Retrospective authority records are to be coded for *AACR2*.

If a heading is in accord with the provisions of AACR2 or is AACR2-compatible, a code indicating the situation is provided in the record for the heading. If the heading is neither AACR2 nor AACR2-compatible, a reference is added and appropriately coded. . . . In all cases in assigning codes, AACR2 or AACR2-compatible will take precedence over ALA or AACR1.[13]

Name files, carrying the authority of principal users of *AACR*, will prove immensely valuable in the interchange of machine records. The establishment of such files early in the life of *AACR2*, whether in an online mode or in batch or on computer-output microfilm, will formalize the use of *AACR2* in an assured manner, a feature which was not possible to provide for *AACR1*.

A combination of *AACR2* and authoritative name files will strengthen the need for the retrospective maintenance of records. Our minds, conditioned by decades of card catalog construction, are still applying to machine-readable records the standards of card catalogs. Machinery of all kinds needs maintenance to ensure acceptable performance. We revise computer systems and formats to utilize the benefits of machines that give higher productivity. We cannot continue to regard our current data banks as immutable records of past bibliographic incidents. We must, at certain points, improve our systems to allow at least for the full exploitation of current and future records.

Having said this, we must accept that there is a widespread and natural anxiety that a thoroughgoing revision, such as has been made in *AACR2* after an interval of only eleven years, will lead to the belief that a further wholesale revision will follow after a similar, or shorter, interval. I trust that it has been clearly understood by all those attending this seminar that *AACR2* is a natural extension of *AACR1*, that what was presented clearly in the earlier code is respected and developed in the later one. However, any change in direction or emphasis between publication and implementation in the early years of the next decade will surely negate all the advantages that can be gained from *AACR2*. For

---

13. *Library of Congress Information Bulletin* 37 (Dec. 1, 1978): 726.

this reason, ongoing revision must be severely limited until we see the success—or otherwise—of our recommendations.

I cannot foretell with calm assurance the future fate of *AACR2*. It is in the hands of those who are present at this seminar, and many hundreds of others on this continent and in many other lands. The example of the ABACUS libraries will be studied and examined, not only in the English-speaking world, but in other countries that also have used *AACR1* as a base. I cannot see that any institution will continue to use *AACR1* to the exclusion of *AACR2*. We have seen that countries with library services in a prime state of development are anxious to follow the example of ABACUS. Let us hope that their firm intent is not shaken by the reaction of the American library community.

Many countries will continue to utilize *ISBD*s, and more will adopt such practices. With *AACR2* demonstrating the comprehensive application of these standards in Part I, we can be certain that libraries that search for solutions to hitherto unanswered problems will expect, and find, some resolution in *AACR2*. We do not seek royalties for such uses but will be satisfied that by such means we are gradually achieving compatible practice in many quarters of the world.

We cannot expect acceptance, total or partial, from all library communities at a particular point in time. Nor can we expect *AACR2* to be applied to a wide range of retrospective records. This will depend upon the magnitude of such operations and the amount of funds available.

Large tracts of what could be considered a bibliographic no-man's-land have clearly been charted in *AACR1* and 2. We have a common and continuing projection which should be employed by as many communities and with as much agreement as possible.

An international policy for author and descriptive cataloging is an inevitable extension of our own local activity, whether it be in the great libraries, the cooperative networks, or elsewhere. Our objective is to bring order out of disorder, placing before the users of libraries and information systems the fruits of their labors (not our own), past and present, in a digestable form that is suited to their needs and appetites.

Let me, in closing, reiterate the essential elements of *AACR2*:

1. A sound basic philosophy
2. A clearly defined set of terms relating to the problems encountered
3. A logical structure
4. A clear and concise method of expression
5. A comprehensive and valid range of examples
6. An effective index.

Appendixes

I. Abbreviations

AA	*Cataloguing Rules: Author and Title Entries* (1908 Joint Code)
AACR1	*Anglo-American Cataloguing Rules* (1967)
AACR2	*Anglo-American Cataloguing Rules* (1978, 2d ed.)
ABACUS	Association of Bibliographic Agencies of Britain, Australia, Canada, and the United States
AECT	Association for Educational Communications and Technology
ALA	American Library Association
ALA/RTSD/DCC	American Library Association/Resources and Technical Services Division/Descriptive Cataloging Committee
ARL	Association of Research Libraries
ASTED	Association pour l'Avancement des Sciences et des Techniques de la Documentation
CCRC	Catalog Code Revision Committee
CIP	Cataloging in Publication
GBN	Geographic Board of Names
GMD	General Material Designation
GODORT	Government Documents Round Table (American Library Association)
GPO	Government Printing Office
IFLA	International Federation of Library Associations and Institutions
ISAD	Information Science and Automation Division (American Library Association)
ISBD	*International Standard Bibliographic Description*
ISBD(CM)	*International Standard Bibliographic Description (Cartographic Materials)*
ISBD(G)	*International Standard Bibliographic Description (General)*
ISBD(M)	*International Standard Bibliographic Description (Monographs)*
ISBD(NBM)	*International Standard Bibliographic Description (Nonbook Materials)*
ISBD(S)	*International Standard Bibliographic Description (Serials)*

ISBN	International Standard Book Number
ISDS	International Serials Data System
ISSN	International Standard Serial Number
JSCAACR	Joint Steering Committee for Revision of AACR
LANCET rules	*Non-Book Materials: Cataloguing Rules* (London: National Council for Education Technology and the Library Association, 1973)
LC	Library of Congress
LCIB	*Library of Congress Information Bulletin*
LRTS	*Library Resources & Technical Services*
MARC	Machine-readable Cataloging
NLC	National Library of Canada
NPC	National Periodicals Center
NSDP	National Serials Data Program
NUC	*National Union Catalog*
NYPL	New York Public Library
OCLC	An online bibliographic services network with headquarters in Columbus, Ohio; originally, Ohio College Library Center
RLIN	Research Libraries Network
RTSD	Resources and Technical Services Division (American Library Association)
SCAULEA	Standing Conference of African University Libraries, Eastern Area
UBC	Universal Bibliographic Control
UNESCO	United Nations Educational, Scientific, and Cultural Organization
WLN	Washington Library Network

II. Selected Bibliography on *AACR2*

1974

"AACR Revision Policy Statements." *American Libraries* 6 (May 1974): 304.

British and Irish Association of Law Librarians. Subcommittee on Cataloguing and Classification. "Memorandum to the Library Association Cataloguing Rules Committee on the Revision of AACR, 1967" *Law Librarian* 5 (April 1974): 9–13.

1975

"AACR New Edition. What Changes Do You Want?" *Feliciter* 21 (March 1975): 10–11.

"AACR—Second Edition." *Catalogue & Index* no. 36 (Spring 1975): 1.

"An ARLIS Submission to the Committee on the Revision of the Anglo-American Cataloging Rules." *ARLIS Newsletter* 23 (June 1975): 14–17.

"Anglo-American Cataloging Rules Grant from the Council on Library Resources." *FLC Newsletter* no. 84 (May 1975): 3–4.

"Anglo-Nordic Cataloguing Seminar on the Revision and International Use of AACR, University of York, 11–14 April 1975." *International Cataloguing* 4 (April/June 1975): 2–3.

"Anglo-Nordic Seminar on the Revision and International Use of AACR, York, 1975." *Catalogue & Index* no. 37 (Summer 1975): 1–2, 8.

"CLR Grant for AACR." *Bookmark* 34 (May/June 1975): 154–55.

"CLR Grant Support Anglo-American Cataloging Rules Revision, Ballots and Library Data Management System." *Information: News and Sources* 7 (July/August 1975): 166–67.

"CLR $111,431 Grant Goes for AACR Revision." *Library Journal* 100 (June 1, 1975): 1054.

"Catalog Code Revision Committee Meets." *Library of Congress Information Bulletin* 34 (May 30, 1975): 225–26.

"Cataloging Rules Development." *Library of Congress Information Bulletin* 34 (June 20, 1975): A103–4.

Chan, Lois Mai. "Years Work in Cataloging and Classification, 1974." *Library Resources & Technical Services* 19 (Summer 1975): 242–59.

Cole, Jim E. "AACR 6: Time for a Review." *Library Resources & Technical Services* 19 (Fall 1975): 314–26.

Edgar, Neal L. "What Every Librarian Should Know about Proposed Changes in Cataloging Rules: A Brief Overview." *American Libraries* 6 (November 1975): 602–7.

Gorman, Michael. "The Current State of Standardization in the Cataloging of Serials." *Library Resources & Technical Services* 19 (Fall 1975): 301–13.

Hagler, Ronald. "Aching Catalogers—Relief Is on the Way!" *American Libraries* 6 (November 1975): 607.

———. "The Development of Cataloging Rules for Nonbook Materials." *Library Resources & Technical Services* 19 (Summer 1975): 268–78.

Hamilton, Geoffrey E., and Christophers, Richard A. "AACR Second Edition: LA/BL Committee on Revision of AACR." *Catalogue & Index* no. 39 (Winter 1975): 4–6.

Hayashikawa, Doris, and others. "Coping with Catalog Code Revision." *Texas Library Journal* 51 (Summer 1975): 74–76.

1976

"AACR Revision Issue: Too Much, Too Fast?" *Library Journal* 101 (Apr. 15, 1976): 959.

"AV Section Using Revised AACR." *Library of Congress Information Bulletin* 35 (October 1976): 461–71.

"Agreement Reached on New Basis for Bibliographical Standard." *Library Association Record* 78 (January 1976): 14.

Anderson, Dorothy. "The Future of the Anglo-American Cataloging Rules (AACR) in the Light of Universal Bibliographic Control (UBC)." *Library Resources & Technical Services* 20 (Winter 1976): 3–15.

"Anglo-American Cataloguing Rules, Second Edition." *British Library Bibliographic Services Division Newsletter* 3 (November 1976): 8.

Buchinski, Edwin, and Hagler, Ronald. "Canadian Involvement in AACR Revisions." *Canadian Library Journal* 33 (February 1, 1976): 7–13.

Buchinski, Edwin. "Developments in the Revision of AACR." *Canadian Library Journal* 33, no. 5 (October 1976): 461–71.

"Code Revision—A New International Standard." *Library Resources & Technical Services* 20 (Winter 1976): 91–93.

"Continuing Reports on the Centennial Conference of the American Library Association. Chicago, Ill., July 18–24, 1976." *Library of Congress Information Bulletin* 35 (September 3, 1976): 525–38.

Croghan, Anthony. "No Sign of AACRimony." *Library Association Record* 78 (August 1976): 367.

Edgar, Neal L. "Some Implications of Code Revision for Serials Librarians." *Serials Librarian* 1 (Winter 1976/1977): 125–34.

Henderson, Kathryn Luther. "Descriptive Cataloging in the United States." *Library Trends* 25 (July 1976): 250–54.

1977

"AACR Revision Controversy Still Smouldering." *Library Journal* 102 (October 15, 1977): 2105.

"AACR Revision—Some Questions Answered." *Catalogue & Index* no. 45 (Summer 1977): 1,8.

"AACR 2nd Edition." *Catalogue & Index* no. 47 (Winter 1977): 4.

"AACR2: Arrangements for Reviewing Final Draft Text." *Audiovisual Librarian* 3 (Summer 1977): 118.

"Anglo-American National Libraries Statement on Adoption of Anglo-American Cataloguing Rules, 2nd Edition, and Dewey Decimal Classification, 19th Edition." *IFLA Journal* 3, no. 2 (1977): 200–201.

Berrisford, Paul D. "Years Work in Cataloging and Classification: 1976." *Library Resources & Technical Services* 21 (Summer 1977): 249–273.

Byrum, John D., and Coe, D. Whitney. "AACR Chapter 6 as Adopted, Applied, and Assessed by Research Libraries." *Library Resources & Technical Services* 21 (Winter 1977): 48–57.

"Catalog Rules Target Date Set." *Feliciter* 23 (February 1977): 1.

Chan, Lois Mai. "AACR 6 and the Corporate Mystique." *Library Resources & Technical Services* 21 (Winter 1977): 58–67.

Gorman, Michael. "Changes in Cataloging Codes: Rules for Entry and Heading." *Library Trends* 25 (January 1977): 587–602.

Hagler, Ronald. "Changes in Cataloging Codes: Rules for Description." *Library Trends* 25 (January 1977): 603–623.

Hinton, Frances. "Anglo-American Cataloging Rules Revision." *Catholic Library World* 48 (May 1977): 412–15.

Jeffreys, Alan. "Management in Cataloguing Services." *Catalogue & Index* no. 46 (Autumn 1977): 2–4.

Maxwell, Margaret F. "The Genesis of the Anglo-American Cataloging Rules." *Libri* 27 (September 1977): 238–62.

1978

"AACR, Second Edition, and DDC Nineteenth Edition: Prospects." *UNESCO Bulletin for Libraries* 32 (March/April 1978): 123.

"AACR 2: Background and Summary." *Library of Congress Information Bulletin* 37 (October 20, 1978): 640–52.

"AACR 2." *Cataloging Service Bulletin* no. 2 (Fall 1978): 3–30.

"AACR 2 Endorsed, Implementation Delayed." *Library of Congress Information Bulletin* 37 (August 18, 1978): 485–86.

"AACR2 Publication Date Named." *Library of Congress Information Bulletin* 37 (December 1, 1978): 725–26.

"ALA Forms New AACR 2 Committee." *Library of Congress Information Bulletin* 37 (May 26, 1978): 333–34.

"Anglo-American Cataloguing Rules, 2nd Edition (AACR2), Some Late Decisions." *International Cataloguing* 7 (January/March 1978): 3.

Berman, Sanford. "Anglo-American Cataloguing Rules—Second Edition." *Hennepin County Cataloging Bulletin* no. 36 (September/October 1978): 1–12.

Bright, F. F. "New Code! A New Catalog?" *Wisconsin Library Bulletin* 74 (November 1978): 278–79.

Byrum, John D. "International Cataloging Consultation Committee." *Library of Congress Information Bulletin* 37 (March 17, 1978): 177–78.

"Can Kilgour Overrule 'the Rules'?" *American Libraries* 9 (May 1978): 254.

"Catalog Closing: Grand Finale Set for New Orleans." *Library Journal* 103 (June 15, 1978): 1216.

Cathro, Warwick S. "Can AACRII Survive the Library of Congress?" *Library Journal* 103 (November 1, 1978): 2163–65.

――――. (Comment by Robert S. Bravard (letter). *Library Journal* 103 (December 15, 1978): 2456.

[Conference on AACR2, October 13, 1978, Buffalo]. *Library of Congress Information Bulletin* 37 (December 1, 1978): 725–26.

Durance, Cynthia J. "AACR 2 Matters" in "Summary Minutes of the Meeting on Cooperative Cataloging of the British Library, National Library of Australia, National Library of Canada, and Library of Congress, Washington, D.C., March 8–10, 1978." *Library of Congress Information Bulletin* 37 (November 3, 1978): 680–84.

Glasby, Dorothy J. "Serials Section AACR Revision Study Committee, Midwinter 1978, Chicago." *Library of Congress Information Bulletin* 37 (March 17, 1978): 181–82.

Gorman, Michael. "And Now, from the Wonderful Folks Who Gave You Superimposition." *American Libraries* 9 (November 1978): 620–21.

――――. "The Anglo-American Cataloguing Rules, Second Edition." *Library Resources & Technical Services* 22 (Summer 1978): 209–26.

Hiatt, Robert M. "AACR 2: Implementation Plans." *Library of Congress Information Bulletin* 37 (November 17, 1978): 710–12.

Jeffreys, A. E. "The Management of AACR2, Its Adoption and Due Consequences." *Catalogue & Index* no. 51 (Winter 1978): 4–6.

Kelm, Carol R. "The Historical Development of the Second Edition of the Anglo-American Cataloguing Rules." *Library Resources & Technical Services* 22 (Winter 1978): 22–33.

Lewis, Peter. "Introducing the Second Edition of AACR." *Catalogue & Index* no. 51 (Winter 1978): 1–4.

Library of Congress. "LC Responds on Serials Headings." *Library of Congress Information Bulletin* 37 (April 1978): 273–74.

Marion, P. C. "*AACR2.*" *Law Library Journal* 71 (November 1978): 673–80.

Martin, Susan K. "An Odd Couple—AACR2 and Automation." *American Libraries* 9 (December, 1978): 689–91.

"Paul Winkler: Editor II of AACR II." *American Libraries* 9 (December, 1978): 649–50.

Pearson, L. R. "LC Bows to Library VIPs: Postpones *AACR2* D–Day." *American Libraries* 9 (September 1978): 450.

Peregoy, Marjorie. "AACR2 and Serials Cataloging." *The Serials Librarian* 31 (Fall 1978): 15–30.

"RTSD Board Seeks Opinions on Cataloging Code Maintenance." *Library of Congress Information Bulletin* 37 (April 7, 1978): 230–32.

Rather, Lucia J. "AACR 2 Options to Be Followed by the Library of Congress: Chapters 1–2, 12, 21–26." *Library of Congress Information Bulletin* 37 (July 21, 1978): 422–28.

"Research Libraries Raising Questions about *AACR2*." *ARL Newsletter* 92 (June 15, 1978): 4–5.

Rosenfeld, H. E. "LC Delays Freezing Its Catalog till 1981." *Wilson Library Bulletin* 53 (September 1978): 18–19.

"Shelving *AACRII*?" *Library Journal* 103 (August 1978): 1477.

Thompson, James. "With the Marriage of LC and AACR2 Postponed to 1981—Ten Ways to Profit from a Long Engagement." *American Libraries* 9 (October, 1978): 538–42.

———. Comment by James R. Dwyer (letter). *American Libraries* 10 (January, 1979): 9.

Tucker, Ben. "AACR2 Introductory Program Committee." *Library of Congress Information Bulletin* 37 (August 4, 1978): 463.

———. "Comparison of *AACR1* and 2." In *The ALA Yearbook*. Chicago: American Library Association, 1978. Pp. 84–85.

"Unique Identification of Serials under AACR2. Photocopy. Washington, D.C.: Library of Congress, 1978(?).

West, Linda, and Weissman, Edward. "AACR Second Edition: A Preliminary View." *Cornell University Library Bulletin* no. 208 (April 1978): 7–12.

1979

"AACR2." *Cataloging Service Bulletin* 5 (Summer 1979): 3–9.

"AACR2." *Cataloging Service Bulletin* 6 (Fall 1979): 2–40.

"AACR2: Corrections." *Catalogue & Index* no. 54 (Autumn 1979): 10.

"AACR2 Corrections." *Music Cataloging Bulletin* 10 (December 1979): 6.

"AACR2 Errata." *Cataloging Service Bulletin* no. 6 (Fall 1979): 2–4.

"AACR 2 Implementation Plans." *Cataloging Service Bulletin* 3 (Winter 1979): 3–7.

"AACR2: A Materiography." *Catalogue & Index* no. 54 (Autumn 1979): 9–10.

"*AACR2* Optional Additions, Options and Alternative Rules: The British Library's Position." *British Library Bibliographic Services Division Newsletter*, 13 (May 1979): 2–7.

"AACR2 Options Proposed by the Library of Congress, Chapters 2–11." *Library of Congress Information Bulletin* 38 (August 10, 1979): 307–16.

Berman, Sanford. "Proposed: AACR2 Options and Addenda for School and

Public Libraries." *Hennepin County Public Library Cataloging Bulletin* 38 (Jan./Feb. 1979): 24–26.

Bindman, Fred M. "Principal Changes in AACR2 for Music and Music Sound Recordings." *Music Cataloging Bulletin* 10 (May 1979): 4–6.

Blei, Barbara. "A Look at AACR2, Chapter 6, from the Cataloguer's Desk at Stockton/San Joaquin Public Library." *Hennepin County Public Library Cataloging Bulletin* 40 (May/June 1979): 31–33.

Bugg, Louise. "AACR2 Training Plans in Michigan." *Michigan Librarian Newsletter* 45 (October 1979): 5.

Butcher, J. E. "Evaluation of AACR2, Part 2: Headings," in *Library Association. Study School and National Conference, Brighton, 1978. Proceedings.* London: Library Association, 1979. Pp. 55–57.

Byrum, John E., and Coe, D. W. "AACR as Applied by Research Libraries for Serials Cataloging." *Library Resources & Technical Services* 23 (Spring 1979): 139–46.

"Catalog Code Revision." *American Libraries* 10 (March 1979): 134.

Clack, Doris. "After the Dust Settles." *Florida Libraries* 29 (Nov./Dec. 1979): 15–19.

———. "The Making of a Code." *Florida Libraries* 29 (May/June, 1979): 8–11.

"Concise Edition of AACR2 Planned." *Library of Congress Information Bulletin* 38 (April 13, 1979): 144.

Coward, R. E. "The British Library and AACR2," in Library Association. Study School and National Conference, Brighton, 1978. *Proceedings.* London: Library Association, 1979. Pp. 67–69.

Daly, Richard R. *The Future Crisis in the Card Catalog: How Libraries Are Preparing for It.* Media, Pa.: Information Associates, 1979.

Decker, Jean S. "Catalog 'Closings' and Serials." *Journal of Academic Librarianship* 5 (November 1979): 261–65.

"Dissolution of AACR2 Committee." *American Libraries* 10 (December 1979): 665.

Dowell, Arlene Taylor. "Living Amid Closed Catalogs." *Hennepin County Public Library Cataloging Bulletin* 39 (March/April 1979): 6–15.

Downing, Joel. "Anniversary and Birth: AA1908 to AACR2." *Library Association Record* 81 (February 1979): 66–67.

Duncan, Winifred E. "AACR2: Implications for School Libraries." *Indiana Media Journal* 1 (Spring 1979): 9–10.

Fasana, Paul J. "Review of Anglo-American Cataloguing Rules Second Edition." *Library Journal* 104 (February 15, 1979): 468.

Fawcett, Trevor. "Anglo-American Cataloging Rules, 2nd ed.: A Review Article." *Art Libraries Journal* 4 (Summer 1979): 23–30.

Fitzpatrick, Kelly. "Closing the Catalog." *Catholic Library World* 51 (December 1979): 226–27.

Fraley, Ruth A. "The Library World According to AACR2; A Cursory Look." New York Library Association. *Bulletin* 27 (September 1979): 1, 6, 9.

"Further Developments on AACR 2." *RTSD Newsletter* 4 (June 1979): 4–9.

Hagler, Ronald. *Where's That Rule?* Ottawa: Canadian Library Association, 1979. (Distributed in the U.S. by the American Library Association)

Hall, A. R. "AACR2 and the Data Bases," in Library Association. Study School and National Conference, Brighton, 1978. *Proceedings.* London: Library Association, 1979. Pp. 61–63.

————— and Massil, S. W. "Study into the Effects of AACR2 on MARC Catalogues: A Preliminary Report: Prepared for the Committees of the Co-operative Libraries Group and the MARC User Group." *Catalogue & Index* no. 54 (Autumn 1979): 4–8.

Hamilton, Geoffrey. "Structure of AACR2 and Changes from AACR1," in Library Association. Study School and National Conference, Brighton, 1978. *Proceedings.* London: Library Association, 1979. Pp. 46–50.

Hewitt, Joe A. "Planning for the Adoption of AACR2 at the University of North Carolina—Chapel Hill." *North Carolina Libraries* 37 (Summer 1979): 5–14.

————— and Gleim, David E. "Adopting AACR 2: The Case for Not Closing the Catalog." *American Libraries* 10 (March 1979): 118–21.

Hunter, Eric J. "A National Training Programme for AACR2," in Library Association. Study School and National Conference, Brighton, 1978. *Proceedings.* London: Library Association, 1979. Pp. 58–60.

————— and Bibby, Joan. "A National Training Programme for AACR2." *Library Association Record* 81 (October 1979): 508.

"Information on AACR 2." *RTSD Newsletter* 4 (October 1979): 6–7.

"International Workshop on AACR2." *Catalogue & Index* no. 54 (Autumn 1979): 10–11.

Jeffreys, A. E. "The Management of AACR2, Its Adoption and Due Consequences," in Library Association. Study School and National Conference, Brighton, 1979. *Proceedings.* London: Library Association, 1979. Pp. 64–66.

Kirby, Steve. "Seminar on AACR2." *New Library World* 80 (March 1979): 50–52.

"LC Name and U. T. Changes for AACR2." *Music Cataloging Bulletin* 10 (December 1979): 6.

Lehnus, Donald J. "AACR2: A Cataloging Instructor's Viewpoint." *Southeastern Librarian* 29 (Fall 1979): 145–51.

Lewis, Peter. "Introduction to AACR2: The Revision and Why It Is Needed," in Library Association. Study School and National Conference, Brighton, 1978. *Proceedings.* London: Library Association, 1979. Pp. 40–45.

"Library Announces Decision to Create Minimum Level Cataloguing Records."*Library of Congress Information Bulletin* 38 (November 2, 1979): 457–60.

Lynch, Mary Jo. "News about AACR II Implementation Studies." *RTSD Newsletter* 4 (January/April 1979): 3–5.

Malinconico, S. Michael. "International Indirection." *Library Journal* 104 (December 15, 1979): 2628–31.

Manning, Ralph W. and Shih-Sheng Hu. "AACR2 from 2 Viewpoints." *Canadian Library Journal* 36 (December 1979): 381–83.

"A National Training Programme for AACR2." *Catalogue & Index*, no. 52 (Spring 1979): 1–2.

"A National Training Programme for AACR2." *Catalogue & Index*, no. 54 (Autumn 1979): 11.

"OCLC Retains Michael Gorman as Consultant on Implementation of AACR2." *OCLC Newsletter* no. 121 (February 8, 1979): 4.

Osborn, Andrew. "The Professional Excellence of AACR2: Its Implementation in Australia." *Australian Library Journal* 28 (September 21, 1979): 301–4.

Payne, Roy. "AACR 2." *New Library World* 80 (November 1979): 219–20.

Ramsden, Michael J. "Travels with a Cataloging Code." *Australian Library Journal* 28 (September 21, 1979): 308–9.

Ravilious, C. P. "Evaluation of AACR2, Part 1: Description," in Library Association. Study School and National Conference, Brighton, 1978. *Proceedings*. London: Library Association, 1979. Pp. 51–54.

"Retrospective Name Authority Records with AACR 2 Information." *Cataloging Service Bulletin* no. 3 (Winter 1979): 7.

Rogers, Jo Ann V. "Nonprint Cataloging: A Call for Standardization." *American Libraries* 10 (January 1979): 46–48.

Sadowski, Frank E. "Initially, We Need Some Definitions: The Problems of Initialisms in Periodical Titles." *Library Resources & Technical Services* 23 (Fall 1979): 365–73.

"Seminar on AACR2." National Library of Canada. *National Library News* special issue (June 1979): 1–32.

"Shank Names *AACR2* Group." *American Libraries* 10 (March 1979): 134.

Shinebourne, J. A. "A Critique of AACR." *Libri* 29 (October 1979): 231–59.

Simonton, Wesley. "An Introduction to AACR2." *Library Resources & Technical Services* 23 (Summer 1979): 1–19.

Smith, Peter. "AACR 2: Another View." *New Library World* 80 (November 1979): 221–23.

Soper, Mary Ellen. "Description and Entry of Serials in *AACR2*." *The Serials Librarian* 4 (Winter 1979): 167–76.

Thompson James. "News about AACR2 Implementation Studies." *RTSD Newsletter* 4 (June 1979): 6–8.

————. "News AACR2 about Implementation Studies." *RTSD News-letter* 4 (October 1979): 7–9.

Turner, Ann. "The Effect of *AACR2* on Serials Cataloging." *The Serials Librarian* 4 (Winter 1979): 177–86.

"Videocassettes on AACR2." *American Libraries* 10 (December 1979): 665.

Weintraub, D. Kathryn. "AACR2: A Review Article." *The Library Quarterly,* 49 (October 1979): 435–43.

1980

"AACR2 Commentary Available." *RTSD Newsletter* 5 (Jan./Feb. 1980): 11.

"AACR 2 Name Changes for Music." *Music Cataloging Bulletin* 11 (January 1980): 4–6.

"AACR2 Serials Cataloging." *RTSD Newsletter* 5 (Jan./Feb. 1980): 2.

Ayres, F. H. "The Code, the Catalog and the Computer." *Library Journal* 105 (Winter 1980): 3–16.

Martin, Susan K. "A Learning Experience: Three Lessons from and Six Points of Action for the Adoption of AACR2." *American Libraries* 11 (February 1980): 117–18.

Potter, William Gray. "When Names Collide: Conflict in the Catalog and *AACR2*." *Library Resources & Technical Services* 24 (Winter 1980): 3–16.

Thompson, Jim. "AACR2; News about AACR2 Implementation Studies." *RTSD Newsletter* 5 (January/February 1980): 1–2.

"University of Illinois Switches to AACR 2." *Library Journal* 105 (January 1, 1980): 12.

III. The Contributors

Joel C. Downing has been Director of Copyright and English Language Cataloguing of the Bibliographic Services Division of the British Library since 1974. Previously employed in public libraries in London, England, and by the Inter Allied Book Centre (Conference of Allied Ministers of Education), he later became Assistant Editor, then Deputy Editor of the *British National Bibliography*. He serves as chairman of the Cataloguing and Indexing Group of the British Library Association, the British Representative of the Dewey Decimal Classification Editorial Policy Committee, and member of the Library Association Cataloguing Rules Committee, the LA/BL Committee on Revision of AACR. He also is the British Library Deputy Representative on the Joint Steering Committee for Revision of AACR.

Neal L. Edgar was born in New York City. He took a B.A. in economics at Trinity College, Hartford, Connecticut, in 1950; an M.A. in education; an M.L.S. at S.U.N.Y, Albany; and in 1965 the Ph.D. in library science at the University of Michigan. Before becoming a librarian, he worked in radio and taught high school English. He has been an Assistant Librarian at S.U.N.Y. and Coordinating Librarian of residence halls at the University of Michigan. From 1965 to 1966 he worked as a serials cataloger at the Library of Congress; then he moved to Kent State University as Acquisitions Librarian, where in 1968 he returned to serials cataloging. He is currently Research Librarian at Kent State University. Dr. Edgar has published widely in professional journals. Active in the Ohio Library Association and in the American Library Association, he served on the Catalog Code Revision Committee.

Barbara A. Gates was born at Worcester, Massachusetts. She earned the B.S.L.S. at Simmons College in 1946 and the M.S. in library science at Columbia University in 1953. She served as a cataloger at Iowa State College from 1946 to 1949, then moved to Vassar College, where she worked as a cataloger from 1949 to 1952. She became Head of Technical Services for the Public Library of Brookline, Massachusetts. Later she became Senior Cataloger of Boston University Libraries until 1962, when she became head of the Serials Department. In 1969 she became

Head of Technical Services at Oberlin College, and later moved to
Brown University. She is very active in the American Library Association, as well as in the Massachusetts Library Association. She has served
as Chairperson of the Council of Regional Groups, and also on the
Catalog Code Revision Committee.

Michael Gorman was born in Oxfordshire, England. He completed the
Library Association (LA) course at the Ealing School of Librarianship
in 1966, winning the Cawthorne Prize for the best results (nationwide)
when he took the intermediate examination. In 1967 he became an
Associate of LA. He has worked in public libraries, and from 1966
to 1972 he served the British National Bibliography as a Research Assistant, then as Author Cataloging Reviser, and later as Head of Cataloging. From 1969 to 1973 he edited *Catalogue & Index*. In addition to
chapters in books, magazine articles, and reviews, he wrote *A Study of
the Rules for Entry and Headings in the Anglo-American Cataloguing
Rules* (1967) and *Format for Machine-readable Cataloguing Motion
Pictures* (1973). The joint editor (with Paul W. Winkler) of the second
edition of *Anglo-American Cataloguing Rules (AACR2)*, he currently
serves as Director of Technical Services at the University of Illinois Library, a position he has held since 1977.

Ronald Hagler is internationally known for his work in catalog code revision. He was Chairman of the Canadian Library Association's committees on the preparation and, later, revision of *AACR1* from 1964
through 1973. A former member of the Canadian Task Group on Cataloguing Standards, he often serves as consultant on descriptive cataloging to the National Library of Canada. Since August 1978 he has served
as chairman of the Canadian Committee on Cataloguing/Comité Canadien de Catalogage, on which he has served since 1974. He is a member
of the Joint Steering Committee for Revision of AACR and is the author
of *Where's That Rule?* (Canadian Library Assn., 1979). Currently, he is
a professor in the School of Librarianship at the University of British
Columbia in Vancouver, Canada.

Frances Hinton was educated at Agnes Scott College and the University
of North Carolina, Chapel Hill. She has served as Young Adult Librarian at the New York Public Library, the South Bend Public Library,
and the Free Library of Philadelphia, as well as Head of the Lowndes-

Echols Regional Library at Valdosta, Georgia. She has been a cataloger for the Kauai Public Library, Lihue, Kauai, Hawaii, and the Free Library of Philadelphia. Presently she is Chief of the Processing Division of the Free Library of Philadelphia. She was a member of the Catalog Code Revision Committee of the American Library Association and is Deputy Representative to the Joint Steering Committee. Currently, she serves as Chairperson of the ALA/RTSD Cataloging and Classification Section.

Åke I. Koel was born in Kuressaare, Estonia, and earned the B.A. degree in psychology from the University of Toronto in 1961. He can communicate in ten languages. He has served as Documentalist-Librarian for A. B. Bahco in Enkoping, Sweden; salesman for Central Scientific Company of Canada; cataloger for the University of Toronto Libraries; and Head of the Serials Section of the Cataloging Department, then Head of the Dutch-Scandinavian Section of the Shared Catalog Division of the Library of Congress. He is presently employed at Yale University. Active in the American Library Association and the Canadian Library Association, he served on the Catalog Code Revision Committee of the American Library Association.

Peter R. Lewis was born in Oxford, England, and was educated at the Royal Masonic School. He became a Fellow of the Library Association in 1955 and received his M.A. from Queen's University in Belfast, Ireland, in 1968. He served on the staffs of the Brighton Public Library, the Plymouth Public Library, and the Chester Public Library between 1948 and 1955, and from 1955 to 1965 on the Board of Trade Library in London. In 1965 he went to Queen's University as Lecturer in Library Studies, and later became University Librarian at Skinner's Library at the City University in London. In 1972 he accepted the post of University Librarian at the University of Sussex that he currently holds.

Lewis wrote a widely used standard text, *The Literature of the Social Sciences* (1960), and has been a steady contributor to professional journals. He was a member of the LA Council in 1971. In 1972 he became Chairman of the Editorial Board of the *Journal of Librarianship,* the quarterly publication of the Library Association.

Chairman of the Joint Steering Committee for Revision of AACR, Lewis represented both the British Library and the Library Association at the Chicago "tripartite meeting" in 1974, which established the project for a revised edition of *AACR.* He subsequently acted as Voting

Representative in the interest of the British Library on the Joint Steering Committee, and was elected to the chair at its first meeting. His experience in the service of *AACR* began in 1964 as a member of the Descriptive Cataloguing Subcommittee of the Library Association Cataloguing Rules Committee (corresponding at that time to ALA's CCRC). When *AACR* (1967) was published, he became Chairman of a new LA Cataloguing Rules Committee and attended annual ALA/RTSD/DCC meetings in that capacity from 1969 to 1973. He was at the International Meeting of Cataloguing Experts in Copenhagen in 1969, where the first *ISBD* was conceived, and in 1972–1973 he chaired the LA Media Cataloging Rules Committee, which in the LANCET rules produced the first British integrated code for nonbook materials. He is currently Vice President of the Library Association.

Seymour Lubetzky was born in Zelwa, Russia. Educated in private schools, he graduated from a Polish science and mathematics gymnasium, attended a teacher-training institute, and later taught in private primary and secondary schools in Poland. In 1927 he moved to Los Angeles. He graduated from the University of California at Los Angeles and the University of California at Berkeley. His first library job was with the National Park Service. He later worked at the U.C.L.A. Library. In 1943 he accepted an assignment with the Library of Congress, eventually becoming Consultant on Bibliographic and Cataloging Policy.

In 1953 his report "Cataloging Rules and Principles" was published and was the subject of a meeting at the ALA Annual Conference that year. In 1955 he was awarded the Margaret Mann Citation, RTSD's most prestigious award. By 1956, the American Library Association, convinced mainly by Lubetzky that the rules of entry were in dire need of revision, had contracted with the Library of Congress for his services to draft a code according to agreed-upon principles. Thus he became the editor of the first edition of *AACR*.

In 1960 Lubetzky returned to U.C.L.A. as Professor in the School of Library Service, a position he held until 1969, when he retired, having given thirty-three years to library service. At the time of his retirement the university awarded him its highest honor, a Doctor of Laws degree. In 1977 he was awarded the Melvil Dewey Medal, with citation, for contributions to bibliography and cataloging as first editor of *AACR*.

S. Michael Malinconico is a native of Brooklyn, New York. He holds degrees from Brooklyn College and Columbia University. He worked for the National Aeronautics and Space Administration as a systems analyst from 1967 through July 1969, and participated in the Apollo project. In August 1969 he was employed by the New York Public Library's Systems Analysis and Data Processing Office as a systems analyst and was assigned to the automated book catalog project. He has held progressively more responsible positions, such as Coordinator of Technical Services Office, Branch Libraries, his current position.

Malinconico was responsible for the design, development, and implementation of the New York Public Library book catalog system and played a major part in the design of that library's authority control system. He was directly responsible for the developments that culminated in the inclusion of nonroman scripts in the automated book catalog system. Also, he converted source cataloging data, expressed in the Cyrillic alphabet, into machine-readable form and was responsible for its publication in the New York Public Library's automated book catalog. Most recently he was responsible for the planning and development of the Library of Congress/Research Libraries Group computer-to-computer link, the first real-time computer-to-computer linkage of bibliographic systems in this country.

Active in the American Library Association, in which he has held various offices, Malinconico has represented that organization at the International Federation of Library Associations' Mechanization Section meetings. The Esther J. Piercy Award for 1978 was presented to him in recognition of his work as an advocate of the application of computer technology as a tool for facilitating the cataloging process, preserving cataloging principles, and improving bibliographic access and control.

Joan K. Marshall is Chief of the Catalog Division, Brooklyn College Library, the City University of New York. She has been a member of the Brooklyn College faculty since 1966. Nationally known for her efforts and views on the need for change in library organization, she is also known for her numerous articles in professional journals. She is the author of the prize-winning book *On Equal Terms*. Active in national, regional, and local professional organizations, she was a member of the Catalog Code Revision Committee.

Gordon Stevenson is Associate Professor in the School of Library and Information Science, the State University of New York, Albany. He teaches courses in subject indexing and classification, cultural and social aspects of libraries, and popular culture. He has held positions at the

New York Public Library as a cataloger, in Kansas City (Mo.) as Head of the Art and Music Department, and in Kansas City (Kan.) as Head of Public Services. He was on the ALA Cataloging Code Revision Committee from 1974 to 1976.

Elizabeth L. Tate was born in Portland, Oregon; graduated from Reed College and Pratt Institute Library School; and in 1963 received the Ph.D. from the University of Chicago. She worked for nine years with the National Bureau of Standards and served as Chief of the Library Division for six years. Most of her library career was spent at the Library of Congress in the Descriptive Cataloging Division, where in 1973 she was appointed Chief. She has taught cataloging at the U.S. Department of Agriculture Graduate School and at Catholic University of America. Also, she served as Information Resources Analyst in the National Referral Center for Science and Technology.

Active in the American Library Association, Tate was elected Chairperson of the Cataloging and Classification Section of the Resources and Technology Services Division—among numerous other positions. From 1974 to 1976 she served as the Library of Congress Representative to the Joint Steering Committee for Revision of AACR. On June 30, 1976, she retired from the Library of Congress, after more than thirty-three years of federal service. She is currently editor of *Library Resources & Technical Services,* the official publication of ALA/ RTSD.

Ben R. Tucker was born September 8, 1935, in Clanton, Alabama. After graduation from Birmingham-Southern College with an A.B. in 1956 and a year of graduate work at Washington University, he earned his M.S.L.S. degree from the University of North Carolina in 1959, and came to the Library of Congress in September as an intern. His entire career at the Library of Congress has been in the Descriptive Cataloging Division, where he started as a Romance-languages cataloger. He served as Principal Descriptive Cataloger from 1974 to 1978. Since February 1979 he has served as Chief of the newly created Office of Descriptive Cataloging Policy at the Library of Congress. From 1976 to 1978 he served as the Library of Congress Representative to the Joint Steering Committee for Revision of AACR.

Index

Prepared by Carol R. Kelm